Robert Morris
The Financier
and
The Finances
of the
American Revolution

Robert Morris
The Financier
and
The Finances
of the
American Revolution

By

William Graham Sumner

Volume I

BeardBooks
Washington, D.C.

Copyright 1891 by Dodd, Mead & Company
Reprinted 2000 by Beard Books, Washington, D.C.
ISBN 1-893122-97-2
(Vol. I)
Printed in the United States of America

THE FINANCIER

AND THE

FINANCES OF THE AMERICAN REVOLUTION

BY

WILLIAM GRAHAM SUMNER

PROFESSOR OF POLITICAL AND SOCIAL SCIENCE IN YALE UNIVERSITY

"It is of the nature of expedients to increase the evils which they postpone"
REPORT OF 1785

"Experience has taught me to be cautious, even in doing good"
R. MORRIS

IN TWO VOLUMES

VOL. I.

NEW YORK
DODD, MEAD, AND COMPANY
1891

THIS book contains a biography of ROBERT MORRIS and a financial history of the period of the American Revolution. Neither of these subjects has heretofore been made the object of thorough investigation. Early in this century, two biographies of Morris were written, — one by Mease, the other by Waln; and numerous short sketches of his career have since been published which simply repeat the contents of those two. The financial history of the Revolution is very obscure. The most important records of the financial administration between 1775 and 1781 are lost. The finances of the Continental Congress had no proper boundary. In one point of view, they seem never to have had any finances; in another, the whole administration was financial.

Neither branch of the subject can be considered as exhaustively treated in the present work. In the "Inventory of Articles found in possession of Robert Morris, in his room, debtors' apartment, Saturday, August 1st, 1801," which is printed with the Account of his Property, is an enumeration showing that he had an enormous mass of papers, letters, account-books, etc., covering his life and business from 1775 to 1800. There were twenty-five letter-

Preface.

books. These books and papers seem to have been scattered; but it is probable that a great many of them may still be in existence. Morris kept a diary during his service as Superintendent of Finance. It was used by Sparks, who published brief extracts from it. From the description of it by Homes, it must be extremely interesting and valuable. Sparks must have neglected his opportunity to secure possession of it and save it; for the present owner, Gen. Meredith Read, of Paris, says that he bought it just in time to save it from the paper-mill. As between my reader and myself, I am called upon to say that I made every possible effort to obtain the use of it for the present work, but that it was not consistent with General Read's views to grant my request. It will remain for myself or another, at some future time, to fill the gaps and correct the errors which are now unavoidable. My book will, I hope, show that it is worth while that this should be done.

Besides searching the printed material for information about Morris's career, I have used all the unprinted papers I could obtain. Of these, the most valuable are the collection of Mr. G. L. Ford, the Dreer Collection in the Library of the Pennsylvania Historical Society, other letters and papers in the same library, and the manuscripts in the State Department. The Ford and Dreer Collections fit into each other for the years 1795-1799. The former also contains a number of letters written in 1785-1787, chiefly on commercial affairs, but which have been very useful to me, especially for Chapter XXV. Mr. Ford put them at my disposal with a generosity for which I make the warmest acknowledgment.

Preface.

As to the other branch of the subject, the financial history of the Revolution, I have only reduced into accessible form the material which is nearest at hand. The careless statements and contradictions of the authorities produce doubts and perplexities, which can only be finally resolved by an appeal to original authorities, which are very inaccessible. Much more remains to be done, therefore, in the study of that subject, before we shall really have at our disposal the amount of knowledge which may even now be recovered.

I wish to acknowledge the valuable aid and suggestions I have received from Messrs. W. C. Ford, Paul Ford, F. D. Stone, G. H. Moore, and Prof. C. H. Haskins; also to acknowledge the courtesies of the authorities of the State Department, and of the New York and Pennsylvania Historical Societies.

In order to use the briefest form of citation of authorities, yet give the reader the full title in the most convenient manner for reference, I have put at the end of the volume a list of books cited, in the alphabetical order of the brief forms of reference used in the course of the work.

W. G. SUMNER.

YALE UNIVERSITY,
   October, 1891.

CONTENTS TO VOLUME I.

CHAPTER I.
MORRIS'S FATHER; HIS BIRTH; MARRIAGE; EARLIEST PUBLIC ACTIVITY 1

CHAPTER II.
THE ORGANIZATION OF THE TREASURY 5

CHAPTER III.
TAXATION UNTIL 1781 11

CHAPTER IV.
PAPER CURRENCIES; PRICE CONVENTIONS; FORCED CIRCULATION; SPECIE IN 1780; THE LOTTERY 35

CHAPTER V.
COMMERCE AS AN ENGINE OF COERCION AND COMMERCE AS A MEANS OF SUPPLY 103

CHAPTER VI.
EMBARGOES 132

CHAPTER VII.
IMPRESSMENT 141

Contents.

CHAPTER VIII.

SUPPLIES FROM EUROPE; HISTORY OF THE MISSIONS THERE UNTIL 1781 156

CHAPTER IX.

1775–77: MORRIS IN THE COUNCIL OF SAFETY, THE PENNSYLVANIA ASSEMBLY, AND THE CONTINENTAL CONGRESS 188

CHAPTER X.

1777–81: MORRIS IN THE PENNSYLVANIA ASSEMBLY; THOMAS MORRIS; SILAS DEANE AND PARTIES IN CONGRESS; THE SHIP "FARMER;" THE COMMITTEE OF PHILADELPHIA; THE FORT WILSON RIOT; THE TENDER LAWS OF PENNSYLVANIA 209

CHAPTER XI.

SPECIFIC SUPPLIES 239

CHAPTER XII.

BILLS ON THE ENVOYS UNTIL 1781 247

CHAPTER XIII.

THE SITUATION IN 1780; MORRIS BECOMES FINANCIER, HIS VIEWS AND THOSE OF OTHERS ABOUT THE OFFICE . . 258

CHAPTER XIV.

THE TASKS OF THE FINANCIER; HIS MEANS, PLANS, AND DEVICES; HIS APPEALS TO THE STATES AND PROPOSALS TO CONGRESS 277

CHAPTER XV.

BORROWING IN EUROPE BY THE STATES; APPEALS OF CONGRESS TO FRANCE; MISSION OF JOHN LAURENS; THE YORKTOWN CAMPAIGN 292

THE FINANCIER

AND THE

FINANCES OF THE AMERICAN REVOLUTION.

CHAPTER I.

MORRIS'S FATHER; HIS BIRTH; MARRIAGE; EARLIEST PUBLIC ACTIVITY.

THE only man in the history of the world who ever bore the title of Superintendent of Finance was ROBERT MORRIS, of Philadelphia. The reader of this book will no doubt admit that he ought to have had a peculiar title, for the office which he filled has never had a parallel. His contemporaries found that this title was somewhat long and clumsy. He was popularly called the Financier, and he is so called on his tombstone.

The father of Robert Morris, also named Robert, was a merchant of Liverpool, England. It is said that he was bred a nail-maker, but had a genius for mercantile pursuits. He is described as having been generous and genial in his disposition toward his equals, but haughty, overbearing, and severe with his inferiors. He became the factor of a Liverpool firm, and took up his residence at Oxford, on the eastern shore of Maryland, when he was about thirty years of age. He was killed at the age of forty by an accident, which is described upon his tombstone in the cemetery at White Marsh, Talbot County,

Maryland. When he was leaving a ship to which he had been paying a social visit, a cannon was fired in his honour. The wadding of the gun struck him in the arm, and the wound proved fatal. His death took place July 12, 1750.

His will is dated April 17, 1749. After leaving legacies to his two sisters, he gave to Sarah Wise, of Talbot County, Maryland, " for the good will and affection I have for her," £250 Maryland currency.[1] He also gave her two silver cans and six silver spoons. To her daughter Sarah he gave £100, and to "the child of which Sarah Wise is now with child," £100. He also gave to Sarah Wise a mourning ring, a silver tankard, and all his wearing apparel. The will then goes on: "I give all my lands and tenements whatsoever whereof I shall die seized, in possession, reversion or remainder, to a youth now living with my friend Robert Greenway in Philadelphia, known there by the name of Robert Morris, Jr., who arrived in Philadelphia from Liverpool sometime in the year 1748; and to him, the said Robert Morris, Jr., now living with Mr. Robert Greenway, merchant, in Philadelphia, I give and bequeath all the lands and tenements I shall die possessed of forever; and I likewise give to the said Robert Morris, Jr., all the rest and residue of my goods, chattels, merchandise, apparel, and personal estate whatsoever." The estate was to be converted into cash and sent in bills of exchange to Greenway as executor, in trust for Robert Morris, Jr., until the latter should demand it. The will was probated August 1, 1750. The personal property was appraised under it at £2,558 18s. 6½d.[2] Robert Morris had a half-brother,

---

[1] Maryland currency was the same as Pennsylvania currency; namely, £1 = $2.66⅔.

[2] Boogher, March, 1883, where there is a portrait of the father. The epitaph is in the " American Review," vi. 69.

Thomas, a posthumous son of his father by a lady whom he married late in life.[1] This wife and son do not appear to be mentioned in the will. Robert assumed a father's responsibilities toward Thomas. Referring to his father, in 1777, Robert wrote: " Whose virtue and whose memory I have ever revered with the most filial piety."

Robert Morris, Jr., was born at Liverpool, January 31, 1734, new style. He was placed in the mercantile house of the Willings at Philadelphia. This house was founded by two brothers, who came from Bristol, England, about 1726. One of them, Thomas, returned to England; the other, Charles, died in Philadelphia.[2]

There are one or two anecdotes about Robert Morris at this period which represent him as very zealous and enterprising. In 1754 the firm was reconstituted, a partnership being formed between him and Thomas Willing, one of the younger generation. This step apparently represents a new infusion of youth and enterprise. In the years immediately following, Morris made several voyages as supercargo. On one of these, during the Seven Years' War, he was captured by the French, and being destitute of money, obtained enough to return home by repairing a watch.[3] He once spoke of having been in Ireland.[4] These voyages offer the only opportunity when he could have been there.

He was married, on the 27th of February, 1769, to Mary White.[5] She was the daughter of Col. Thomas White,[6] was born at Philadelphia April 13, 1749,[7] and was a sister of the first Bishop of Pennsylvania of the Protestant Episcopal Church. She figures with high honour in a poem

[1] Laurens Corresp. 71. [2] Balch, Philadelphia Papers, ciii.
[3] Delaplaine, 143. [4] Carey's Debates, 88.
[5] Pennsylvania Marriages, Second Series Penn. Archives, ii. 211.
[6] Account, 59. [7] Penn. Mag. ii. 157.

attributed to Joseph Shippen, about the belles of Philadelphia.[1]

Morris first appears active in public affairs in connection with the resistance to the Stamp Act. He signed the non-importation agreement in 1765, and was on a committee of citizens to force John Hughes, collector of the stamp tax, to desist from the administration of his office, in October of that year.[2] Hughes's account of this affair is that he had obtained the office on the recommendation of Franklin. On the arrival of the stamps a mob collected; a meeting was held at the State House, and a committee was sent to Hughes to ask his resignation. He refused, because he could not discharge his sureties, who had given bonds for his faithful performance of the duty; but he finally consented not to act until further orders, or until the Act was enforced in other colonies. A few hours later he received a peremptory demand to resign, to which he submitted two days afterward.[3]

Morris was warden of the port of Philadelphia in 1766.[4]

It will be perceived that he was forty-one years old when the Revolution began. His career as a public man then began. He took part in all the great enterprises of the United States which were not military, and he was not without influence on those. The Financier, as we shall see, had to undertake a number of functions which no modern Secretary of the Treasury ever thinks of executing. It will be our most convenient method of dealing with our subject to investigate, first, the facts in regard to the plans and proceedings, under each of the important topics of finance, which were pursued at the beginning of the Revolutionary period.

[1] Penn. Papers, lxxii.
[3] Prior Documents, 45.
[2] Hazard's Register, ii. 247.
[4] Penn. Colon. Rec. ix. 293.

CHAPTER II.

THE ORGANIZATION OF THE TREASURY.

THE object of a system of public finance is to draw from the resources of the country so much as must be employed for the work of the state, to obtain it promptly and without waste, and to cause the burden of providing it to be distributed among the citizens in the proportion which the institutions of the country provide for as just.

Public finance, therefore, deals with the methods and apparatus of obtaining resources for the support of the state and expending them for its maintenance. Its leading topics are taxation, public loans, and the fiscal system. Banking and currency enter into it if they are made an integral part of the apparatus by which the fiscal operations are carried on. The finances of the American Revolution were peculiar, from the fact, among others, that they scarcely had a definable limit. The regular, normal operations of taxation and public loans did not exist. There was no proper fiscal system for the collection of revenue and disbursement of expenditures. There was only a simulacrum of a treasury. On the other hand, the financial officers and the financial apparatus were forced to include in their scope currency, banking, transportation, and commerce.

One instance is found of a man who retired from public life because he disapproved of raising an army without providing for its maintenance. It is Samuel Dexter, who was a member of the first Provincial Congress of Massachusetts.[1] It is not a very strong mode of action to retire from the public service out of dissatisfaction with what is done; but the instance is noticeable because it stands entirely by itself, as an argument or protest against the line of conduct which was adopted by Congress and by the several States. It seemed to be accepted by everybody as a rational and correct view of the situation, that, of course, taxes could not be laid, because the fight was against taxation. We have not met with a single case in which anybody undertook to point out the distinction between resisting all taxation and resisting taxation which was not levied upon due authority; nor have we found one case in which anybody argued that the people had intelligently undertaken to resist the authority of Great Britain, and that they could or would subject themselves to the necessary cost of it, in money and military effort, like men.

June 2, 1775, Congress resolved that nobody should sell any supplies to the British, or advance them money, or negotiate bills of exchange for them.[2] The next day they voted to borrow £6,000, with which to buy gunpowder, and that they would make full and ample provision for repaying it. A week later they voted to take up the question of ways and means.[3] December 26, they recommended the colonies to take a census, having in view the apportionment of expenditures.[4]

It was not, however, until February 17, 1776, that they provided any permanent or regular organization for the treasury. A standing committee of five was then appointed to superintend that department.[5] April 1, they attempted an organization of the treasury office under this standing committee. James Duane was made chairman,

---

[1] Mass. Papers, 22.
[2] Journ. Cong. i. 105.
[3] Secret Journ. i. 14.
[4] Journ. Cong. i. 284.
[5] Ibid. ii. 64.

and it was resolved "that all Assemblies, Conventions, Councils and Committees of Safety, Commissaries, Paymasters, and others entrusted with public money should, within a reasonable time after being called upon for that purpose by the Committee of the Treasury, produce their accounts at the treasury office, in order to their being settled and adjusted."

October 3, 1776, Congress established the loan-office system. The immediate object was to borrow five millions of continental dollars at four per cent, for the payment of which the faith of the United States was pledged. The certificates were in the shape of an acknowledgment of the receipt of so many dollars, which the United States promised to pay to bearer. There was to be a loan officer in each State, appointed by the State, and responsible for the faithful discharge of his duty, — although the record does not say to whom he was to be responsible. Accounts were to be sent to the continental Treasurer once a month. No certificate was to be for less than $300. The sums borrowed were to be repaid in three years. The Commissioners were to receive as their sole remuneration one eighth of one per cent on all the loans issued.[1]

During 1777 we find Congress voting all sorts of petty appropriations,—for instance, $16.39 for ferriage; $11.78 for meals supplied to troops; $22 for supplies to two sick men in the hospital; $16 for a lost rifle; and so on all through that year and part of the next.

February 6, 1778, on the ground of a scheme drafted by the Committee who were sent to Valley Forge to confer with Washington, a new attempt was made to regulate the accounts of the army. The States were called upon to report the advances which they had made, from which we must infer that the records of the treasury were then very

[1] Journ. Cong. ii. 374.

imperfect in regard to the expenditures which had been incurred.[1]

In July, 1778, Gerard reported that Congress was occupied with measures against the tories. He thought that they relied on confiscation as the chief financial resource.[2]

In September financial affairs had reached such a point as to demand once more the special consideration of Congress. The Committee of Finance made a report, but the revelations were such that it was put under a strict injunction of secrecy.[3]

One result of it, however, was that, September 26, the treasury was remodelled with five distinct bureaus.[4] This was an attempt at more efficient organization; but we presently find that the bureaus quarrelled, from which it appears that the organization was clumsy and excessive. In November Congress resolved to devote themselves to the business of finance day by day until it should be finished. They were still entirely unconvinced that finance is a matter of executive administration, and that the line between its functions and those which are suitable for a deliberative and enacting body is very distinct. They still clung to the system of administration by a committee of the legislative body, and they thought that fidelity to the maxims of civil liberty required that they should not only lay down rules, but also administer. Their proceedings repeatedly manifest this inexperienced misconstruction of civil liberty and the "great principles of the English Constitution."

April 22, 1779, the Committee on the Treasury reported that the public business could not be conducted under the present arrangement. This led to an attempt to reorganize the system; and July 30, Congress adopted an ordinance for establishing a new Board of Treasury, to consist

---

[1] Journ. Cong. iv. 58. [2] Doniol, iii. 273.
[3] Journ. Cong. iv. 395. [4] Ibid. 404.

of three commissioners, not members of Congress, and two members of Congress, any three of whom might do business.[1]

May 26, 1779, Congress called for forty-five million dollars in addition to the fifteen million already called for for that year, and added a long proclamation to try to stimulate zeal and patriotism.[2] The Board of Treasury reported that one cause of the alarming expenses in the quartermaster's and commissary's departments arose from allowing commissions to the numerous persons employed in purchasing for the army. This had caused great dissatisfaction, and those departments should be put on a different footing with respect to the expenditure of public money.[3]

February 25, 1780, Congress made a call on the States for specific supplies; and, November 4, they apportioned a tax of six million silver dollars, to be paid partly in specific articles. It is asserted that the apportionment of taxes among the United States of the Netherlands furnished the model of the requisitions by the Continental Congress.[4]

A system of requisitions assumes a high organization of society and strong political vitality. Some of our States still have a system of requisitions upon counties and towns, which amounts to the same thing, and is executed without any trouble. The failure of requisitions in the Revolutionary period must be referred to the all-pervading lack of organization and the low political vitality of the Union.

June 17, 1780, all the States except Georgia were called on to report what action they had taken on the resolutions of Congress since January 1, 1779, calling for men and supplies.[5]

[1] Journ. Cong. v. 228.   [2] Penn. Packet, May 29, 1779.
[3] Journ. Cong. v. 176.   [4] Temple's Works. i. 67.
[5] Journ. Cong. vi. 61.

In his report of 1785, Robert Morris said: "Genius and judgment have undoubtedly been displayed by the Board to whom Congress entrusted their affairs; yet genius and judgment will always leave open to experience a large field for improvement."

At the beginning of 1781, the devices which have been mentioned having all proved wasteful and inadequate, it was found necessary to select a competent man and entrust the business to him. Robert Morris was chosen.

CHAPTER III.

TAXATION UNTIL 1781.

THE history of taxation in the colonies, and the attitude of the minds of the people toward taxation when the war broke out, give the key to the financial history of the war.

The citizen of a modern well-organized state regards taxation as one of the normal experiences of life. He can scarcely imagine what life would be without it, and he hears with astonishment of people who were civilized, yet did not need to be taxed, were not taxed, and refused to be taxed as passionately as we refuse to be robbed. The situation, however, is not difficult to realize.

In a country which had no civilized neighbours, and in which the population was scattered in isolated farms and plantations, each household lived upon its own piece of ground. In the northern colonies each farmstead almost sufficed for itself. In the southern colonies, where indigo, tobacco, and rice were produced, there was more constant and direct intercourse with the rest of the world, and dependence upon it. For this reason the English writers spoke of the northern colonies as poor or as useless to the empire. In either case, however, upon the farmstead or the plantation the owner lived in slight relations with any of his fellow-men but his immediate neighbours. If he and they needed defence, they had to defend themselves; they could not without difficulty and with little result call upon any larger political body for protection. As a matter of fact, therefore, a man got nothing from the Commonwealth of which he was a member, except the regulation and enforcement of contracts and the settlement of disputes under general regulations of law and by established tribunals.

Outside of the farm production and the household mechanical industries, the school, the church, and two or three mechanical employments, like blacksmithing and wagon-making, were the only social ties of the industrial organization. It was when it became necessary to obtain supplies of iron and other metals, salt, spices, tea, coffee, and sugar, that the freeholders were forced into exchange operations for their supplies.

Such being the general characteristics of the situation, the individual saw little reason why he should pay anything to the Commonwealth, which to him was only an abstraction, or, if he tried to make it concrete, was only a group of office-holders whom he never had seen. They appeared to come to him, or to enter into his life, for no other purpose than to take a part of his product for which he received no return. Hence we find the American colonies resisting taxation in a way which to the modern man seems childish and ignorant. In the quarrel with Great Britain a great deal was made of the principle of taxation; but, as usual, the declaration about the principles only covered the real question of interest. What they objected to was parting with their products.

As to the modes of taxation, the first and most obvious kind of tax for such a community as has been described, where all were on a level of social condition and education, and as nearly on a level with respect to property as a human society ever can be, would be a poll tax. A poll tax would easily develop, as it did in some of the colonies, by a little gradation, according to professional occupation, into a sort of income tax. The next tax must be on land, which, where the land bore no rent, would be a property tax, and could be easily expanded, by putting in stock, buildings, and chattels, into a complete property-tax system, which therefore seemed the fairest of all.

In 1692, in New Hampshire, the Selectmen and a special Commissioner in each town were directed to make a census of the males over sixteen, and to assess all the real and personal property of every description. All males except the members of the Council, ministers, and schoolmasters, were to pay a poll tax. For common labourers it was eighteen pence. For artisans and other industrial classes it was higher "proportionately to other men for the produce of their estates." Wage-earners were to pay threepence in the pound. The assessors were to rate merchants according to their stock, at discretion.[1]

In 1756 New Hampshire laid an excise on rum, wine, and cider, also a tax on tea and a tax of one penny per acre on land.[2]

The grand list of a Massachusetts town for 1767, which is given, shows an inventory of all the kinds of property which existed at the time, including money at interest. It was upon such a list that taxes were levied for town purposes, within the scope of which nearly all the life of the citizen was passed.[3] Beyond that, the Colony or Commonwealth had but a vague and unimportant existence. Its political vitality was exceedingly low. It is most instructive to notice in Weeden's "New England," in which the economic and social phenomena are most carefully and exhaustively collected, what a very small place is occupied by the sub-

[1] N. Hamp. Prov. Papers, iii. 165.   [2] Weeden, 647.   [3] Ibid. 730.

ject of taxation. It is simply maintaining an illusion to carry back into the colonial days the notions of "Massachusetts" and "New York" which we have to-day, and to suppose that anything corresponding to them existed before the Revolution. Much more is it maintaining an illusion to endeavour to find the organs and functions of a modern state in communities, each of which consisted really of a congeries of co-operative land companies. It has often been fondly imagined that examples of the communal state, or of some pet notion about village communities, had been found in these little townships, which were simply amorphous political bodies. Taxes in them were really nothing but the subscriptions of a club.

Modern systems of taxation under a high organization reach commodities in transfer. The colonists could not use those taxes except for tobacco, and spirits, or salt; that is, commodities which could not be produced in households economically. All these taxes, however, were inquisitorial and direct; and the collection of them, in a country with a sparse population, was very expensive and difficult. Morris wrote to Jefferson in 1784 that the expense of collecting taxes in this country was greater than in almost any other.[1] These were very serious obstacles to the imposition of any taxes of the kind we have described, so that, in a sense, it might be said that taxation did not pay. A further difficulty was that a community of the kind we have described had very little occasion for the use of money. A tax, however, was a direct call for money; that is, it called for what the farmer had not. Hence we find that paper money was constantly called for and excused on the ground that it was needed to pay taxes, and currency and taxes appear in a constant combination.

[1] Dip. Corr. Rev. xii. 475.

There were therefore real reasons for the social friction which was always produced by taxation, and it required ingenuity to devise means of obtaining a revenue from a colonial community. The easiest and best means was by import duties on spices, sugar, tea, coffee, wine, and spirits. The next best plan was by some means which should reach those operations of the courts of justice in the enforcement of contracts and settlement of disputes, which, as we have seen above, were real services rendered by the Commonwealth. The colonists were always extremely litigious. The transfers of freeholds were very frequent, conveyancing being very simple. The Stamp Act Congress alleged this fact as an argument why the stamp tax was oppressive, but it was also the reason why the tax was effective for revenue purposes. Import duties, however, had the great convenience and the great advantage, in a political point of view, that they could be levied in bulk at the seaports, and that the tax-collector and the tax-payer never came face to face. The English government laid import duties by a number of Acts from the 25th of Charles Second on, so that in the controversies at the beginning of the Revolution some of the writers on the English side declared that the American assertions that they had never been taxed but by themselves, were false.[1] In the Congress of 1774, R. H. Lee reckoned the revenue actually raised from America at £80,000 sterling.[2] When first a federal revenue was necessary, import duties presented themselves immediately as the most convenient way to get it.

Of course the colonies were not able to go on without some taxes. It would require a great amount of labour, which has not yet been performed, to find out the tax history of the separate colonies; but the following brief

[1] Civil War in America, 98; Stedman, i. 11.
[2] Adams, ii. 363.

notes may serve to give an idea of the position and attitude of the people with respect to taxation, when the war broke out.

In a scheme to reduce New England,[1] we find it written: "A race of men free as air from all subordination, no barons, no magistrates but among their companions, no taxes but of almost individual voluntary constitution, not one in one hundred perhaps in the country districts paying half a crown per annum, though wholesome food and apparel be found in comfortable plenty in every family," as a description of the New England people. The writer says also that great frauds have prevailed in Massachusetts under the exemptions allowed from taxes and militia duties. When the Provincial Congress of Massachusetts assumed the government, one of their first acts of usurpation was to direct the collectors and constables no longer to pay the taxes to the colonial Treasurer, but to a Treasurer whom they appointed.[2] They seized with amusing eagerness on the report that there was a man at Salem who had £500 which he was willing to lend to the Province. "It would be of the greatest importance to pay the soldiers, and might prevent the greatest mischief." This was a fortnight before Bunker Hill.[3] They did not lay new taxes until after the State government was organized, and at the end of March, 1775, as the collectors and constables had not paid the money to their Treasurer, they published an address in which they say that they, "earnestly attentive to the ease of the inhabitants of the colony, are desirous of completing the preparation so essentially necessary to the public safety without calling on them for other moneys than such as are now due to the colony."[4]

In Rhode Island the government of the colony went

---

[1] Stevens, 2.   [2] Mass. Journ. 260, 286, 451.
[3] Ibid. 296.   [4] Ibid, 113.

over directly to the Revolution, it being only necessary to depose the Governor. Taxation was carried on, therefore, just as before. In February, 1777, a committee of the Assembly made an assessment of the towns of Rhode Island, taking as a basis, the last previous estimate, which was in 1767. Their total estimate for the State was just over seven million dollars.

A tax of £32,000 was laid in Rhode Island in March, 1777, and another of the same amount in August, to be paid December 1.[1]

It was the custom in Rhode Island to levy a poll tax of sixpence for every £1,000 levied on property. In December a tax of £48,000 was levied, to be collected by March 1. From a protest against taxation, which was made in this last case, we learn that the representatives of Providence, in order to induce the Assembly to consent to begin taxation, in March, 1777, agreed to have £100,000 added to the assessment of that town.[2] In March, 1778, some town treasurers, having failed to collect taxes, had been put in jail. The Assembly ordered the State Treasurer to sue them on their bonds.[3]

In June, 1778, the Rhode Island Assembly laid a tax, in which they included a one-fourth part of the requisition on the State which had been voted by Congress on the 22d of November, 1777. That tax was payable on the 1st of October. In October they laid another, payable January 1, 1779. In February, 1779, they laid another to pay the requisition for that year, half of it payable in May and the

---

[1] When this tax was under consideration, a protest was entered against it on behalf of some towns then held by the English, "because taxation and representation ever ought to go hand in hand, — an idea Americans ought never to depart from." This is a good illustration of the confusion of mind produced at the time by the facile use of the dogma, "No taxation without representation."

[2] R. I. Col. Rec. viii. 331. [3] Ibid. 382.

other half December 1. In June, 1779, still another tax was laid; and another special tax, to be paid before August 1.[1] In a protest which was made on behalf of some towns which had been injured by the enemy, and therefore could not afford to pay as much as the rest, we meet with some interesting statements of principle about taxation. The protestors give as the first reason: " Because liberty and property are the essential matters that constitute a freeman, that as long as an individual enjoys those essential matters, he considers himself as a member of society worthy to contend for them and risk his all in their preservation; that whenever an individual or a community at large are deprived thereof, they are no longer to be considered as freemen, but the abject slaves of despotism. . . . In order to support government, taxation is necessary. He that receives protection ought to contribute to the support of his protectors. Taxation, or contribution for the support of government, ought to be free and voluntary, and equal upon every part which receives protection, agreeably to the abilities of the individual or towns at large who receive benefit thereby."[2]

In Connecticut, all male persons from sixteen to seventy, except those exempted by law, were liable to taxation. Lands, dwelling-houses, ships, warehouses, mills, shops, cattle, horses, and swine, and occasionally other things, were taxed. The grand list of the colony in 1775 was six million dollars.[3]

In April, 1775, £50,000 in bills of credit, not bearing interest, were issued by Connecticut, payable two years later; and a sinking-fund tax of seven pence on the pound was levied on all polls and ratable estate, to be paid by the time that the bills would be payable. In May another

---

[1] R. I. Col. Rec. viii. 503, 554, 568.   [2] Ibid. 569.
[3] Hinman, 14.

issue of the same amount was made, with a similar tax, the time of expiration being three years later.¹

In May, 1776, the Connecticut Assembly issued more bills of credit, payable January 1, 1781, with a tax of eight pence on the pound to sink them. In December a tax of fourteen pence on the pound was laid, and in May, 1777, a tax of twelve pence.² In August, a tax of a shilling on the pound was laid, payable in November; and in October a tax of twelve pence on the pound, payable April 15, 1778. In February, 1778, a tax of a shilling on the pound, payable June 1, and another tax of the same amount, payable November 1, were laid to pay the quota of the State under the requisition of November 22, 1777.³

Thus it will be seen that the two States which enjoyed complete self-government did set about taxation in good season.

In New York there was an excise on beer and wine as early as 1650. It produced great complaint, as a tax on "what they eat and drink."⁴ In 1677 a poll tax was proposed, because it was so difficult to assess and collect the property tax. In 1713 an excise was levied on all strong liquors sold at retail.⁵ In 1734 Governor Cosby proposed a stamp tax: "If any branches of your trade be overladen with duties, I wish some effectual method could be taken to ease them by an imposition on some other part better able to bear it, or on something that may not at all affect trade. For my own part, I think a duty upon paper to be used in the law and in all conveyances and deeds of every denomination may, if rightly managed, bring a considerable sum of money yearly to the treasury; and if, upon trial, you find it will answer your expectations, you may then ease such branches of trade as most want it of so much as

---
¹ Hinman, 170, 173. ² Ibid. 99, 266. ³ Ibid. 287, 293, 309.
⁴ Schwab, 21. ⁵ Ibid. 51.

the duty will amount to. I propose it as an experiment." In 1755 Governor De Lancey again proposed a stamp tax. He thought that such a tax "will be so diffused as to be in a manner insensible." The next year the plan was taken up again, and the tax was adopted December 1, 1756. The act is entitled "An Act for Erecting and Establishing a Stamp Office in this Colony for Stamping all Vellum, Parchment and Paper charged with the several Duties therein mentioned." It was renewed in 1757 and 1758, and expired in 1760.[1]

Dawson says that the first proposition that the mother country should tax the Colonies by means of stamped paper was made in 1744, by an aspiring New York politician, Lieutenant-Governor Clark.[2]

In the ten years before the Revolution the revenue of New York from auctions and hawkers' and peddlers' licenses averaged £1,000.[3] By the tax law of March 19, 1774, the assessors were to go from house to house, and make a list with an appraisal of all real and personal property.[4]

In 1774 Tryon made a report on the revenue of New York, in which he said that there were import duties on slaves, wines, distilled liquors, cocoa, and all European and East India goods if they came from the British islands in the West Indies; also two per cent on auction sales of certain goods, and licenses on peddlers. The average annual revenue was £5,000, New York currency. There were bills of credit out for £120,000, which, at 5 per cent, would bring in, until 1776, £5,602 per annum. After that one tenth of the principal was to be paid in annually. [When 1776 came, the repayment was postponed.] Tryon

---

[1] Journ. Gen. Ass. i. 654; ii. 453, 506, 1277, 1289; Livingston & Smith, 106, 139. The notes on the Stamp Act are communicated by Mr. Schwab.
[2] Sons of Liberty, 42.   [3] Schwab, 52.   [4] Ibid. 62.

goes on to say that the revenue from duties is appropriated to salaries, and the interest on the bills of credit is appropriated to the support of His Majesty's troops and the forts, arms, and the Governor's house. Then there is an excise on spirituous liquors which is expected to produce £1,000 in the city and county of New York. That income is appropriated to hospitals, streets, and the encouragement of the fishery off the coast. In the other counties the excise revenue is appropriated to roads. He puts the expenses of the colony in 1773 at £17,567.[1]

Jay urged McDougal, in the New York convention of 1775, "to impose light taxes, rather with a view to precedent than profit."[2] The Provincial Congress wrote to the delegates at Philadelphia, July 28, 1775: The large expenses "show us the necessity of laying a tax on our colony, but prudence or policy will impress as strongly on your minds, as on our own, the propriety of doing this in the manner least liable to popular disgust, or perhaps opposition." They proposed a tax of a shilling a pound on sales of tea.[3] August 5, a Committee of Ways and Means was appointed. They reported, August 30, that at least £15,000 ought to be raised by tax. An amendment was carried that the expenses should be met by bills of credit redeemable in 1776, 1777, and 1778.[4] September 2, they voted to issue bills, which were to be allotted in quotas on the counties for redemption; but the quotas were left blank.[5] February 13, 1776, the Tryon County Committee asked for a loan of £500 for the expense of scouting-parties and guards. The association would be hurt or broken if they should raise a tax.[6] March 9, 1776, the Convention called on the Provincial Treasurer to lay before them the state of the treasury. They voted to

[1] Doc. Hist. N. Y. i. 519.   [2] Pellew's Jay, 52.   [3] N. Y. Journ. i. 92.
[4] Ibid. 101, 128.   [5] Ibid. 133.   [6] Ibid. 296.

advance money to the counties, because "the imposition of taxes on the inhabitants of this colony to enable the county committees to pay the said contingent charges may be very inconvenient at this time."[1] Gouverneur Morris proposed that revenue should be raised by tax. It was referred to a committee, but they were discharged the next day.[2]

The Provincial Congress of New Jersey voted, June 3, 1775, that it was absolutely necessary to establish a fund; and "being persuaded that every inhabitant is willing and desirous to contribute his proportion of money for so important a purpose," they resolved to apportion and raise £10,000. They apportioned that sum on the counties. Committees were to apportion the tax on individuals in the townships. October 9, a petition was presented from inhabitants of Gloucester County that those who had refused to pay this tax might be compelled to do so. October 24, after reciting that many had not paid this tax, it was ordered that it be collected by distress.

February 20, 1776, an act was passed to issue £50,000 in bills of credit, and an elaborate system of taxes was connected with it to sink the same. The assessors were authorized to assess merchants, ferries, and vessels, within limits. A hired man who worked with a horse was to be assessed not under four nor over ten shillings; one who had no horse, not under two nor over six shillings. Slaves, cattle, horses, and vehicles were taxed a few shillings each. Land was to be put in at one twentieth of its real value if improved, at one fortieth if not improved. Bonds and notes at interest were to be assessed at one twentieth. Peddlers must pay for a license in each county.[3]

In 1740 in Pennsylvania there was no land tax, and had

---

[1] N. Y. Journ. i. 356. In August, 1776.   [2] Ibid. 559, 562.
[3] N. J. Prov. Cong. 181, 203, 225, 419.

been none for nearly forty years. The expenses of the government were paid by an excise and by tavern licenses.[1] In his examination before the House of Commons, in 1766, Franklin said that there were taxes in Pennsylvania on all estates, real and personal, a poll tax, a tax on all offices, professions, trades and businesses, according to their profit, an excise on all wine, rum, and other spirits, and a duty of £10 per head on all negroes imported, with some other duties. The poll tax was 15 shillings on every unmarried free man over 21 years of age. The taxes on real and personal estates were 18 pence in the pound at a full assessment; and the tax on profits, with other taxes, he thought amounted to fully half a crown in the pound.[2] He put the revenue of Pennsylvania at £20,000 sterling.

In 1775 the Pennsylvania Assembly voted that those who did not associate should pay a money tax equivalent to the time spent by the associators in drill. This became the beginning of militia fines for non-service.[3] All white males between sixteen and fifty were ordered to associate, and those who did so were ordered to tax the non-associators £2 10s. The tax was raised in April, 1776, to £3 10s.[4]

The Pennsylvania Assembly, by the same Act by which it constituted the Council of Safety, June 30, 1775, voted a tax to be raised on all real and personal property in the same manner as by the laws then in force. This tax was to begin "immediately after the sinking of the bills of credit now remaining to be sunk of those sums granted to the King during the course of the last war." This adjourned the tax so far that it probably was neglected. The proper officers were not ordered to collect it, but were en-

[1] Stille's Dickinson, 47.
[3] Stille's Dickinson, 167.
[2] Franklin, iv. 162, 167, 182.
[4] Votes and Proc. 660, 713.

joined to do so, "as they regard the freedom, welfare, and safety of their country." What was the practical effect of such a piece of legislation?[1]

Mention is made of a tax on liquors and slaves in Virginia in 1706.[2] In 1714, in a petition to the King, it was stated that the King had two shillings per hogshead on tobacco exported and tonnage; but the income appears to have been appropriated to the expenses of the colonial government, and the petitioners go on to say that the quit-rents of the colony were appropriated to the support of its government until about nine years before, when they were called into the exchequer of England. They ask that they may be re-applied to the expenses of the colonial government.[3]

In the three southernmost colonies it appears that taxation was suspended, whatever it may have been before. In 1779 it was said that taxation had lain dormant for four years in South Carolina.[4]

When the war broke out, the payment of the import duties, tonnage taxes, and port dues to Great Britain, which amounted, as we have seen, to £80,000 per annum, speedily ceased. In the States which underwent a revolutionary change the revolutionary legislatures did not venture on any taxation for two or three years. Therefore the outbreak of the war caused the cessation of that little taxation which had existed, and it was not until after the Federal Constitution was adopted that the people of the United States paid a tax for federal purposes equal to the import duties which they had paid under the British rule.

A modern writer has said: "As to taxation, it was ridiculous to believe that the people would submit to the creature of their own making the powers which they had denied

[1] Penn. Col. Rec. x. 282.
[2] Va. Papers, i. 106.
[3] Ibid. 178.
[4] Laurens Correspondence, 150.

to Parliament; and even an attempt at such a measure might at this stage have proved of so unpopular a nature as to be attended with the downfall of Congress."[1] Although it may sound strange that a modern writer should sympathize with the revolutionary standpoint, the statement undoubtedly expresses the view of Congress in the early years of the Revolution. The Americans would not pay any taxes which were levied upon them by a Parliament in which they were not represented, and they would not pay any which were levied by a "creature of their own making;" that is, they would not pay any at all. This describes the situation faithfully.

Adam Smith states the expenses of the civil establishment of the colonies before the Revolution in sterling as follows: Massachusetts, £18,000; New Hampshire, £3,500; Rhode Island, £3,500; Connecticut, £4,000; New York, £4,500; Pennsylvania, £4,500; New Jersey, £1,200; Virginia, £8,000; South Carolina, £8,000; Maryland and North Carolina not known. We may take it to have been, in round numbers, $300,000 for them all.

January 14, 1777, Congress made a vague recommendation that the States should tax, but nothing came of it. The price Convention at Yorktown, in March, 1777, voted down a proposition to recommend a tax for extinguishing the paper currency.[2]

In August, John Adams was convinced that it was necessary to proceed to taxation.[3]

September 10, Morris was on a committee of Congress to urge the States to proceed to taxation, and to prepare an estimate of the quotas that should be raised by each.[4] November 22, Congress issued a circular prepared by this Committee. They say that they have got along so far by

[1] Phillips, ii. 14.
[2] N. J. Corr. 40.
[3] Letters to his Wife, i. 246.
[4] Journ. Cong. iii. 307.

means of the continental currency, sparing the people from taxation. They now ask for five million dollars for the year 1778, which they apportion between the States, subject to an ultimate rectification. The States are requested to issue no more bills of credit, and it is recommended that local conventions shall regulate wages and prices and charges at inns, and also take away from the engrossers and forestallers any excess beyond what they need for their own consumption, paying them only the assize price. These conventions are also to fix prices for supplies for the army.[1]

November 14, Congress urged Washington to obtain necessary supplies from the disaffected inhabitants, believing that the well-disposed people would be rather pleased than dissatisfied if their enemies were compelled to supply the army.[2]

This recommendation quite fell in with the spirit of the times, and it appears that such taxes as were obtained were extorted from tories. This produced added bitterness between whigs and tories; and the outlaws, like Fitzpatrick and Moody, made a merit of offsetting this by their outrages on the whigs. In a circular of Congress to the States, September 13, 1779, it was stated that three millions had been paid in up to that time. This was no doubt the face value of continental paper.[3]

In October the Council of Safety of Pennsylvania ordered that militia fines and dues for substitutes should be collected by distress, there being large arrears.[4]

In August, 1778, the City Wardens of Philadelphia informed the Council of Safety that the lamp and watch tax of the city had not been collected for two years. Debts had been contracted, and no tax could for some

[1] Journ. Cong. iii. 415.
[2] Ibid. 395.
[3] Ibid. v. 259.
[4] Penn. Col. Rec. xi. 333.

time be collected. They asked for and obtained a loan from the Council.[1]

With respect to two taxes which were levied by Pennsylvania in 1778, the Commissioners of Chester County reported to the State Council that they had no return of assessments of property for one third of the townships, the township assessors having refused or neglected to act. The assessors were fined, and writs were issued to the sheriff, but they were not served.[2]

In Franklin's instructions, which were prepared in October, 1778, excuses are made for the neglect of taxation. It is said that America had never been much taxed, nor for a continued length of time, " and the contest being upon the very question of taxation, the laying of imposts, unless from the last necessity, would have been madness." [3] This extract from a serious document, intended to be read by the French authorities, throws the strongest light on the state of mind in which the public men of the country were at that time with respect to taxation. The alliance had then been formed, and Frenchmen were liable to taxation in order to execute its purposes.[4] Congress, instead of resolutely taking the necessary measures for success, presents an excuse, which could not have been valid unless it had been assumed that taxation was an arbitrary and unnecessary exaction which might be escaped altogether.

February 5, 1779, the Council of Pennsylvania sent to the House of Representatives a message in which they proposed more taxes, especially on pleasure-carriages, plate, slaves, and servants. General taxation should be

---

[1] Penn. Col. Rec. xi. 559.   [2] Futhey & Cope, 98.
[3] Secret Journ. ii. 118.
[4] On the state to which French finances were reduced ten years later, partly on account of the war in alliance with the United States, see Arthur Young in Pinkerton, iv. 401.

" adapted to the present value of money." They recommended that the forfeited estates of tories should be sold speedily, both for pecuniary and political reasons; also that fees and licenses should be adjusted to the value of the currency. They thought that the penalties for refusing office were not high enough, and ought to be raised.[1]

January 2, 1779, Congress called upon the States for fifteen million dollars in that year, and for six million dollars annually for eighteen years after 1780, in order to sink the loans and emissions. May 21, they called for forty-five million dollars more within that year. October 6, they called for fifteen million dollars monthly from February, 1780, for nine months, and they fixed the exchange for these taxes at forty for one. The object of these requisitions was to try to get the enormous amount of continental paper out of the way. Pelatiah Webster says that although the amount demanded sounds large, a quarterly tax of one bushel of wheat on each soul would be sufficient, for there are three million souls, and wheat is $20 a bushel. If some were so poor that it was necessary to excuse them, still the middling farmer who has ten in his family, would have forty bushels of wheat to pay in the year. That is a great deal. It is equal to $40 in the old time, and forty silver dollars would pay it now ; but that would not be heavy on every farmer.[2] He was now writing in favour of taxation, and argued that the taxes which he proposed were not more than two thirds of the taxes in Great Britain, which he reckoned at about six dollars a head. He made a long enumeration of the incidental losses and hardships of the war, in order to prove the real strength of the States, and he argued that they could have borne taxation for the same result much better.[3]

[1] Minutes Penn. House Rep. i. 305.
[2] Webster, 22. [3] Ibid. 93.

Some people were paying taxes. For instance, we find in Marshall's Diary, November 6, 1779, that he paid his taxes, £57 8s., being State, county, and old man's taxes.[1] The collection, however, was so irregular and imperfect that there was no equality or uniformity in the burden.

January 29, 1777, it was reported to the Pennsylvania Assembly that there were great arrears of taxes; that some counties had paid and some not, and that there was great inequality.[2] It is well known that nothing hinders the collection of taxes so much as faults of collection by which some pay and others do not.

December 28, 1779, Connecticut having applied to Congress for permission to retain part of the federal taxes and expend them in its own way, Congress refused to allow it, on the ground that it was inconsistent with the public interests.[3] This was an illustration of the rate at which the little system which had existed was falling to pieces, and of the way in which the financial mistakes were disintegrating the Union. The inequality of the burden on the States was analogous to the inequality on individuals, which has just been noticed.

In a letter by Hamilton which is supposed to have been written to Morris, probably in the fall of 1779, he proposed a tax in kind as the only one by which the farmers could be made to bear their proper share of the burden.[4] One of the New Jersey Congressmen, writing to the Governor in November, argues that every man should be taxed according to his ability; but as it is not possible to attain that result accurately, he seeks an approximately just standard. He finds it in the plan of taxing a man according to his family. "The whole debt of the Union

[1] Marshall's Diar7, 232, 261, 275.
[2] Penn. Journ. i. 106.
[3] Journ. Cong. v. 246.
[4] Hamilton's Works, iii. 61.

does not amount to a hundred dollars a head, and, if set off on the scale of strict justice, would not perhaps, to the poor, be more than the price of three or four days' work on a taxable."[1]

September 13, 1779, Congress issued a circular to the States in regard to the finances. The amount borrowed in America before the 1st of March, 1778, the interest of which was payable by bills of exchange on the Envoys in France, was seven and a half million dollars. The amount borrowed since then, the interest of which was payable here, was a little over twenty-six million. Taxes have as yet brought in only three million, so that the people of America, in loans and taxes, have provided only $36,700,000. There is due abroad an uncertain amount, probably four millions.[2]

In March, 1780, Webster wrote another essay in favour of taxation. It should be equal to the expenses. However, this frightens everybody, and they say it is impossible. Then they have recourse to the most ruinous measures.[3] Paine also was writing in favour of taxation. "Taxation occasions frugality and thought, and depreciation produces dissipation and carelessness."[4] In No. 10 of the "Crisis," October 6, 1780, he made a calculation that the English were taxed forty shillings sterling for a head of the population. He reckoned the war taxation of America, State and federal, at thirteen shillings four pence a head, and the peace taxation at five shillings. The quota for the State of Pennsylvania for 1780 was £64,280 sterling, specie value, or three shillings five pence sterling per head. The old quit-rents of one penny sterling per acre on only one half of the State amounted to £50,000, which are now discontinued. Therefore quit-

---

[1] N. J. Corr. 202.
[2] Journ. Cong. v. 259.
[3] Webster, 119.
[4] Paine's Works, i. 324.

rents and taxes, taken together, before the war, were more than taxes without quit-rents now are.[1] He estimated the army expense at £1,200,000; the continental civil expenses at £400,000; the expenses of the State governments at £400,000, making £2,000,000 sterling for the total expense. He says that the militia fines were more than all the taxes in Pennsylvania. The muster-roll was 60,000 men. Two thirds of these did not turn out, but paid the fine, which he estimated at £1 10s. per head, and 15s. on each £100 of property.

In Connecticut, in 1780, thirteen taxes were laid in ten months, amounting to 87s. 5½ pence in the pound, 84 shillings of which was in continental currency, worth a hundred for one. About two fifths of the amount was collected on polls. Houses were not included, and the assessment on land was arbitrary. In 1784 houses were put in at an assessment of 15 shillings for each fireplace. There was also a tax on faculty, — £50 for lawyers, £5 for mechanics, and others at various rates.[2] In 1783 one penny in the pound produced £6,250. Bronson thinks that the list may have been one twenty-fifth of the true valuation of the real and personal property of the State. If, then, a man had property worth at a fair market $100, his list would be $4; his tax would be $18, nearly all of which he would pay in a currency depreciated to sixty or one hundred for one, so that his tax would be from 18 to 30 cents in specie.

The taxes in Massachusetts, in 1780, were $2,000,000 on about 300,000 people; that is, $6⅔ per head. The taxation was reduced one sixth in 1781.[3] De Chastellux says that there was an excise and license tax, and a tax on

[1] Paine's Works, i. 198.
[2] Bronson, N. Haven Hist. Soc. Papers, i. 113.
[3] Hamilton's Works, iii. 92.

wealth assessed by twelve assessors in Boston, who were elected at a town meeting. They estimate the daily profits of a business by the amount of bills drawn, etc., and assess accordingly.[1]

January 2, 1781, President Reed of Pennsylvania sent a circular to the Commissioners of taxes in the counties. An Act has been passed putting a penalty of £500 specie on a Commissioner who fails in his duty, and £100 on an Assessor or Collector. Fines have also been laid for not furnishing recruits. He made an earnest appeal to the Commissioners to bring in the taxes. There are four thousand persons in the State suffering for lack of provisions. In July he made another appeal, saying that some Commissioners had as yet done nothing; and in December he made still another.[2] Here we see the action of a Governor who was trying to comply with the requisitions of Congress.

We have the means of following this appeal to the counties in the same State, in order to find out what was going on there, and we may thus realize how it was that all this effort was like water spilt upon the sand. In point of time, it is true that the statement now to be given belongs to the year 1780, but the state of things underwent no change.

A committee was appointed, in September, 1780, to visit the counties, find out why revenue failed, and propose remedies. Reed was on it. October 5, 1780, he writes that the deficiency of taxes is due to the neglect of the officers. The excises, fines, licenses, etc., would in a few years have been lost to the country. Not one third of the taverns take out a license. Continental property is sold by appraisement. The officers gratify a friend with a good

[1] Chastellux, ii. 293.
[2] Second Series Penn. Archives, iii. 453, 493, 498, 538.

team at a third of its value. He writes from Bethlehem, where he says that there is a Commissary on full pay, with an assistant, to supply six Hessians who work about the town. A mulatto under the Deputy Commissary has acquired a handsome fortune, some say £10,000 specie. There have at times been twelve deputy-quartermasters on full pay, with clerks, etc., in this one county. Had a suitable inspection taken place twelve months ago, thousands, if not millions, might have been saved.[1]

December 23, 1780, an Act of Pennsylvania laid a duty on spirits, wine, coffee, cocoa, tea, sugar, and molasses for the State.[2]

June 19, 1781, Reed sent a very peremptory message to the Assembly about the need of revenue (see p. 238). He wrote to Washington immediately afterward that they went home, at the April session, without doing anything except forcing every buyer of flour to allow one third of his purchase to be taken for the army; but that the merchants would not give flour for paper.[3] However, the Assembly repented, and on June 22 passed a revenue Act, apportioning requisitions on the counties.[4]

We constantly meet with statements in respect to taxation which show that it occasioned great hardships to individuals or to districts. A case is given of a man in Pennsylvania, with a small farm, whose militia fines amounted to £21 10s. The collector took away two horses and seven cattle.[5] The people of Northumberland County, Virginia, declared that they could not pay taxes, being ruined by the raids along the coast. They were defenceless, because their arms had been taken away. The Collector of Caroline County, Virginia, reported that

[1] Reed's Reed, ii. 281.   [2] Penn. Packet of Jan. 9, 1781.
[3] Reed's Reed, ii 297, 301.   [4] Penn. Packet, June 26, 1781.
[5] Penn. Archives, ix. 495, February, 1782.

the people would willingly pay the tax, and have cheerfully given up their property, which has been exposed for sale; but the scarcity of money prevents anybody from purchasing it.[1]

Congress ordered the Board of Treasury, March 6, 1781, to report the arrears of public taxes previous to March 18, 1780, and the arrears of the quotas of the States under the resolution of that date; also the names of the Commissioners of the loan officers who had neglected to make proper returns, according to order. They set apart Tuesday, Thursday, and Saturday of each week for the subject of finance.[2] In a committee report of this time it is stated with reference to the end of 1776: "As the governments of the several States were not yet sufficiently organized and in vigour, and as the expenses of arranging and equipping the militia were great, and the resources from commerce were cut off, it was not thought proper to proceed to taxation."[3]

July, 1781, Morris wrote to the Governor of Havana that the United States had more strength in men and arms and ammunition than when the war began; that the means of subsistence were ample, but that the paper money had collapsed and another medium of exchange must be found. "Our people are not enured to taxation, neither has the revenue which this country is capable of affording been drawn fairly or fully into use."[4]

When it was feared that the English would invade New Jersey, or even attack Philadelphia, during the siege of Yorktown, Thomas Paine proposed to Morris to levy a tax of one fourth or one third of the rental of Philadelphia as an emergency tax. At a guess, he estimated the rental of the city at £300,000, or $800,000.[5]

[1] Va Papers, iii. 236, 373, in 1782.
[2] Journ. Cong. vii 47
[3] App. to vol vii Journ Cong [Patterson]
[4] Dip. Corr. Rev. xi. 385.
[5] Letters to Morris, 470.

CHAPTER IV.

PAPER CURRENCIES; PRICE CONVENTIONS; FORCED CIRCULATION; SPECIE IN 1780; THE LOTTERY.

THE financial arrangements of Congress all involved a queer inversion of the proper course of financial devices.

A treasury is only a reservoir which must be fed by revenues on one side, and thus maintain currents of expenditure on the other. The revenue can come only from the products of individuals; and it must be collected in districts, combined in counties, and carried up to the central treasury. From this it finds its way back again by expenditures to individuals. The continental treasury was peculiar in that all streams flowed out from it, none into it.

In July, 1775, Governor Trumbull wrote to the Connecticut delegates to obtain part of the continental paper and forward it to him.[1] It was not issued until August.

At the end of 1775 the Provincial Congress of New York applied to Congress for a loan of £45,000 on the credit of the colony. This was the colony which had proposed the issue of continental paper money, to be sunk by taxes in the States, when issued by Congress for general purposes in its own enterprises. The first and common-sense answer to this was made by Congress,

[1] Hinman, 545.

that, although the credit of the colony of New York was unquestionable, yet it was inexpedient to make the loan. Nevertheless they gave it immediately afterward.[1] March 19, 1777, Congress advanced to New Jersey and to Pennsylvania each $100,000, each State "to be accountable." During that and the following year Congress went on making advances to the States, and also to various officers in enormous amounts, the phrase being always added that the recipient was "to be accountable."[2] In March, 1779, Congress loaned to Pennsylvania $2,000,000 at six per cent, until the taxes should come in, especial difficulty being caused by the fact that their revenue consisted almost entirely of the two emissions which Congress had called in because they had been counterfeited.[3]

If we follow this a step further, we find also cases in which the States were making advances to the counties.[4] We can even go further, and find some cases on record where the counties made advances to individuals.[5]

It is still more remarkable to find the New York Congress soliciting a loan from General Washington. In one case he declined to lend because he had no funds. In another case the general in the field advanced money to the Committee of Safety, which held the powers and authority of one of the constituent bodies which were carrying on the war.[6] January 1, 1776, the Governor of Rhode Island sent blankets which he had collected to Washington, and sent the bill with them.[7]

In 1781 the agent of Virginia wrote to Washington that the Virginia troops were so naked that they could not leave their quarters. After all the impressments, it

---

[1] N. Y. Journ. I. 244. [2] Journ. Cong. iii. 71, etc.
[3] Minutes Penn. House Rep. i. 330; Journ. Cong. v. 79.
[4] N. Y. Journ. I. 296, 551. [5] Ibid. 577.
[6] Ibid. 422, 527, 533. [7] R. I. Col. Rec. vii. 446.

had not been found possible to clothe them. Congress cannot do it. He appeals to Washington.[1]

In the relations with Europe also, as will be seen below, although at first the plan was a normal and reasonable one to buy supplies by the exportation of American products, things speedily took such a form that there was a flow this way and none the other. The Commissioners, instead of being supplied from America, were called on to supply America. After the inflow from France began, it to the extent of its magnitude supplied the want of the other; but how were the remaining wants of the treasury to be supplied? It must act like a fountain; and Congress, instead of being a mode of organization of the strength of all, must take the position of a Providence or Beneficent Power toward the members of the Union. So long as the continental notes could be printed and circulated, this appearance could be kept up. Congress created and poured forth. It enjoyed an easy popularity so long as this *rôle* lasted. It had released the people from taxation. It now conducted a war for them, and paid all the bills. The trouble of it was that there must come a catastrophe, after which the disgust and contempt would be proportionately great.

To understand these proceedings and the notions which led to them, it is necessary to keep in mind the state of the political and social organization, especially in those points, already mentioned, in which they were different from the state of things in our time. The legislatures dealt with the towns and counties by recommendations and requisitions. The whole country was under a " nightmare of liberty," and was thrown into agonies of fear the moment that any vigorous action was apprehended, in the way of organizing civil power. When Congress recom-

[1] Va. Papers, i. 524.

mended to the States, and they to the counties or towns, all civil energy was subjected to a constant operation of dissipation. All American history has been a process of development in which, as the country has filled up with population, the towns and counties have merged in the States as true commonwealths, and the States have merged in the Union, until a true confederated state has grown up where there were in the eighteenth century only little groups of farmers scattered along the edge of a wilderness.

May 10, 1775, Congress resolved to issue bills to an amount not exceeding two million Spanish dollars, and the colonies were pledged for their redemption. Later the phrase was " the faith of the colonies." The form of these bills was that the bearer was entitled to receive blank Spanish milled dollars, or the value thereof in gold or silver.[1] Attention was immediately directed to the probable consequences of this issue of paper in the Provincial Congress of New York. May 26, a committee was appointed to take into consideration the expediency of emitting a continental paper currency, and a letter was prepared to the New York delegates in the Continental Congress. It has occurred to the New York Congress " that an uncommon levy of money will soon be necessary for continental service, and that therefore an universal paper currency may probably become the subject of consideration in your respectable body. To this scheme it may naturally be objected that it will be imprudent in one colony to interpose its credit for the others. On the other hand, it is clearly impossible to raise any sum adequate to the service by tax, and the necessary intercourse of expenditures throughout the colony will be obstructed by separate emissions on the respective credits of the several colonies, which cannot in their nature gain universal circulation." They therefore

[1] Journ. Cong. 1. 117.

have the matter under consideration, and ask the Continental Congress to delay action in regard to it until they can communicate their opinion.[1]

A public session of the New York Provincial Congress was held on the 30th of May, when the report of the Committee on the continental currency was presented. It asserted that the proportion of gold and silver in this colony (New York), compared with others, varied with the price of bills of exchange in the several colonies, " owing to the relative quantity of paper money circulating amongst them, their several debts, and the several balances of their trade; but that, upon the whole, there is a smaller proportion of gold and silver in this colony than in several others." Connecticut and New Jersey are indebted to New York. Hence a large proportion of a general paper currency will flow into New York. The emission of paper will exclude gold and silver, causing it to be exported or hoarded. If the emissions are great, the paper will depreciate, which will make people less willing to receive it. Therefore, whether it be a currency or not will depend upon the security which can be given for the repayment of it. Gold and silver being excluded, paper will supply its place, provided it can obtain a general credit. There are but three ways to issue a general paper currency: "first, that every colony should strike for itself the sum apportioned by the Continental Congress; second, that the Continental Congress should strike the whole sum necessary, and each colony become bound to sink its proportionable part; or, thirdly, that the Continental Congress should strike the whole sum, and apportionate the several shares to the different colonies, every colony become bound to discharge its own particular part, and all the colonies to discharge the part which any particular colony shall be unable to pay." As to the second

[1] N. Y. Journ. i. 14.

plan, the Committee think that if any default occurs it will be by Connecticut or New Jersey, or both, which will hurt New York. They therefore prefer the third plan, because it will force other colonies to help them bear their loss by Connecticut or New Jersey, or both. [Their whole argument about it is how it will affect New York.] There are two difficulties about an emission of paper money: first, to give it an immediate and ready currency; second, to provide ways and means for sinking it. If it is issued by Congress for general purposes, it will be received, and will be a bond of union. This report was sent to the delegates in the Continental Congress for their information; but they would readily see that it was improper to lay it before the Continental Congress [because the arguments were all from the standpoint of New York].[1]

The author of this project was Gouverneur Morris.[2]

June 30, the delegates of New York wrote from Philadelphia: "We have the pleasure to acquaint you that a continental currency is forming, and when completed, you will be immediately supplied with a sum adequate to your exigencies."[3]

The act of Congress for issuing the paper and regulating it was passed July 29.

Each colony was to provide ways and means to sink its proportion of the bills issued by Congress in its own way. The quota was to be determined by the number of inhabitants of all ages, including coloured; but as this was not known, an estimate was made. If the common denominator was 300, the proportionate numerators would be, New Hampshire, 12; Massachusetts, 43; Rhode Island, 7; Connecticut, 24; New York, 24; New Jersey, 16; Pennsylvania, 37; Delaware, 3; Maryland, 31; Virginia, 49; North Carolina, 24; South Carolina, 24; fractions or decimals

[1] N. Y. Journ. i. 18. [2] Sparks's Morris, i. 38. [3] Ibid. 64.

being omitted. Connecticut, New York, North Carolina, and South Carolina were all four rated exactly equal. Each colony was to pay its quota in four annual instalments; namely, on the last day of November, 1779, 1780, 1781, and 1782. Each colony was to lay taxes, payable in these bills or in gold and silver. If in the latter, then the bills were to be bought up and cancelled by punching a hole in them, and returned to the treasurers appointed by Congress, then to be burned and destroyed. All silver and gold turned in on these quotas was to be held to redeem the notes. Their plan was that the taxes should be equal to the quotas, and the quotas should amount to the entire issue.[1]

The plan of the continental paper was to put it in the power of the Continental Congress to make such expenditures as they saw fit for the common cause, without asking the previous consent of the States, and to bind the States to meet those expenditures by taxation, which would retire and destroy the notes. This assumed that taxation was going on, or would be immediately begun, which, as we have seen, was by no means the case. It also assumed a responsiveness of the States to political demands made upon them by the Union, which by no means existed. The plan also clearly shows the idea which prevailed at the time, that the difficulties with Great Britain would be brought to a speedy solution. We may safely believe that no one then supposed the colonies to be at the beginning of a seven years' war. For this reason they put the date of redemption so far off. These faults all belong to the circumstances of the case and the practical administration of the system; but it is very important to observe, for a just appreciation of the plan, that it contains no fundamental financial absurdity. The Continental Congress never entered on the issue of paper money with any notion whatever that debt

[1] Journ. Cong. i. 174.

could be paid with scraps of paper which might be made as numerous as leaves on the trees. In financial character the notes which they issued were neither bonds nor currency; they were more like exchequer bills, although they bore no interest. In the language of the time, they were "anticipations." They anticipated taxes yet to be raised, and were receivable for the taxes. If promptly paid in and destroyed, they would clear the way for another issue of anticipations in the following year. If they were not promptly retired, they would accumulate until the movement of trade was arrested and public credit destroyed.

Whenever we come upon statements of the doctrine of currency held by the men of the revolutionary period, we find that the doctrines which they professed were substantially correct. Pelatiah Webster starts from the notion of the specie requirement of the colonies. There was a general notion, he says, that the current cash of the thirteen States was about thirty million dollars. In 1776 he thought it was about twelve millions.[1] In 1780, taking the rate of depreciation as a basis, he calculated that it was not over four millions.[2] Hamilton started from the supposition that it was thirty millions.[3] In his letter to Morris of April, 1781, he said that the stock of specie was not over six millions.[4]

It is evident that they did not know what it was, and that the oft-repeated assumption that it was thirty millions was sheer guesswork. All the colonies had used depreciated paper for so long that the specie requirement had been entirely lost sight of and was unknown. Theoretically, however, the attempt to define it or to use it as a basis of calculations showed that they were quite free from wild ideas about paper money.

[1] Webster's Essays, 6, 114.
[2] Ibid. 142.
[3] Hamilton's Works, iii. 64.
[4] Ibid. 103.

Among Franklin's papers was found a set of propositions about paper currency, probably written by him: "Gold and silver will always rise and fall very nearly in proportion as exchange rises and falls, being only wanted in those colonies that have a paper currency for the same use as bills of exchange; that is, for remittances to England."[1] General Greene, in June, 1776, showed that he understood that depreciation is due to an issue beyond what is necessary for a circulating medium.[2] In a resolution of Congress, November, 1777, it is stated: "No truth being more evident than that, where the quantity of money of any denomination exceeds what is useful as a medium of commerce, its comparative value must be proportionately reduced."[3] Tench Francis, writing on paper currency, says that the value of land, labour, and commodities in one country compared with others shows whether money is superabundant. Maryland put a fund in England at four per cent, which would have been worth six at home, and issued paper money on it, which depreciated to one half.[4] Silas Deane incidentally expressed the opinion that depreciation must begin as soon as paper exceeds the amount of specie which would be necessary in circulation.[5] An anonymous writer, "Conti," in September, 1776, wrote: "When paper money circulates in the common course of trade, its value gradually rises and falls according to its quantity, when relatively considered with the value of the real effects of a country, such as houses, lands, provisions, gold, silver, and merchandise of every kind; for though paper merely has not any significant value in itself, and has only such nominal value as we place upon it, a single dollar bill

---

[1] Franklin, vii. 322. [2] Greene against Bancroft, 15.
[3] Journ. Cong. iii. 415. [4] Pownall, Admin. ii. app. 279.
[5] Deane's Narrative, 43.

being as large as an eight-dollar bill, yet as, by general consent, we agree to receive and pass this as one and that as eight, so long as this mutual confidence and resolution continues, they are to all intents and purposes of as much real worth as so much actual gold and silver, which are of themselves of no other absolute value than what mankind have been pleased to fix on them." So far he seems to have adopted the fundamental fallacy of paper money; but he adds: "It must be granted that the issuing large sums will gradually decrease the value of the emission in the same proportion as the introduction of an over quantity of any article of merchandise would affect its price and sale."[1] Webster maintained that the value of the currency of any State has a limit beyond which it cannot go. If the nominal sum is extended beyond that limit, the value will not follow. No human wisdom or authority can stretch the nominal currency beyond such real value. "The value of the current money in any country cannot be increased by any addition made to its quantity." However, we find him maintaining at the same time, as a maxim, that no State can be ruined or much endangered by any debt due to itself only.[2]

It is a more correct statement of the doctrine of money, which is not even yet by any means adequately discussed in the text-books, and much less popularly apprehended, that the amount of money required is a case of supply and demand, and has all the complications of any other case of supply and demand; but for all practical purposes, and especially under the commercial and industrial organization which existed in the colonies, the doctrine as apprehended by these writers was correct. Especially it was

[1] 5th Series Am. Archives, i. 430.
[2] Webster's Essays, 2, 6, 27.

correct at the point at which the sound doctrine of money comes in collision with the fallacies of paper money.

The separate provinces were also driven to the issue of paper as the exigencies of the war were felt by one after the other. Massachusetts was therefore the first to take this step. She had been on a specie basis since 1749; but May 1, 1775, the Committee of Safety resolved that, whereas Connecticut and Rhode Island were helping them, and had brought some paper currency of their own, which had not of late had a currency in Massachusetts, such currency should be paid and received in Massachusetts in the same proportion to silver as in the colonies where issued.[1] May 20, 1775, in order to make the necessary advance payment to the Massachusetts soldiers, the Receiver-general was directed to issue on the credit of the colony £26,000. They are bills of credit in the old form, payable into and out of the public treasury of the colony, and signed by the Receiver-general; so that by this step the Provincial Congress assumed full authority as to finance for the colony.[2] May 24, 1775, the Provincial Congress published an exhortation to the people to lend their money on the Receiver-general's certificates, payable in June, 1777.[3] June 28, 1775, the Provincial Congress passed a resolution that the bills of all the colonies, except Nova Scotia and Canada, should be a good and sufficient tender in the payment of all debts and damages on contracts, and receivable into the public treasury, Rhode Island bills at six shillings and nine pence for an ounce of silver, and the others at six shillings and eight pence an ounce; and if anybody should refuse these notes, or demand a premium for receiving them, he should be deemed an enemy of the country; and the local committees were directed to report the names of such.[4]

[1] Mass. Journals, 530. [2] Ibid. 246. [3] Ibid. 255. [4] Ibid. 414.

Massachusetts thus early began the system of terrorization in support of paper issues.

In May and June, 1775, Rhode Island issued bills at the rate of six shillings and nine pence for an ounce of silver, to be paid within five years, with interest at two and a half per cent. In October the Assembly issued bills which bore no interest. Both were legal tender, and any one who refused to receive them was to be boycotted by the good people of the colony.[1]

In January, 1776, bills bearing no interest, to the amount of the interest-bearing issues of the previous May and June, were ordered to be printed; and the holders of the interest-bearing notes were ordered to bring them in and exchange them for the non-interest-bearing notes within one month after the end of the session of the Assembly. The reason alleged was the burden of the time, and the fact that Congress and the other colonies had emitted bills which bore no interest. In March the Assembly voted that the interest on all bills of the colony which bore interest should cease one month later.[2] In September the College at Providence petitioned the legislature that interest might be continued on their funds, which had been loaned to the State. An exception was made in favour of the College.[3] In December, 1776, the Assembly voted to borrow bills and give the Treasurer's notes for them, bearing interest at six per cent.

In July, 1776, the notes of the State and Continental Congress were made legal tender. If the notes were tendered in the presence of two witnesses, the creditor was allowed one month in which to accept them, after which he was precluded from recovering on the contract, and the principal sum was to be lodged in the treasury of the State, for the use of the State, within three months from the time

---

[1] R. I. Col. Rec. vii. 321, 374, 389.   [2] Ibid. 470.   [3] Ibid. 607.

that the tender was made.[1] They also laid a penalty of £50 on any one who should buy specie with paper, or discriminate between specie and paper in prices. No one was to receive execution upon any judgment until he should take an oath that he had never received gold or silver at a higher rate than six shillings for the dollar.[2]

August 23, 1775, a New York committee returned from Philadelphia with $175,000 of continental paper money.[3] This may be taken as the date when it began to be issued.

December 9, the New York Congress wrote to their delegates at Philadelphia that New York had £45,000 of paper money ready for emission, but that it was thought better that all paper should be continental; therefore New York would not issue this if Congress would advance an equal amount. Congress refused this. Hence it was resolved that the emission was necessary. However, we find that they received paper at the same time from Philadelphia.[4] December 26, 1775, Congress established quotas for sinking new issues of continental paper, which were to become due on the last day of November in 1783, 1784, 1785, and 1786.[5] February 21, 1776, they ordered notes to be issued in the form of one half of a dollar.[6]

If the continental paper had borne interest, it might have been treated like exchequer bills, and would not have become currency. This was then supposed to be a conclusive reason why it ought not to bear interest. Paine argued that a debt was no burden if it bore no interest. It would have been more correct to regard depreciation as interest than as taxation, which was then the custom. It would have been seen that the paper bore an incredible rate of interest. As the case was, the continental notes immedi-

[1] R. I. Col. Rec. vii. 584.
[2] Ibid. 591.
[3] N. Y. Journ. i. 116.
[4] Ibid. 212, 239.
[5] Journ. Cong. i. 284.
[6] Ibid. ii. 69.

ately became currency. Then the limit to which it could have been issued without depreciation would have been set by the specie circulating at the time in the thirteen colonies. As this was very small, large amounts of colonial paper being already in circulation, the amount of room for the circulation of continental paper was exceedingly small. Depreciation, therefore, must have begun almost immediately. It was regarded as the highest crime against patriotism to depreciate it, or to recognize and admit that it was depreciated. Hence all evidence on this point was suppressed, as far as possible. The official tables of depreciation which were afterward adopted were notoriously and grossly untrue.

Nourse gives a table of depreciation for each of the States. Some of them recognized depreciation from January, 1777, others from April or July, others not until September. The scale adopted by Congress for loan-office certificates, June 28, 1780, begins with September.[1]

We seek such incidental mention of facts as can be found showing the truth on this matter. The earliest in date which we have found is the case of Robinson and Price, who were charged before the Provincial Congress of New York, November 3, 1775, with advancing the price of blankets.[2] This is not clearly a case of depreciation of the currency. In fact, it is more probably an advance due to the state of the market for the goods named under the non-importation. March 9, 1776, Robinson and Price, having been published as enemies of their country, expressed contrition and prayed to be restored. Congress ordered them to be restored, and gave them a copy of the order, that they might have it published in the newspapers.[3] There is ample evidence that in those days it was no trifling penalty to be advertised as an enemy of one's country. January 30, 1776, a hatter at

[1] Philips, ii. 210.   [2] N. Y. Journ. i. 193.   [3] Ibid. 349.

Philadelphia was summoned before the Committee for refusing continental money on grounds of conscience. He was censured, and remanded for a week to think it over. Two other persons were summoned on the following day for the same fault. These were probably not cases of depreciation, but of refusal by Quakers, who refused to handle the continental money because it was issued for the purposes of war.[1] They were punished for it, however.[2]

March 9, 1776, the whig committee of Queen's County, Long Island, in gathering evidence against some tories, specify in regard to one of them that he asserts, "I take no continental currency unless for a bad debt."[3] May 28, 1776, Thomas Harriot was reported to the Provincial Congress of New York for refusing to take continental bills. He did not care whether he was held up as an enemy of his country or not. The Congress advised the Committee of New York City to send him to jail. As he persisted, they summoned him to appear, June 6, and he was ordered to be published as an enemy of his country.[4] May 25, William Newton was convicted of refusing to receive continental paper in payment, but he recanted. Another very important case, which is reported in full, was that of Andrew Gautier. The city Committee of New York declared him an enemy of his country. He appealed to the Congress. The Continental Congress had limited the price of tea to six shillings per pound. The accused in this case did not charge more, but he refused to sell tea at all, except for gold or silver. The most important fact for our present purpose is that it was incidentally asserted by the witnesses in this case that six shillings in silver would buy more than eight shillings in continental paper. This establishes an important depreciation in the continental paper,

[1] Marshall's Diary, 59. [2] 4th Ser. Amer Arch. iii. 1388; iv 564.
[3] Onderdonk's Queens, 50. [4] N. Y. Journ. i. 465, 480, 488.

at New York City, in May, 1776, without the presence of the enemy, or any other political or military element to affect it.¹ Gautier, having been convicted, made a submission, and was pardoned.

June 14, the Committee of New Windsor, New York, reported that Mrs. Jonathan Lawrence sold tea at eight shillings per pound, and that "her husband made Fort Constitution an asylum for that useless herb." The Congress replied: "We are surprised at his conduct, and make no doubt you will treat him and all others according to their demerits after a fair hearing." ²

June 1, 1776, the Committee of New York City petitioned the Provincial Congress to forbid any one to ask for gold or silver in preference to continental bills.³ Action was postponed. An investigation of alleged depreciation was made in Virginia in the same month. It was denied that prices had been raised; but it was found that there was a difference of twelve and a half per cent between Virginia paper and continental paper, against the former, on the 2d of July, 1776. There is no explicit statement about the relation of continental paper to specie.⁴

September 19, 1776, a quartermaster in New Jersey wrote to the Governor that his agents could get no grain near Hackensack, because the people would not sell it except for gold and silver. The enemy were then in the neighbourhood.⁵

October 9, the Council of Safety of Pennsylvania was informed that a cargo of salt had been monopolized, and that the price had been advanced. They ordered it seized and sold at prime cost.⁶ The difficulty of obtaining salt is one of the leading social features of the period. By this action

[1] N. Y. Journ. i. 461, 465, 473.   [2] Ibid. 494.
[3] Ibid. 470.   [4] 4th Series Am. Archives, vi. 1551-1606.
[5] N. J Corr. 11.   [6] Penn. Col. Rec. x. 749.

the Council of Safety entered on the line of policy which was pursued with the greatest persistency for the next five years. If merchants who brought salt to the market had made great gains upon it, they would speedily have increased the supply until the price declined; but after one cargo had been seized no more were brought, and the scarcity and dearness of salt continued. October 31, John Baldwin, a cordwainer, who had refused continental bills, was declared an enemy of his country, precluded from trade and intercourse with the inhabitants of these States, and committed to jail.[1] November 6, Colonel Bull reported that the Treasurer of the hospital refused continental paper. This seems to have been passed over. The next day Colonel Matlack reported that Colonel Hare, a continental officer, ostentatiously bought three silver dollars at a large advance in continental paper. The case was referred to a committee to consider and consult with the continental Board of Treasury.[2]

One of the very first acts undertaken by the Assembly under the new Constitution was a tender law. It was finally passed January 29, 1777, having been delayed by the reluctance to act under the new Constitution, and by the threatening invasion.[3]

William Ellery, delegate to Congress from Rhode Island, wrote to the Governor from Baltimore, December 26, 1776, that he was paying six dollars a week for board. The prices of articles of ordinary living had doubled within a year or two.[4] Up to this time there had been no blockade or important interference with commerce.

The effect of the advance of the English across New Jersey toward Philadelphia was to cause a rapid depreciation of continental paper at that city. General Putnam,

[1] Penn. Col. Rec. x. 774.   [2] Ibid. 779, 780.
[3] Penn. Journ. 100.   [4] R. I. Col. Rec. viii. 169.

who was in command there, issued a proclamation that if any one refused continental currency his goods should be forfeited and he should be imprisoned.[1] Benjamin Rush wrote to R. H. Lee that Putnam's action produced only a temporary remedy. Those who had goods refused to sell them, and creditors refused to give up the bonds or kept out of the way when continental money was about to be tendered to them. Rush proposed that Congress should recommend the States to declare the debt forfeited, and should fine the creditors severely for refusing the currency. "This will be more effectual than imprisonment, which, from becoming so common for tory practices, has now lost its infamy. . . . I tremble every time I think of the danger of the further progress of the refusal of our money."[2] We find Robert Morris, who was left in charge of things at Philadelphia at this time, inveighing against the depreciation. He said that one silver dollar was then worth two paper ones. December 27, Congress recommended the Council of Safety of Pennsylvania to take the most vigorous and speedy measures to punish such as refused continental currency, and suggested that Washington should help them.[3] Thereupon the Council ordered that if any one refused it, or charged a higher price in it than in specie, he should be considered a dangerous person, and should forfeit the goods offered for sale, or the debt, to the other party, and should be fined £5 to the State. At the same time it was ordered that all persons whose shops had been shut up for refusing continental currency should be allowed to begin business again.[4] The application of "legal tender" here to compelling a person to sell for the specified currency goods which he had put upon the market is to be noted.

[1] 5th Ser. Am. Arch. iii. 1214.   [2] Lee's R. H. Lee, ii. 160.
[3] Journ. Cong. ii. 475.   [4] Penn. Col. Rec. xi. 70.

Another device which we find employed over and over again with persistent faith is the price tariff. As soon as legal tender means anything more than a specification of that thing in the shape of currency which shall be a "good delivery" in the discharge of a debt, just as custom or law determines what shall be a good delivery under the terms of a contract on the side of goods, it becomes necessary to use other names for it in order to avoid confusion. The best designation for the abuses of legal tender is "forced circulation." The price tariffs and price Conventions were devices for giving a forced circulation to the continental paper, against fact and truth and right. On account of the legal, financial, and political vices of the continental currency, in the shape which it had taken by the end of 1776, it failed of its purpose because it encountered the resistance of persons whose interests were imperilled by it. The price Conventions were intended to bear down this resistance in the hope of still attaining the purpose, in spite of it.

As early as September 15, 1774, a Convention of delegates from the towns of Hartford, New London, Windham, and part of Litchfield counties was held at Hartford, Connecticut, which favoured a non-consumption agreement, and denounced monopoly and forestalling, which "then prevailed to a great degree among the mercantile portion of the community." They resolved that if any merchant should engross any unusual amount of goods, in order to forestall the non-importation agreement, they would "find ways and means, without violating his private rights, to defeat this view, and to make him sensible that virtue and public spirit will be more for his interest than low selfishness and avarice can be."[1]

March 27, 1776, the Committees of Inspection of fifteen

[1] Hinman, 20, 77.

towns in Hartford County met at Hartford to consider the alarming prices of West India goods. They set prices for rum, molasses, sugar, coffee, and salt. No licenses to purchase tea should be given except for the sick; the name of the person, and the quantity wanted, being entered in the permit. The price was set at four shillings and sixpence a pound.[1]

In March, 1776, the Treasurer of Connecticut doubted the propriety of receiving continental bills in payment of colony taxes; but the Governor and Council of War "considered it necessary to support the union of the colonies in the free circulation and credit of continental bills," and ordered him to do so.[2]

In June, for fear that pork might be engrossed by individuals, a committee was appointed in Connecticut to buy all there was in the colony at the market price and store it for the use of the army. If any person who had more than he needed for his own use should refuse to sell it, or should refuse to take bills of credit for it at the market price, he was to forfeit the value of it, to be recovered in any proper court.[3] In October it was enacted that if any one should discriminate between paper and specie in prices or contracts, he should forfeit the value of the money exchanged or the commodities sold. There was at that time great complaint of engrossing. In November the Assembly established a price tariff for wages and goods. Any one who charged more than the rates set was to suffer the penalties of the law against oppression. Acts were passed against engrossing, especially salt; and the Selectmen were authorized to seize stocks and distribute them among the people at the price set by law.[4]

December 4, the Governor of Connecticut wrote to the

[1] Hinman, 83.   [2] Ibid. 349.
[3] Ibid. 228.   [4] Ibid. 232, 244.

Governor of Rhode Island that Connecticut declined to attend the proposed price Convention, because Congress had the subject under consideration, and Connecticut feared that the step would occasion jealousy and endanger union.[1] However, delegates were afterward appointed.[2]

The first price Convention was convened at Providence, December 25, 1776, and sat until January 2, 1777. It was formed of delegates from the four New England States. Its conclusions were transmitted to Congress, and by them sent out to the different States. The high prices were attributed to avarice. Fatal consequences were apprehended from the extravagant price of labour, which made soldiers discontented with their pay. Hence a price tariff was adopted for New England.[3] The price of farm-labour was put at three shillings and fourpence per day in summer, and the rest of the year to correspond. In the Massachusetts Act, the wages were set at three shillings and found, as usual.[4] There was great complaint at this time that the high gains of privateering raised wages and made recruiting impossible.[5]

The Providence Convention complained that imported goods were sold at an advance of five or six times the prime cost, and were retailed at a further advance of forty or fifty per cent. They set prices for imported goods. Textile fabrics were not to be sold for more than 275 for that which cost 100 in Europe ; other goods at not more than 250 for 100, except munitions of war, and the retail advance was not to exceed twenty per cent. It was left to the States to fix the price of wood, hay, lumber, leather, cotton, linens, meat, and flour, and rates for carting.

This price Convention also recommended that no further

[1] Hinman, 70.
[2] Ibid 260.
[3] R. I. Col. Rec. viii. 85.
[4] N. Y Journ. ii 327, 371.
[5] See page 133.

emissions of paper money be made; that taxes be laid, and that if in an exigency bills must be issued, they bear interest at four per cent, and be redeemable in not more than three years.[1] It will be noticed that the price Conventions repeated this recommendation. It may be believed that the people would have submitted to taxation much earlier, and much more willingly, if their leaders had had more moral and political courage.

Congress approved the measures proposed by the Providence Convention, except a recommendation to strike bills bearing interest, which, they thought, would depreciate all other currency. The other States were recommended to adopt measures for regulating wages and prices, and it was proposed that similar conventions should be held of the Middle States at Yorktown, Pennsylvania, and of the Southern States at Charleston. All were recommended to restrict their paper issues.[2]

Rhode Island took up the propositions of the price Convention with great zeal. The penalty of demanding more than the tariff price was set at the value of the article, — half to the State, and half to the informer. Any one who refused for his commodities the tariff price, and afterward sold them for any other goods, was to forfeit the value thereof, half to the State and half to the informer. If complaint was made that articles necessary for the army or navy were withheld by monopolizers, the State officers and Judges or any two Justices of the Peace might issue a warrant to impress and seize the same, breaking open buildings. The goods were to be appraised by two indifferent men at prices not to exceed those of the tariff. Anybody who contracted to receive for labour or goods more than the tariff rates was to be counted an enemy of his country, and fined twenty shillings for every article sold of the price

[1] R. I. Col. Rec. viii. 97.   [2] Journ. Cong. iii. 50.

of twenty shillings or under, and a sum equal to the value of the article, if it was worth more than that.[1]

The effect of the commercial war, as we shall see in Chapter V., was to prevent the importation of those supplies which were indispensable for an armed resistance to Great Britain. A merchant speculated on the probability of war. If he thought that it would ensue, he made large importations. Then, when it was found necessary to go to war, and the commercial war had to be dropped, the only stocks in the country were those which these merchants had brought in; but when they sought that profit which was their legitimate reward for a foresight which no one else had exercised, and without which the country would have been still more destitute, they were abused as engrossers and forestallers, and measures were taken to rob them.

The price Convention also recommended that additional bounties should be given to stimulate recruiting, and that the pay and allowances of the New England militia and the continental army should be equalized.[2]

In February, 1777, another Act against monopolies was passed in Rhode Island, a committee being appointed in each seaport town to determine whether European goods were sold according to the price tariff limitation. In March it was found necessary to explain the price tariff, and it was amended as to wages and some of the prices. It was also enacted that if some people were in want, while others had a superfluity, Justices of the Peace might order constables to break open the buildings of the latter and supply the former at lawful prices.[3] In May, another Act against monopoly was passed. In June all the restrictions on the price of salt were repealed; and it appears that in many towns no committees had been appointed to enforce the price law.[4]

[1] R. I. Col. Rec. viii 90.
[2] Ibid. 103, 105.
[3] Ibid. 124, 174, 183.
[4] Ibid. 262, 271.

In August the Acts to prevent monopoly and engrossing were repealed.¹

In January, 1777, Connecticut passed an Act against monopoly and oppression, according to the recommendation of the Providence Convention. It was also forbidden to distil spirituous liquor from grain, under penalty of forfeiting four times the value of the grain.² At the May session, it was found necessary to pass another Act, extending and amending the Act against monopoly, and in August both Acts were repealed; so that the course in Connecticut was very closely parallel with that in Rhode Island.³

In May, 1777, it was enacted in Connecticut that no bills should be current in that State except those emitted by Connecticut or by the United States, under a penalty of not more than £50 and not less than £2.⁴

In August it was reported to the Connecticut Assembly that a pamphlet was in the press at Hartford, called " A Discourse upon Extortion," which reflected on the government, and would endanger the public peace. The sheriff was ordered to seize it.⁵

In October, 1777, the Connecticut Assembly passed an Act to punish sharpers and oppressors. After the 12th of November no person should purchase except in small quantities a long list of enumerated articles, covering all the necessaries of life, unless he had a license from the Selectmen, which license should be granted only to men of good character and friends of independence. If any person so licensed should charge unreasonable prices, or refuse to sell for bills of credit, he should forfeit his license. A person applying for a license to sell articles which he had engrossed must make a list of them, and no Commissary should purchase for the army until he produced his

---

¹ R. I. Col. Rec. viii. 289.   ² Hinman, 253.
³ Ibid. 269, 284.   ⁴ Ibid. 269.   ⁵ Ibid. 287.

authority from the Governor or an Assistant. Any person who should purchase without this authority should forfeit three times the value of the article and be liable to imprisonment not more than six months.[1]

Agreeably to the recommendation of Congress, Commissioners from New York, New Jersey, Pennsylvania, Delaware, Maryland, and Virginia met at Yorktown, Pennsylvania, in March, 1777. A committee prepared a preamble and resolutions. In the preamble it is stated that disaffected persons have monopolized the necessaries of life in order to raise prices, thereby distressing the army and discouraging the struggle for liberty. The States were therefore recommended to fix prices and enforce the sale of necessaries. An engrosser or monopolizer was defined, at least negatively. He is *not* one who keeps an open shop for retail trade, and takes gold, silver, and paper without distinction. This report was recommitted, and in the second revision of it it was asserted that the great quantity of paper currency which had been brought into circulation for the purpose of supporting the war had produced the result that the medium greatly exceeded the quantity of transferable property. Hence it had decreased in value to those who wanted it only for the purchase of necessaries. The non-importation agreement and the war risk had made imported commodities scarce and dear. The inimical persons had refused to take the paper currencies, and had bought gold and silver at high rates. A resolution is therefore proposed that the legislatures be recommended to tax so as to withdraw the paper money. This resolution was promptly disagreed to. A maximum price tariff was then proposed for such things as were needed for the army and navy, and the legislatures were recommended to rate other things by proportion to these, and manufactured goods in the same

[1] Hinman, 289.

proportion to present wages which they bore to wages before the war. It was also recommended that the legislatures should forbid sales at public auction, except for goods condemned in the admiralty court, or taken by process of other courts, and then that no large lot should be sold; also that commerce with foreign parts should be encouraged by premiums, except in the case of luxuries, the importation of which should be discouraged. The delegates from Pennsylvania, Delaware, and Maryland voted to reject this report; those from New York, New Jersey, and Virginia voted to adopt it. The reason of the opponents was that they, "conceiving that such regulations will be productive of the most fatal consequences to these States, are for adopting measures which, in their opinion, will in their operation tend to counteract the causes which have occasioned the evils so justly complained of." Being thus unable to agree, the Convention resolved to send certified copies of their proceedings to Congress and the constituent States.[1]

July 30, 1777, a Convention was held at Springfield, Massachusetts, of delegates from the four New England States and New York. The President, Stephen Hopkins, reporting its proceedings to the President of Congress, said that the four New England States in the previous winter passed acts to prevent monopoly and oppression, and to support the paper currency; "but the other United States, not judging it expedient to enact similar laws, hath in a great measure prevented their answering the good purposes for which they were intended, and has rendered it very difficult, if not impracticable, fully to execute the same." The Convention were impressed with the importance of redeeming the bills issued by the States, and with the necessity of large and frequent taxation, which they

[1] N. J. Corr. 34.

have recommended to the States. The whole United States should adopt the same measures.¹ This Convention showed some reaction against the policy of price regulation. In June, John Eliot wrote from Boston: "We are all starving here, since this plaguy addition to the regulating bill. People will not bring in provision, and we cannot procure the common necessaries of life. What we shall do I know not."²

The President of the Massachusetts Council wrote to the Governor of Rhode Island, July 2, 1777, that the laws to regulate prices had not succeeded.³

At the beginning of 1777 Congress also made enactments to try to give forced circulation to the continental paper. In order to resist the pernicious artifices of the enemies of American liberty, who try to impair the credit of bills by raising the value of gold and silver, *Resolved*, That said bills ought to be equal to Spanish dollars, and whoever shall ask, offer, or receive more in said bills for gold, silver, houses, or goods than of any other kind of money, or shall refuse to receive such bills for goods, ought to be deemed an enemy and forfeit the value of the money, or goods, or house and lands; and the States are recommended to enact laws to this effect. Also to make the bills legal tender, extinguishing the debts when they are refused. The debts payable in sterling money ought to be discharged with continental dollars at four shillings and sixpence per dollar. The States are also recommended to draw in and sink their quotas, and to raise by taxes such sums of money as they think will be most proper in the present situation of the inhabitants, and to remit to the continental treasury.⁴

[1] Hinman, 589.
[2] Belknap Papers, 124.
[3] R. I Col. Rec. viii. 280.
[4] Journ. Cong. iii. 16.

John Adams declared that he did not believe in the proposed remedies for depreciation. The only way to do was to stop the emissions and lay taxes.¹

Evidently the effects of the commercial war and of depreciation on prices are confused with each other; but that there was true depreciation from the summer of 1776 seems to be beyond doubt.

R. H. Lee, upon the depreciation of the currency, converted his rents into rents in kind. This raised a storm against him. He was charged with being a Tory, with refusing the State money, and with favouring New England. In 1777 he was left out of the delegation to Congress.² In January a letter which Colonel Philemon Dickinson received from his brother was submitted to the Council of Safety of Pennsylvania, on account of a passage which read: "Receive no more continental money on your bonds and mortgages. The British troops having conquered the Jerseys, and your being in camp, are sufficient reasons. Be sure you remember this. It will be better for you."³

The legislation against monopolizers and refusers of the continental currency was, at least in some of the States, no dead letter. The Committee of Safety of New Jersey proceeded very energetically in this line. January 26, 1777, a person was before them for speaking contemptuously of the law to regulate prices. He was forced to give bonds to appear when wanted. Another, who had charged more in paper than in specie, was given two days to repay to the buyer the surplus exacted and produce a receipt for the same.⁴ In October a man was sum-

---

¹ Adams's Letters to his Wife, i. 183. For his doctrine of depreciation, see below.
² Lee's R. H. Lee, i. 192. ³ Penn. Col. Rec. xi. 92.
⁴ N. J. Cong., etc. 196.

moned for selling salt for more in continental paper than in specie. He was fined £6 and the costs of sending for him. He refused to take the oath, and was imprisoned until he could find bail to appear for trial.[1] In January, 1778, the Council of Safety voted that the Governor should advise magistrates to enforce strictly a State act for the regulation of prices, which had been passed December 11, 1777. Very many cases follow during that winter and spring in which the law was rigorously enforced.[2] One who sold shoes above the tariff was fined £6 and the price at which he sold the shoes; namely, $4.50. Another was fined £6 for each of two offences; namely, selling flour above the tariff, and discriminating between continental and specie. Another, who had sold a number of different articles, was fined the value of each, and £6 penalty on each, making in all £69 7s. 6d. Another, who seems to have been an innkeeper, was fined the penalty of £6 for each item in his bill, making a total fine of £37 2s. 6d. Those who could not pay were sent to jail.

October 13, 1777, the Pennsylvania Assembly reconstituted the Council of Safety so that it consisted of the Executive Council of the State, with some additional persons. This council entered on its business by issuing a proclamation against forestallers and engrossers. All persons were exhorted not to sell to such, but to sell to the army.[3] November 7, they passed an ordinance that any one who engrossed iron, leather, salt, wheat, cattle, or other merchandise or food, should forfeit the same; for the second offence, should be imprisoned three months, besides the forfeit; for the third offence, the same as for the other two, and the pillory besides. It was explained

[1] N. J. Cong., etc. 147. [2] Ibid. 195-257.
[3] Penn. Col. Rec. xi. 325.

that this did not apply to those who manufactured or improved the goods before selling again.[1] At the same time they set the price of whiskey at eight shillings sixpence per gallon, to discourage the manufacture of it, because it raised the price of corn.

In October, 1777, Connecticut instructed her delegates in Congress to propose that Congress should recommend each State to draw in and sink the outstanding bills of credit emitted by them, except for fractions of a dollar, and to tax themselves amounts to be apportioned to each State by Congress, sufficient to pay the current annual expenses of the war, and to pay part of the continental bills; also that Congress should apportion the whole issue of continental bills between the States, recommending to each to provide funds for sinking the same within a reasonable time.[2]

November 22, 1777, Congress, encouraged perhaps by this proposition, resolved that the depreciation was due to the excessive quantity of the paper, together with " the arts of our open and secret enemies, the shameful avidity of too many of our professed friends, and the scarcity of foreign commodities. The consequences to be apprehended are equally obvious and alarming. They tend to the depravity of morals, the decay of public virtue, a precarious supply for the war, debasement of the public faith, injustice to individuals, and the destruction of the honour, safety, and independence of the United States. Loudly, therefore, are we called on to provide a seasonable and effectual remedy." They evidently regarded depreciation as an evil which had independent and extraneous causes, and not as flowing by direct consequence from the issues themselves. They "earnestly recommended" taxation, and apportioned five million dollars between the States. Then they urged

[1] Penn. Col. Rec. xi. 337.   [2] Hinman, 291.

the States to make no more State issues, and to retire by taxes those already out. They declared their confidence and hope in the loan offices, and recommended that three conventions should be held, — one at New Haven, one at Fredericksburg, Virginia, and one at Charleston, — to ascertain and regulate prices.[1]

December 3, Congress, reciting that the tories had agreed to support the credit of the paper money which was struck under the authority of the King, in order to hurt the continental money, urged all the States to compel the former kind of money to be brought in and exchanged for continental paper or the later paper issues.[2]

January 15, 1778, the Price Convention met at New Haven. Instead of following the policy recommended at Springfield in the previous year, this Convention regarded itself as called to set prices, and it prepared a complete tariff.[3] Thomas Cushing, President of the Convention, transmitted its proceedings to Congress.[4]

In February, 1778, the Assembly of Connecticut enacted a tariff of wages and prices, according to the recommendation of the New Haven Convention. Wages were not to be over seventy-five per cent higher than in 1774, and the prices were generally put, for domestic products, at about seventy-five per cent advance on those of 1774. Foreign merchandise imported by capture or otherwise was to be sold at not more than one dollar continental currency for each shilling prime cost in Europe. All vendors of imported articles were held liable to produce an authentic invoice of prime cost. Retail prices were not to exceed wholesale prices by more than twenty-five per cent, and the cost of land carriage. The Selectmen in the towns were to make rates for articles not mentioned in the tariff. Any one who

[1] Journ. Cong. iii. 415.
[3] New Haven Hist. Soc. Coll. iii. 39.
[2] Ibid. iii. 431.
[4] Journ. Cong iv. 73.

should charge more than the tariff rates was to forfeit for each article the value of which did not exceed forty shillings, a penalty of forty shillings; and for each article of greater value, a penalty equal to the value. No person could begin a suit in law or equity until he should have taken an oath that he had not charged or taken more than the rate established by this law for wages and prices; but if he had done so, he might purge himself by confessing and paying double the surplus. Proof of probable guilt was made sufficient to convict, unless the accused should make oath that he was not guilty.[1]

In 1778 and 1779 the chief interest of Rhode Island in the price Conventions was to induce the other New England States to provide quotas of militia to help to defend Rhode Island. The help which was promised was never given.

On the report of the delegates to the New Haven Convention, in February, 1778, a committee was appointed in Rhode Island to draft a bill embodying its recommendations; but no action was taken. The Governor of Connecticut wrote in May, expressing his regret at this, because the laws recommended by that Convention were the only means of stopping depreciation until taxation could be employed. The Governor of Rhode Island replied that the relations of Rhode Island with Massachusetts were such that it could only act in concurrence with that State.[2]

In June the Governor of Connecticut wrote to the President of Congress that the recommendations of this Convention had been ineffectual. Rhode Island, Massachusetts, and New Hampshire had not complied with the recommendations.[3]

In March following, James Lovell, for the Committee

[1] Hinman, 306.   [2] Ibid. 361, 423, 425.   [3] Phillips, ii. 243.

of Foreign Affairs, wrote to the Commissioners at Paris: "The manners of the Continent are too much affected by the depreciation of our currency. Scarce an officer, civil or military, but feels something of a desire to be concerned in mercantile speculation, from finding that his salary is inadequate to the harpy demands which are made upon him for the necessaries of life, and from observing that but little skill is necessary to constitute one of the merchants of these days." [1]

The complaints against General Greene as quartermaster show that he was largely a victim of depreciation.[2]

In May the Pennsylvania Assembly passed a law suspending for a time the act regulating prices.[3] The suspension was to last until the next meeting of the Assembly.

In the instructions that were given to Franklin, as sole minister to France, in October, 1778, there was included an elaborate disquisition on the condition of the finances. It is there said that the necessaries of life were cheap at the beginning of the war, compared with other articles which rose more rapidly [obviously the effect of the non-importation, which did not act upon the food products raised at home, but on the manufactured articles which were imported]. This discouraged industry; but the husbandmen being often called to arms, the means of subsistence became dearer. The tender laws produced monopoly. The several States, instead of laying taxes, issued paper money in great variety, in addition to that issued by Congress. This variety made counterfeiting especially easy, of which the enemy took advantage. The paper cannot be reduced by taxation while the war lasts, because the emission must continue to supply what is

[1] Dip. Corr. Rev. i. 375.   [2] Reed's Reed, ii. 241.
[3] Minutes House Rep. i. 211.

necessary over and above the taxes. The military operations also interfere, and the government is weak, lacking method and firmness. Neither is it possible to borrow, because the depreciation would make the principal and interest worth less a year hence than the principal is now. Loans in Europe are the only plan for reducing the paper; but America cannot give security, and she cannot expect subsidies from allies who are themselves engaged in war.[1]

December 16, Congress voted that it was necessary to take out of circulation the emissions of May 20, 1777, and April 11, 1778.[2] This was much more easily voted than done. It produced very great inconvenience. In the following April the Council of Pennsylvania appointed commissioners of exchange in each county to exchange the notes of these emissions for others, on account of the great inconvenience to the people who lived at a distance from the centres of commerce.[3]

It appears that even public officers found it difficult to distinguish counterfeits.[4]

We find ample evidence that the bills of credit were counterfeited in large numbers. In May, 1776, a party of counterfeiters were arrested in Queen's County, Long Island. They were counterfeiting Connecticut and continental bills.[5] The standing penalty for counterfeiting bills of credit was death; but it seems to have been very rarely, if ever, inflicted. In Pennsylvania, however, it was held that the law setting the penalty of death upon the crime of counterfeiting continental notes applied only to those emitted before the Act was passed.[6]

The Pennsylvania Act was passed by the Convention,

---

[1] Secret Journ. ii. 119.
[2] Journ. Cong. iv. 513.
[3] Penn. Col. Rec. xi. 736.
[4] Phillips, ii. 227.
[5] N. Y. Journ. i. 443, 461.
[6] Penn. Packet, Nov. 17, 1779.

August 1, 1776. Any one who should counterfeit the paper currency of Congress or of any State was to suffer death. The informer was to have £50 from the estate of the counterfeiter, if he had any; if not, £20 from the treasury of the State. Any one who uttered counterfeit money was to stand in the pillory, have his or her ears cut off and nailed to the pillory, and receive thirty-one lashes on his or her bare back " well laid on," besides making good any damages to the person to whom the counterfeits were given. If there was no property out of which the damages could be paid, the culprit was to be sold to service for not more than seven years.[1]

The counterfeiters in New York were imprisoned, and for a while lay in irons, but later escaped from jail and disappeared. In June three continental soldiers were arrested at New York for passing counterfeit continental bills, of which the back was genuine and the face counterfeit.[2] In 1777 counterfeiters were arrested in Pennsylvania who were operating both on State and continental bills. They had bills in their possession for $4 on one side and $30 on the other.[3] We have not been able to find that any counterfeiter suffered as much as the tories, especially if the latter were persons of position and property.

In June, 1780, Congress offered a reward of $2,000 in old continental to any one who would prosecute to conviction a counterfeiter or utterer of counterfeits, and several persons won the reward.[4]

In December, 1778, Marshall, who was a very stern whig, had reached the point where he made a contract for pork in hard money. He did it continental fashion, however, for he borrowed two silver dollars of the butcher and gave

[1] Penn. Journ. i. 60.
[2] N. Y. Journ. i. 495.
[3] Penn. Col. Rec. xi. 234.
[4] Phillips, ii. 229.

them back to him for earnest money.[1] In that month the Council of Pennsylvania appointed two committees — one to investigate north of Market Street, Philadelphia, and the other south, — whether there was any engrossing. Nothing came of it.[2] This measure, however, led Washington to express to Reed his pleasure that the Assembly was going to bring to punishment the monopolizers, forestallers, and engrossers; "those murderers of our cause."[3]

The amount of continental currency issued in 1775 was six million dollars; in 1776, nineteen million dollars; in 1777, thirteen million dollars; in 1778, sixty-three million dollars.[4]

October 2, 1778, Congress recommended the States to pass laws for the seizure and forfeiture of all grain and flour purchased up or engrossed, with such exceptions and under such limitations and restrictions as they should think most expedient.[5] December 29, citing a report in circulation that Congress would never redeem the bills, but would suffer them to sink in the hands of the holders, they resolved, "That the said report is false and derogatory to the honour of Congress."[6] January 13, 1779, they adopted a circular letter to the States which had been prepared by the Board of Treasury. They seem to accept the quantity doctrine of value for currency, for they say that "the paper currency multiplied beyond what was competent for the purposes of a circulating medium." They affirm that it will not be difficult to raise the value of the paper, "it being evident that our ability to sustain a tax must increase in proportion to the quantity of money in circulation."[7]

In April, according to the admitted scale of deprecia-

---

[1] Marshall's Diary, 206.
[2] Penn. Col. Rec. xi. 640, 687.
[3] Reed's Reed, ii. 41.
[4] Nourse.
[5] Journ. Cong. iv. 414.
[6] Ibid. 533.
[7] Ibid. v. 16.

tion, a paper dollar was worth five cents. In May, Congress issued an Address to the inhabitants of the United States. Depreciation, they said, was partly " owing to the artifices of men who have hastened to enrich themselves by monopolizing the necessaries of life, and to the misconduct of inferior officers employed in the public service." [1]

In many respects the year 1779 marked the lowest ebb in politics and morals, as well as in finance, which was reached during the war. Congress was split up by factions and cabals.[2] It seemed to have adopted, in respect to the currency, the recklessness of a hopeless bankrupt. The public had also fallen under the wretched delusions of a period of inflation, and seemed to be rendered savage whenever these delusions were exposed. Innumerable efforts, some of them of a very extravagant character, were made, to try to deal with the miseries of the situation, and all sorts of suggestions were made in the effort to account for the troubles or to provide remedies for them.

There was a quite widespread belief, at the end of 1778, that the British were about to withdraw, and that there would be no campaign in 1779.[3] This may account, in part, for the recklessness of the continental issues in 1779. Joseph Reed, in fact, in 1780 expressed this opinion. He said that Congress expected peace. "And a few landed men, apprehensive of the taxes on their estates, poured out the public money with such profusion as to force the public bankruptcy, while they frustrated every measure for restoring public credit, either by a foreign loan, or a vigorous internal exertion."[4]

In April, 1779, an Act was passed by the Pennsylvania Assembly that Justices of the Peace might authorize the

---

[1] Journ. Cong. v. 171.   [2] See pages 210, 218.
[3] Leake's Lamb, 216, 219; Va. Papers, i 311.
[4] Reed's Reed, ii. 249; to Washington.

seizure of provisions, if informed that any person held more than he would need for his personal use before the next August. The committees to execute the seizure were to be appointed by the Justices. Any person who needed supplies might apply, within forty days, for a part of what had been seized. If it was not thus called for within that time, the Commissary might take it for the military service. Property thus seized was to be appraised by the Committee at the rate then current in the neighbourhood. If the owner refused the money offered in payment, it was to be deposited with the Justice of the Peace, and this was to discharge the buyer from liability.[1]

In May a handbill was posted on the coffee-house at Philadelphia, with the signature " Terra Firma," in which it was declared that the militia would bring before the civil magistrates those who raised prices.[2]

This threat of a popular movement caused the authorities of Pennsylvania to present a memorial to Congress, proposing joint action to deal with the difficulty in anticipation of such popular action. This called out another "Address" to the public by Congress. It contained new exhortations to pay taxes; but the only part of it which won attention was unfortunately that in which Congress fell in with the popular delusion of the moment, that depreciation was due to monopolizers and extortioners.

May 25, a great mass-meeting was held at which it was resolved to appoint a committee to fix a tariff of prices, and to take steps to carry the same into execution, "throughout the United States."[3] This is the same meeting at which the Committee was appointed to investigate the proceedings of Robert Morris.[4] June 1, the

[1] Penn. Packet, April 20, 1779.
[2] Smith's Hist. Curios., Series 2, Plate xii.
[3] Penn. Packet, May 27, 1779.   [4] See page 228.

Committee appointed at that meeting advertised that they had set prices as of May 1, and were investigating to find out what the prices were on April 1, in order to introduce those on July 1. They would also investigate the rent of houses. In the "Packet" of June 29 they published their tariff for July. They also published an Address to the citizens of the United States about the currency. They want a comprehensive policy adopted for fixing prices. In the same paper is a copy of a broadside published at Boston, June 16, against monopolizers and extortioners, who are reducing the currency to waste paper by refusing to take it for their commodities. They are called upon to lower their prices, and the people of Nantucket are especially denounced because they "first introduced the accursed crime of refusing paper money." This Boston movement, according to a reference in the handbill, was stimulated by the Philadelphia movement of May. The Philadelphia Committee hold up the Boston movement to imitation, and exhort the people of Philadelphia to put down monopoly.

The artillery company at Philadelphia passed resolutions that if the Committee needed support, they would give it with their arms.[1] In August a plan was formed, in connection with this same movement, and submitted to the Executive Council, that subscriptions should be sought by a canvass of the wards of the city of Philadelphia, which subscriptions should act as a prepayment of taxes and prevent further emissions of paper money.[2] This was only one of numerous schemes for dealing with depreciation which appear in the "Packet" during that summer.

July 15, the cordwainers and curriers of Philadelphia published an address to their fellow-citizens, complaining

[1] Penn. Packet, July 1.
[2] Packet, July 10, Penn. Archives, vii. 621.

that the Committee had fixed the prices of their products, and not of those of others, or had set the prices of their products disproportionately low. They argue that the Committee, by their tariff, hinder goods from being brought to market. A Whig shoemaker in the same paper denounces this protest, however, as a tory move. July 20, the cordwainers and curriers return to the attack. They say that it is one thing to raise the credit of a currency, and another to fix prices, and that the Committee have mistaken one for the other. July 29 the Committee of Newcastle County, Delaware, adopted a tariff of prices.

In September a committee of a Philadelphia town meeting prepared a memorial to Congress asking them to make no further emissions.[1]

In August Washington wrote to his agent not to accept any more paper on contracts made before the war. He had made and would make any sacrifices for the cause, but did not feel called upon to take a shilling in the pound on his credits, and was sure that no honest man would try to pay in that way.[2]

June 24, a great mass-meeting to deal with the same subject was held at Boston. The merchants joined in resolutions to sell goods at prices that were named, and resolved that they would not buy and sell gold or silver, or buy and sell goods for hard money. They submitted these resolutions to the town-meeting. The depreciation was charged to hawkers and monopolizers, who pretended to be merchants. It was resolved that high prices were a grievance, into which a free people had a right to enquire. A committee was appointed, to whom complaints against monopolizers were to be submitted.[3]

A Convention was held at Concord, Massachusetts, July

---

[1] Penn. Packet, September 18.   [2] Washington, vi. 321.
[3] Penn. Packet, July 13, 1779.

17, at which "a large number of delegates" were present. Azor Orne was President, and Samuel Ruggles, Secretary. The object was to find out the cause of high prices. They adopted a tariff, and resolved that any one who charged more should be deemed an enemy of his country. The towns were to establish rates for labour, transportation, mechanical work, etc., and were to prevent buying and selling silver, or demanding specie for goods. It was recommended to the people to lend to the government of the State all the money they could spare, and to pay taxes promptly. It was voted that another Convention should be held in October. In the address which they adopted, they denounced the tories, as well as the jobbers, harpies, and forestallers.[1]

A price Convention of the State of Rhode Island assembled at East Greenwich August 10. There were full delegations from all the towns. They adopted resolutions following closely those of the Concord Convention, and called another Convention to meet in November.[2]

The adjourned Convention met at Concord October 6; and on the 19th a meeting was held at Faneuil Hall, Boston, presided over by Samuel Adams, which adopted and approved its action. It was to the same effect as before.[3]

There was great scarcity in Boston in 1779. In March we find it stated: "The miseries of famine are now mingled with the horrors of war. The poor people in the almshouse have been destitute of grain and other necessaries these many days. Many reputable families are almost starving." In October the same writer said: "We are likely to be starved throughout Boston. Never such a scarcity of provision."[4]

October 20, a Convention of the New England States

[1] Penn. Packet, August 12, 1779.
[2] Ibid September 2, 1779.
[3] Ibid. October 30 and November 2.
[4] Belknap Papers, 139, 152.

and New York was held at Hartford. It was an adjournment of the Convention at New Haven in 1778. Massachusetts now instructed her delegates "to agree on a mode of internal trade and commerce in consistency with the general welfare." "It was impossible for the Eastern States to continue their regulations without the co-operation of those to the southward." She proposed a larger meeting, to win a larger constituency for common action, in the hope of accomplishing the result.[1]

It is evident that these conventions were, on the one hand, an attempt to introduce the element of social organization which was such a great need of the time, and on the other hand, that they were pursuing the chimera of a combination wide enough and close enough to realize impossible aims in opposition to fact and right. At the same time that this Massachusetts recommendation reached New York from the east, the legislature of New Jersey made a proposition to New York for a limitation of wages and prices.[2] New York referred the matter to Congress. November 19, Congress, acting upon these suggestions from the Eastern States, passed a set of resolutions. The estimates had been made on a basis of twenty-fold prices, and must be raised if prices rise. The States were recommended to pass laws fixing prices, both for domestic produce, wages, and transportation, not to exceed twenty-fold the prices of 1774, and for imported articles in proportion, excepting salt and military stores. The acts of the Hartford Convention were approved, and the States were recommended to pass laws against engrossing and withholding. A resolution that the legal tender laws should be revised in such a way as to prevent injustice was postponed.[3]

Pennsylvania had already acted in this direction. Octo-

[1] Penn. Packet, November 18.   [2] N. J. Corr. 195.
[3] Journ. Cong. v. 317.

ber 8, an Act was passed to prevent engrossing and forestalling. Forestalling was defined in the old mediæval sense, of buying goods before they were brought into the general market. The penalty for this was to be a fine of a thousand pounds, or imprisonment for not more than a year. Engrossing they defined in the sense of the old regrating; that is, buying to sell again in the same market, without change. The penalty for this was to be the forfeit of the articles, and the same penalty as for the former offence. Retail profit was not to exceed twenty-five per cent. No one except the first importer or producer was to be allowed to expose goods for sale without obtaining a permit; and before a permit could be obtained, oath must be taken to comply with this act. The penalty for violation of this was double the value of the goods. Justices of the Peace might give warrants for the seizure of engrossed goods for the army. Protection was extended against prosecution for any acts done in obedience to this Act. Commissioners of trade were appointed in the counties. Special provisions were added about merchants and millers.[1] An Act was also passed, which had long been pending, prohibiting the manufacture of whiskey from grain, lest grain might thus be made dearer.[2] November 26, an Act was passed to prevent sales at auction, because they raised prices, and to prevent male persons capable of bearing arms from peddling.[3] That peddling and sales at auction raised prices, were among the generally current notions at the time.

A Boston minister wrote in October: "I doubt whether Egypt during the seven years of famine was in greater distress than this unhappy town. We can procure nothing

---

[1] Penn. Packet, October 12, 1779.
[2] Ibid. October 30; cf. also May 8.
[3] Ibid. December 4.

for money. Barter is the only method of commerce which now prevails. You will therefore readily believe that the circumstances of such as have neither salt, sugar, etc., beggar all description." [1]

The record furnishes some illustrations of the injustice, loss, and inconvenience which were produced.

In April, 1779, a young lady wrote to the "Packet," stating that her trustee had taken advantage of the depreciation of paper money to pay to her the principal of her inheritance on her coming of age, in that currency. He had held the property for six years, and now proposed to pay her the same number of dollars which had been entrusted to him.[2] In June a man wrote that he had bought a hogshead of sugar and sold it at a large profit, but the currency which he obtained for it would buy only a tierce. He sold the tierce at a profit, but the currency would buy only a barrel.[3] In a letter of Timothy Pickering of December 13, it is stated that the price of a pair of shoes is a hundred dollars. Flour is from £90 to £100 per hundred weight; beef, 22 shillings 6 pence per pound; salt, 75 cents per bushel; rum, £25 per gallon; sugar, £150 to £200 per hundred weight.[4] In May R. H. Lee wrote to Jefferson that the depreciation of the paper currency had nearly transferred his entire estate to his tenants. The rents of 4,000 acres would not pay for twenty barrels of corn. When a tenant agreed to give £6 for a hundred acres, he could not sell his tobacco for more than 16 or 18 shillings a hundred; now he sells it for £10 or £12. Lee favours a conversion of money rent into produce rent.[5]

Two foreigners — one French, the other English — expressed opinions about depreciation as follows. Chastel-

---

[1] Pickering's Pickering, i. 242.   [2] Penn. Packet, April 17.
[3] Ibid. June 5.   [4] Pickering's Pickering, i. 245.
[5] Lee's R. H. Lee, ii. 45.

lux says: "This depreciation of the paper is not felt in those places where it remains the same; but Philadelphia is, so to speak, the great sink wherein all the speculations of America terminate and are confounded together. . . . Two classes of men, Quakers and tories, equally dangerous, one from their timidity and the other from their bad intentions, are incessantly labouring to secure their fortunes. They lavish the paper for a little gold or silver to enable them to remove wherever they may think themselves in safety. From these reasons, the paper money is more and more decried, not only because it is too common, but because gold and silver are extremely scarce, and difficult to be obtained."[1] The translator adds: "The variety of the depreciation at different periods and in different parts of the continent, whilst it gave rise to great temporary abuses, had been so divided and balanced by alternate profit and loss amongst all classes of citizens that, on casting up the account, some very unfortunate cases excepted, it seems to have operated only as a general tax on the public; and the universal joy on its annihilation, with the satisfactory reflection on the necessity under which it was issued in the critical moment of danger, seemed to conciliate all minds to a total oblivion of its partial mischiefs. Here and there great fortunes are to be seen reared upon its now visionary basis, and families reduced from opulence to mediocrity by means of this now destructive medium; but these instances are by no means so frequent as they have been represented in Europe, and were often the result of ill-judged but avaricious speculations."

In the summer[2] there appeared a series of papers on the currency in the "Penn. Packet" by "A Farmer of Virginia," which were probably written by R. H. Lee. There was an active discussion of the doctrines of currency. "Wal-

[1] Chastellux, i. 329.   [2] 1779.

singham" maintained that gold and silver were not true standards of value, because they were subject to monopoly. Land, he said, was the only true barometer of value.[1] In the same year, also, Franklin wrote about the paper, especially as a resource for carrying on the war: "This effect of paper currency is not understood on this side the water, and indeed the whole is a mystery, even to the politicians, how we have been able to continue a war four years without money, and how we could pay with paper that had no previously fixed fund [*i. e.* revenue] appropriated specifically to redeem it. This currency, as we manage it, is a wonderful machine. It performs its office when we issue it; it pays and clothes troops, and provides victuals and ammunition, and when we are obliged to issue a quantity excessive, it pays itself off by depreciation." He asserted that the depreciation acted as a tax according to the time that each man kept the money in his hands; hence that it taxed the richest most.[2]

At the beginning of 1780, however, an effect of paper currency had been realized which he neglected to mention. It had produced a social palsy. The effect of an excessive inflation of the currency is the same as having no currency at all; for the channels of circulation are entirely clogged, and all real money is held at a distance. A return to barter is therefore enforced. So much for commerce; but in respect to the State which issues the paper, there is no resource to be reached except by violent seizure, forced loans, and impressments. The national resources are therefore removed beyond the reach of the government, except by action which destroys the good will of the people. As to the notion that depreciation acts only as a kind of tax, because it is accomplished with a loss of a few cents on the dollar in the hands of each successive holder over a

---

[1] Penn. Packet, February 16, 1779.   [2] Franklin, viii. 328; ii. 421.

period of time, nothing could be more childish. The law reports of the last twenty years of the eighteenth century are full of cases to prove that the depreciation entered into and vitiated every pecuniary relation between man and man. The vice of it could not be eliminated. The courts could not do justice, because the depreciation introduced a fraud into the very essence of the case, and the agent of the fraud was almost always innocent, so far as his intention was concerned. If, therefore, the court undertook to release the victim of the fraud from all effect of the fraud, the injury was simply thrown back on the perpetrator, who, being innocent, suffered as much wrong as the victim would have suffered if nothing had been done. There were innumerable relations into which this vice entered, which were not contract relations, but arose unavoidably out of social relations, family relations, trusts, partnerships, and joint interests of long standing. Even when the relations were contract relations, it was impossible to draw the stipulations in such a way as to throw out the effect of depreciation. When the attempt was made to do this, the interpretation of those stipulations subsequently gave rise to interminable differences of opinion and contradictory decisions, especially in regard to the method of calculating depreciation, between different courts, arbitrators, etc. Ample proof of this may be found in the course of the present volume.

We have seen above,[1] that depreciation prevented the sale of loan-office certificates, because, before the interest became due, the depreciation would more than offset it. Who would become a lender on a depreciating currency? We shall also see[2] that depreciation forced the State to order that taxes be not paid until some measure to deal with it could be adopted, — which never was done,

[1] Page 68.   [2] Page 95.

because there is no such way. When the currency was depreciating, every day that a man could delay payment of his taxes was a gain of so much per cent. The tax collectors won by depreciation, because they could discharge their dues to the treasury with a fraction of what they had collected. Allegations that they had done this are constantly met with.

September 1, 1779, $160,000,000 of continental bills being out, Congress declared that they would on no account emit more than $200,000,000, and that they would not emit the other $40,000,000 if they could help it.[1] September 13, they issued a circular to the public. Depreciation, they say, is either artificial or natural. The artificial "is our case. The moment the sum in circulation exceeded what was necessary as a medium of commerce, it began and continued to depreciate in proportion as the amount of the surplus increased, and that proportion would hold good until the sum emitted should become so great as nearly to equal the value of the capital or stock on the credit of which the bills were issued." If, then, $30,000,000 was the specie requirement, and there were $150,000,000 out, the natural depreciation should be only as five to one. The excess of the actual depreciation, which was then over thirty for one, they declared to be artificial. This artificial depreciation, they said, arose from a doubt as to the ability or willingness of the United States to redeem the bills. That, however, depended on success in the war and the resources of the country. Assuming that the country should come out of the war with a debt of $300,000,000 on 3,000,000 people, or $100 per soul, they asked who doubted that the people could pay this in eighteen or twenty years, within which time, moreover, the population would greatly increase? They speak of the £3,000,000

[1] Journ. Cong. v. 253.

sterling per annum profits, which it was reckoned that the English had made out of the colonial trade, as an annual tax paid to Britain; but when America should become independent, the whole world would be open to her. "Let it also be remembered that paper money is the only kind of money which cannot 'make unto itself wings and fly away.' It remains with us; it will not forsake us. It is always ready and at hand for the purpose of commerce or taxes, and every industrious man can find it."[1]

In opposition to all these notions, Webster maintained that depreciation was the most inconvenient kind of tax. He wanted hard money received at the treasury at a ratio against paper which would stop the depreciation, and he wanted loan-office certificates to be paid off at the exchange between paper and specie which ruled at the date of their issue. On the other hand, he wanted to prevent an appreciation of the currency, which he saw would be a hopeless and disastrous undertaking.[2]

In the letter which Hamilton wrote, probably at the end of 1779, containing his first bank scheme, and addressed, as it is supposed, to Robert Morris, he says: "The object of principal concern is the state of our currency. In my opinion, all our speculations on this head have been founded in error. Most people think that the depreciation might have been avoided by provident arrangements in the beginning without any aid from abroad, and a great many of our sanguine politicians till very lately imagined the money might still be restored by expedients within ourselves. Hence the delay in attempting to procure a foreign loan." He ascribes the depreciation, or high prices, to the strain of the war, especially in respect to the number of labourers drawn off into the army. In fact, he

[1] Journ. Cong. v. 261.
[2] Webster's Essays, 29, 46.

contributes nothing of value to the discussion, but uses the facts as an argument in favour of a foreign loan.[1]

The amount of continental currency issued in 1779 was $140,000,000.

January 29, 1780, another price Convention met at Philadelphia, in consequence of a call issued by the one at Hartford in the previous October. The four New England States — New Jersey, Pennsylvania, Delaware, and Maryland — were represented. The absence of New York and Virginia prevented those present from taking any important action. They appointed a committee to regulate prices. The President of the Convention was directed to write to the Governor of Virginia and ask him to give the earliest notice of the determination of Virginia as to meeting the other States in Convention. The co-operation of New York was expected; but there had been no meeting of her Legislature since October, 1779. The Convention adjourned until February, and then until April. Then a further adjournment was taken until August. March 4, Virginia expressed the opinion, in regard to a proposition for taxation, that it would fall on the slave-owners.[2]

Under date March 29, 1780, we find a letter of John Eliot: "The town of Boston is really poor. If some brighter prospects do not open, it is my opinion that we cannot subsist. You are sensible how much depends upon our trade. Let this one instance of our going downward convince you. An outward-bound cargo cannot be purchased for the whole amount of the vessel and cargo returning safely to the wharf. . . . Most of the ready money which was in the town the country people have drained, such was the necessity of obtaining fuel at any price. One effect these things have upon all

---

[1] Hamilton's Works, iii. 61.   [2] Hamilton's Republic, ii. 81.

orders of men in the seaport, — a hearty wish for peace, which sentiment did not pervade the mobility till the present time. Did the country farmers *feel* like the Bostonian mechanic, I don't know what would be the consequence." He tells a story of one of the latter who wanted peace at any price.[1]

In March, 1780, an attempt was made to introduce an entirely new system of currency. In the old colonial currencies, at a certain stage, notes of a "new tenor" were generally introduced in order to try to begin again, without doing anything to get rid of the old notes. The present attempt was of that kind. The Act of March 18, 1780, thus became a point of new departure for certain purposes, although the new issue did not succeed, and the old paper kept on its course. According to this Act, the States were to bring in their quotas monthly, as heretofore provided, for twelve months, silver and gold being taken at the rate of one to forty. All bills which came in in this way were to be destroyed, and other bills were to be issued for not more than one twentieth of those destroyed, to be redeemable in specie within six years, and to bear interest at five per cent in specie, payable at the redemption of the bills, or, if the holder prefer, in sterling bills of exchange annually on the Commissioners in Europe at four and six pence to the dollar; which was promised on the faith of the United States, in case the States on whose funds they were emitted should, by the events of war, be rendered incapable of redeeming them. These notes read that the holder should be paid by the State of blank, according to an Act of the Legislature of such State, and they were indorsed with the guarantee of the United States. They were to be struck under the direction of the Board of Treasury for each State, in propor-

[1] Belknap Papers, 177.

tion to the monthly quota, and lodged in the loan offices in the respective States, and signed by Commissioners of Congress and of the State, in the proportion only of one to twenty of the old bills destroyed. As fast as they were signed the State was to have six tenths of them, and the remainder was to be at the disposition of the United States, but credited to the States on their requisitions. The States were to provide funds for their quotas of the new bills adequate to sink one sixth of them annually after the 1st of January, 1781.[1]

Pelatiah Webster thinks that this plan would not have been a bad one if it had been supported by taxes, but that the people had been so worried by the various attempts to give forced circulation to paper, and by all the heterogeneous schemes which had been put forward, that they were dull and unresponsive to new propositions.[2] On the 20th of March Congress recommended the States to revise their tender laws, and amend them "in such manner as they shall judge most conducive to justice, in the present state of the paper currency."[3]

In May, 1780, when this new paper was issued, there was at first great opposition and clamour against it among the merchants; "but Mr. Morris, having expressed himself in its favour, stemmed the tide, and it met with an uncommon approbation, or at least a trifling opposition."[4] The depreciation of the continental paper had not, however, been assumed in accordance with truth, and the notes issued under the Act of March 18 depreciated during the summer nearly one half.[5] "Congress expected that the new would regulate the old, but it goes the other way."[6]

[1] Journ. Cong. ix. 32.
[2] Webster, 116.
[3] Journ. Cong. vi. 34.
[4] Reed's Reed, ii. 200.
[5] Letters to Washington, iii. 157.
[6] N. J. Corr. 268.

By the Act of March 18, 1780, Congress abandoned all hope of ever paying the notes, and committed an act of bankruptcy. It was indeed inevitable; but it was a cruel blow to those who had maintained their faith in Congress, and had obeyed its often repeated behests with respect to the paper. As in all cases of currency abuse, it was the simple, honest, uninstructed people who suffered most. A man of small means, who found himself left with a bundle of worthless continental notes alone to represent his surplus in the world, was sure to feel very bitterly against all the authorities who had recommended it or forced it on him. He was earnestly in favour of more paper issues until he could pay his debts or buy goods with the paper which he possessed.

When this Act was known in France, it caused consternation among those who had engaged in transactions with America.

In June, 1780, Chaumont reported to Vergennes a conversation which he had had with John Adams about the depreciation of the American currency. Adams asserted that but for America there would have been no general alliance against England. Hence the obligation was from the European powers to America. The currency had been scaled down because the allies in Europe would not supply money to America. These notions astonished Chaumont, and also Vergennes.[1]

The latter addressed a letter to Adams, taking as his text a newspaper which the latter had sent to the Minister, containing information that the Assembly of Massachusetts had scaled the paper money down to forty for one, in compliance with a resolution of Congress. Vergennes protested against this, so far as it affected foreigners: "Americans alone ought to support the expense which

[1] Durand, 226.

is occasioned by the defence of their liberty. . . . They ought to consider the depreciation of their paper money only as an impost, which ought to fall on themselves, as the paper money was at first established only to relieve them from the necessity of paying taxes."[1]

Adams replied in a long letter, in which he undertook to elucidate the doctrine of money and the philosophy of depreciation. " A certain sum of money is necessary to circulate among the society, in order to carry on their business. This precise sum is discoverable by calculation, and reducible to certainty. You may emit paper or any other currency for this purpose until you reach this rule, and it will not depreciate. After you exceed this rule it will depreciate, and no power or act of legislation hitherto invented will prevent it. In the case of paper, if you go on emitting forever, the whole mass will be worth no more than that was which was emitted within the rule. When the paper therefore comes to be redeemed, this is the only rule of justice for the redemption of it. The Congress have fixed five millions for this rule." He says that those who have violated the public faith are those who have demanded more paper money for goods or labour than they were worth in silver. Congress, therefore, cannot pay two hundred millions of silver dollars to the present possessors of the bills. "The social compact being between the whole and every individual, and between every individual and the whole, every individual, native or foreign, who uses this paper, is as much bound by the public faith to use it according to the terms of its emission as the Congress is, and Congress have as good a right to reproach every individual who now demands more paper for his goods than silver, with a breach of the public faith, as he has to reproach the public or their representatives. . . .

[1] Dip. Corr. Rev. v. 210.

When Congress issued their bills, declaring them in effect to be equal to silver, they unquestionably intended that they should be so considered, and that they should be received accordingly. The people or individuals covenanted in effect to receive them at their nominal value, and the Congress in such case agreed on their part to redeem them at the same rate. . . . Upon the whole, as the depreciation crept in gradually and was unavoidable, all reproaches of a breach of public faith ought to be laid aside, and the only proper inquiry now is, What is paper honestly worth? what will it fetch at market? And this is the only just rule of redemption." He says that to make an exception as to foreigners would open the door to frauds. Very few bills are owned out of America. Then he quotes prices to show that people who carry goods to America have made big profits. He asserts that when twenty-five dollars in paper were given for one in silver, not more than twelve in paper were given for one in bills of exchange. Also that the depreciation was unequal at different places, and that an importer could make gains by selling his goods for paper in one place, and using the paper to buy with in another.[1]

June 26, 1780, Adams sent to the President of Congress an account of his controversy with Vergennes about the paper money. "I am determined to give my sentiments to His Majesty's ministers whenever they shall see cause to ask them, although it is not within my department, until I shall be forbidden by Congress; and to this end I shall go to court often enough to give them an opportunity to ask them, if they wish to know them."[2] On the 30th Vergennes complained to Franklin that Adams had sent him a long dissertation on the scaling down of the American currencies, full of abstract reasoning, but with no foundation.[3]

[1] Dip. Corr. Rev. v. 215.   [2] Ibid. 227.   [3] Ibid. iii. 152.

The same day he sent Adams a dignified note, declining further discussion. He thought that France deserved some preference before other nations. Adams replied that he thought so too; but he repeated, as if it was the main point of his contention, that the depreciation of the bills and certificates " being more the act and fault of their possessors than the government, was neither a violation of the public faith nor an act of bankruptcy."[1]

Franklin replied to Vergennes that he did not fully understand the matter about the currency, but he was sure that Congress would rectify any injustice to foreigners, especially to Frenchmen, on the ground that "inconvenience ought to fall wholly on the inhabitants of the States, who reap with it the advantages obtained by the measure." He promised to lay the matter before Congress, and assured the Minister that the Americans did not agree with Adams's opinion.[2] Adams's correspondence with Vergennes was continued in the next month. Adams volunteered the opinion that France ought to send a fleet and army to America, without which Washington could not reduce New York. This gave offence, and he was told that Franklin was the only one who bore credentials to the King of France.[3] Franklin attributed the fault, in a letter to Vergennes, to Adams's indiscretion: "I live upon terms of civility with him, not of intimacy."[4]

In a conference with a Committee of Congress, June 18, 1781, Luzerne took notice of the discussion between Adams and Vergennes about the depreciation of the currency. He urged Congress to recommend the States to take action which should prevent the tender laws from acting against foreign merchants.[5]

It is difficult to characterize properly the argument that

[1] Dip. Corr. Rev. v. 232. [2] Ibid. 246. [3] Ibid. 302.
[4] Durand, 231. [5] Secret Journ. ii. 450.

depreciation was due, not to the act of the authority which issued, but to the misdoing of the people who used, the currency. Even among Americans such an argument would be in the highest degree sophistical and false. Addressed to foreigners, to those of whom the United States had been begging, and who had been responding with a generosity soon to prove ruinous to themselves, it was something far worse than that. The most important point about it was that foreigners did not understand the use of paper money or the phenomena of depreciation. They did not live in the midst of it. They could not watch it, learn its mysteries, or guard themselves against it. They were not bound to understand it. They had a right to suppose that dealings with America and Americans were on the usual basis of transactions between civilized men, and that the Americans, if they invented any devices for use among themselves, would not force the consequences of those devices on foreigners who dealt with them.

The most important consequences of Adams's quarrel with Vergennes were political, and lie beyond our subject. The fundamental difference was as to the point of view. Was France indebted to America for helping her to cripple England, or was America indebted to France for helping her to win independence? Adams's sturdy and offensive maintenance of the former view[1] was serviceable to his country, for it prevented the United States from falling into dependence on France.

April 10, 1780, Congress resolved to make good to the army the deficiency produced in their original pay by depreciation.[2] June 28, they adopted a scale of depreciation, and resolved to apply it to the notes which had been loaned to the loan office.[3] According to a table in the

---

[1] Dip. Corr. Rev. iii. 164. [2] Journ. Cong. vi. 37.
[3] Ibid. 69.

"Penn. Packet" of January 2, 1781, the depreciation in July, 1780, was as sixty-four and a half to one.

August 3, the adjourned meeting of the price Convention was held at Boston. Delegates were present from New Hampshire, Massachusetts, and Connecticut. A series of very important resolutions were adopted, — that the States should fill their quotas of men; that State agents should correspond with each other about prices and supplies; that the States should undertake to transport the supplies to the army; that they should prevent extortion in the market, where goods were offered to the soldiers; that they should repeal all embargoes except on goods transported by water; that they should sink the continental paper by taxes, if possible; that they should provide revenues to sink regularly all new issues; that they should not issue State notes; that sick soldiers should be cared for, and account should be kept against the State to which they belong; that the transmission of intelligence to the enemy should be prevented; that the States should not enlist each other's men; that men and magazines should be prepared before January of the next year.[1] These resolutions bore a very different character from the price tariffs and terrorism of the previous price Conventions, and there were suggestions in them which bore useful fruits. The most important of all, however, was the one which has not yet been mentioned, — "That the Union of these States be fixed in a more solid and permanent manner; that the powers of Congress be more clearly ascertained and defined; that the important national concerns of the United States be under the superintendency and direction of one supreme head; that it be recommended to the States to empower their delegates in Congress to confederate with such of the States as will accede to the

[1] New Haven Hist. Soc. Coll. iii. 37.

proposed Confederation, and that they invest their delegates in Congress with power competent for the government and direction of all those common and national affairs which do not, nor can, come within the jurisdiction of the particular States."

Another Convention was held at Hartford, November 2, 1780, and another was attempted in 1781, but a quorum was not obtained.[1] The Articles of Confederation contained a prohibition of combinations between any number of States less than the whole. Hamilton, Madison, and others took alarm at such combinations for any purpose whatever, and discouraged them.[2] It is worth noticing that, in so doing, they justified the disapproval which Great Britain had expressed of the Continental Congress as a device for constitutional redress.

The price Conventions, however, seem to have paved the way for the conventions about commerce out of which grew the Constitutional Convention of 1787 and the federal Constitution. They helped to consolidate the Union.

In 1780 Paine wrote that the worse the times, the less the depreciation; that the currency never depreciated by any advantage obtained by the enemy.[3] When the proposition to repeal the tender laws was before the Assembly of Pennsylvania, on a motion for leave to bring in the bill, Bayard, the Speaker, gave a casting vote for it. "I give my vote," said he, "for the repeal, from a consciousness of justice. The tender laws operate to establish iniquity by law." When the bill was brought in, it was lost.[4]

In December Stephen de Lancey, the tory, published an appeal to the Americans, in which he argued that the Revolution was foolish and was a failure. All his points

[1] R. I. Col. Rec. ix. 153, 161.   [2] Madison Papers, i. 429, April, 1783.
[3] Paine's Works, i. 206.   [4] Ibid. 407.

were drawn from depreciation and the abuse of paper money.[1]

As late as January, 1781, Major Wertz was put under bonds to appear and answer for refusing to take Pennsylvania State money at a rate equal to gold and silver.[2]

At last, on the 16th of March, 1781, Congress (probably under the influence of Robert Morris) resolved that all debts now due from the United States which have been liquidated in specie value, and all debts which have been or shall be made payable in specie, shall be paid in specie or its equivalent, at the current exchange between specie and other currency; and the States were recommended to amend their legal tender laws so that the bills should be a tender only at their value in gold and silver. Only one man, Clark of New Jersey, voted against it.[3] The method in which this system was applied is shown by the case of Kalb.[4] Each payment which had been made was extended in specie at the depreciation per cent set in the scale for the date.

At this time George III. expressed the opinion that the help of France could not enable America to restore the paper currency. "If that is not effected, it is impossible the rebellion can long subsist."[5] Instead of its restoration, the same effect was about to be produced by its final annihilation.

The Council of Pennsylvania was charged with the duty of publishing official rates of depreciation month by month.[6] In the spring of 1781, the custom grew up of rating the State paper, called "Island Money," at three to one in specie. The Council published the rating of continental to island money. This was then multiplied by three to get the rating

[1] Laurens Corr. 202.
[2] Marshall's Diary, 267.
[3] Journ. Cong. vii. 49.
[4] Dip. Corr. Rev. xi. 188.
[5] George III. ii. 369.
[6] See page 236.

of continental to specie. On the 1st of May the Council, instead of rating continental to island, rated continental at 175 to one against specie. The public multiplied by three, as before, and rated continental at 525 to one.[1] This rating held firm in spite of all explanations, remonstrances, and protests. It was the death-blow of continental.[2] The quotation of continental previously made by the Council must have been far above the truth of its value. A writer in the "Packet" asserted that the market-rating on the 1st of May was from 175 to 225.[3]

As soon as this collapse of the currency took place, it was found necessary to order that no more taxes should be received except from those who were willing to pay at the old rate of 75 for one; because otherwise those who paid after this date would pay only about one seventh as much as those who had paid before, and the collectors would be tempted to buy the depreciated paper and pay with it what they owed for previous collections.[4]

On the downfall of the paper, in May, 1781, at Philadelphia, it is related that a procession marched through the streets with the paper notes fastened in hats as cockades, and that a dog was tarred and plastered over with the notes.[5]

In Rhode Island a mock burial of the continental paper was celebrated with a funeral oration. The State of Rhode Island had just issued a new kind of paper. Holding up a bundle of this, the orator exclaimed, "Be thou also ready, for thou shalt surely die."[6]

The continental paper, however, continued to circulate in Virginia and North Carolina a year longer than north of the Potomac. Jefferson thought that the reason was

[1] Webster, 174.
[2] Reed's Reed, ii. 295.
[3] Penn. Packet, May 12.
[4] Ibid. May 5, 1781.
[5] Moore's Diary, iv. 425.
[6] Waln, 229.

because the French gold and silver came into use in the North, which was an exact inversion of cause and effect. He says that the depreciation went on in the South until it was a thousand for one.¹ May 5, 1781, it is stated that soldiers in Virginia had received their pay in paper at forty for one, but could not buy anything with it at less than three hundred for one.² May 18, wagoners there refused to go any farther because of the depreciation in continental money, in which they were to be paid. It had fallen to four or five hundred for one within a few days. It is evident that the depreciation was now so rapid that a man might lose all his wages while he was earning them.³

In June General Gates wrote that there were general execrations in Maryland and Virginia at the downfall of the paper money, directed against Congress, the Executive Council, and others.⁴ August 1, in Virginia, the lowest depreciation was said to be five hundred for one.⁵ According to a memorial of the Virginia officers, the pay of continental officers and soldiers began, in 1776, at $90 for a colonel, $45 for a captain, and $7 for a private. In May, 1778, by depreciation, this was worth $18, $9, and $1.54. Then Congress raised it; but the new pay was worth, in August, 1779, $6.50, $3.50, and, for a private, 33⅓ cents for rations. It was raised again then; also a year later. In November, 1781, it was worth $3⅓, $1.66, and 20 cents.⁶ September 27, it was reported from Williamsburg that paper currency had entirely ceased to circulate.⁷ This fact — that paper circulated many months longer south of the Potomac than north, or that the North obtained specie many months sooner than the South — helps to

---

¹ Jefferson, ix. 249.   ² Va. Papers, ii. 86.   ³ Ibid. 107.
⁴ Letters to Robert Morris, 459.   ⁵ Va. Papers, ii. 280.
⁶ Ibid. 629.   ⁷ Ibid. 500.

account for a certain embitterment in the South, which had important political effects, and of which Robert Morris was, to a certain extent, a victim.[1] In 1788 Charles Biddle recorded that, according to his information, Virginia paper money was at forty for one against continental, and continental at sixty for one against silver, so that a Spanish dollar would pay $2,400 of debt, in Virginia paper.[2]

On the other hand, the so-called "island money" of Pennsylvania became as good as specie or better, because it bore interest, and the amount of it which was issued was not equal to the value of the tract of land which was pledged as security for it.[3]

November 27, 1781, Robert Morris wrote to Franklin that he had received not over a hundred thousand dollars in hard money during his administration. Taxes have been laid and are being collected in most of the States to sink the paper money, which "will bring in all this useless load by the middle of next summer. I have some expectation that the States of Massachusetts, Connecticut, Pennsylvania, and Delaware will be entirely rid of it by the spring. If I could buy anything with it, I would not until the last necessity; but it will buy nothing, so that it must be burnt as soon as it honestly can."[4]

According to a statement prepared by Joseph Nourse in January, 1786, the total issue of continental notes was $241,562,775. The amount then outstanding was $130,127,419.[5] In a statement which he made in 1828 he reduced the amount issued by about $10,000. He left out an issue of $500,000 which was made, November 2, 1776, in notes of one ninth, one sixth, one third, and two thirds

[1] See vol. ii. pp. 52, 60, 81. [2] Biddle, 237.
[3] Ibid. 238. [4] Dip. Corr. Rev. xii. 31.
[5] State Dep. MSS., Reports Board of Treas., No. 139, 77.

of a dollar, of which no specimens exist.[1] However, we find that counterfeiters in Pennsylvania, in 1777, had a plate for printing notes for two thirds of a dollar.[2] These were continental notes. It is not probable that they would counterfeit an issue which had never been made. Jefferson estimated the continental issues at $200,000,000, and their value at $36,000,000.[3] This estimate has no value. The figure for the total amount was evidently controlled by the vote of Congress that they would not issue more than $200,000,000, and the value is put far too high, because it is derived from a scale of depreciation which never admitted the full truth. In the "American Almanac" for 1830, the amount of continental issues is put at $357,000,000. In the "Merchants' Magazine"[4] it is put at $387,000,000. These high estimates include re-issues. In a treasury report by Levi Woodbury, in 1843, the total is put at $242,100,176. Bronson, who made a careful and independent re-examination of the record, put the amount at $242,052,780, omitting the issues which were re-called, etc.[5] In 1791 the amount outstanding was put at $78,000,000.[6] In the report of 1843 the amount never redeemed was put at $73,000,000. In the Act of August 4, 1790, it was provided that the continental bills of credit might be funded at one cent on the dollar; the amount so funded was $6,000,000.[7]

Jefferson put the State issues at $200,000,000.

Hard money began to be plentiful in 1779, through the disbursements of the English and the French, and through importations from Havana.[8] In 1780 Webster argued from

---

[1] Phillips, ii. 57, Nourse's Report in 20th Congress, 1st Session, State Papers, xx. 107.
[2] Penn. Col. Rec. xi. 234.
[3] Jefferson, ix. 259.
[4] See vol. viii. p. 84.
[5] New Haven Hist. Soc. Papers, i. 113.
[6] Annals of Cong. i. 1217.
[7] Elliot's Funding, 12.
[8] Webster, 75.

this that the paper ought to be got out of the way.[1] Pownall had information, at the same time, that there was more than three millions of English money in gold and silver locked up in America which would come out when the paper should be destroyed.[2] A writer in the "Packet" undertook, in February, 1781, to make an estimate, although it was only a guess, of the amount of plate in the colonies. The total which he reached was two million dollars' worth, besides which he thought that five million dollars in specie was hoarded. He wanted the ports opened to trade, but a prohibition on the export of specie.[3] In 1782 specie was very scarce in the circulation of Virginia. Imported articles were one hundred per cent higher than in Philadelphia.[4]

In spite of the notion that it was treasonable to trade with the enemy, and the attempts which were made to stop that trade, it went steadily on. In 1782, describing the trade of New York, Hamilton said that the interior of the State traded with the city to the amount of £30,000 per annum.[5] The city was like a free port outside of the State, and the trade with it was the body of the trade of the State with Europe.

"The prodigious quantity of French money brought into America by their fleets and armies, and the loans made to Congress, together with the vast return of dollars from the Havana, and the Spanish, Portuguese, and English gold which found its way into the country from the British lines, rendered specie very plentiful toward the conclusion of the war; and the arrival of the army of the Count de Rochambeau was particularly opportune, as it happened at the very distressing crisis of the

[1] Webster, 143.
[2] Pownall, 55. See also, Brissot, i. 262; Jefferson, ix. 259.
[3] Penn. Packet, February 17, 1781.   [4] Jones's Letters, 88.
[5] Hamilton's Works, viii. 65.

death of the paper currency. The French money alone in circulation in the United States in the year 1782 was estimated, after very careful calculations, at thirty-five million livres, or nearly one and a half million pounds sterling." [1]

In 1783, the paper having been swept away in Virginia, a tax collector complained of the inconvenience and trouble of keeping the money which he had collected, because it was all silver.[2]

Lord Sheffield said that very little money was sent to America by the British authorities after the first year of the war, or possibly the second. During those years Portuguese gold was sent. Afterward only a little specie was sent, — just enough to control the exchanges. The English army was supported by goods exported and sold in spite of all restrictions. British subjects in New York had a great deal of specie. The Dutch and Germans had hoarded it. That which went into the American lines to buy provisions came back to buy English goods. Since the war much specie had passed from America to Europe.[3]

The farmers on Long Island hoarded great quantities of specie obtained from the English. In November, 1777, a plan was organized by which they could loan it to the State of New York. The possession of it caused a constant succession of robberies and outrages during the war. Hence an opportunity to invest it was no doubt welcome. Before 1782, large sums had been loaned. The bonds were signed by George Clinton.[4]

There is among the Stevens Facsimiles, in the handwriting of Paul Wentworth, a plan of a lottery for twenty

[1] Chastellux's Trans. ii. 30.   [2] Va. Papers, iii. 465.
[3] Sheffield, 169.
[4] Onderdonk, Suffolk, and Kings, 109, 201 ; Queens, 175.

million livres, which was apparently proposed at Paris to be made on behalf of America, in the spring of 1777.[1]

November 18, 1776, Congress adopted the scheme of a lottery. There were to be a hundred thousand tickets, each one consisting of four coupons, and there were to be four classes. The coupons of the first class cost $10; of the second, $20; of the third, $30; and of the fourth, $40. The prizes were of greater value in the successive classes. They consisted of bonds of the United States, payable five years from date, with four per cent interest. In lieu of the interest on the prize, the winner might have the pre-emption of such coupons in the next succeeding class as should not be renewed within the limit of time which was set. Every one who started in the first class had a right to go through the other classes, but was not obliged to do so. If he did not, the coupons for the subsequent classes were to be sold, priority being given, as just stated, to those who drew prizes in the former class. Those who drew $50 in the last class were to receive their money; those who drew larger prizes were to receive bonds, payable as before. There were seven managers under oath. Money received for the tickets was to be paid into the continental treasury. The first class was to be drawn at Philadelphia March 1, 1777. The tickets were to be sold for cash, and each manager was to have one tenth of one per cent on the sale of the tickets, as remuneration.[2]

During 1777 many of the tickets remained unsold; and the occupation of Philadelphia having interfered, the drawing of the lottery was deferred. The last postponement was until the 1st of May, 1778, when the drawing appears to have taken place; for on the 2d of May Congress authorized the managers of the lottery to draw on the money received for tickets to pay the prizes. The

[1] Stevens, 148. [2] Journ. Cong. ii. 433.

interest on the bonds to be issued for prizes of the second class was raised to six per cent, and the drawing of the second class was set for the 1st of January following. Loan-office certificates at four per cent were to be printed to pay the prizes drawn in the first class. June 3, Congress ordered the list of prizes drawn in the first class to be published as soon as possible. September 29, they ordered the loan officer in Pennsylvania to issue a warrant in favour of the managers of the lottery, to enable them to pay the high prizes in the first class.[1]

October 30, 1779, the managers of the lottery were ordered to sell tickets for the third class. The drawing was to take place March 1, and six per cent certificates were ordered issued for the second-class prizes.[2] January 28, 1780, Congress ordered that only the prizes should be drawn in the lottery, and not the entire number of prizes and blanks. On the 8th of February, they voted that the managers of the lottery should be allowed $12 a day from the 28th of November, 1778, to the 29th of June, 1779, when the second class was drawn.

December 20, 1781, there is an entry in the accounts of $173 paid to the managers of the lottery to enable them to draw the fourth class.[3]

[1] Journ. Cong. iv. 182, 234, 409. [2] Ibid. v. 300. [3] See vol. ii. p. 88.

CHAPTER V.

COMMERCE AS AN ENGINE OF COERCION AND COMMERCE AS A MEANS OF SUPPLY.

IN his Report of 1785, Morris said that the accounts of America differed from those of other countries. "It may be laid down as a general rule that governments should never be concerned in mercantile operations. The business of government is of itself too complex, and prudence dictates that it should be simplified. But if the attention of the public servants be required to numerous objects, some must be neglected. But although these observations be just in the general, yet the particular circumstances of America were such as to render exceptions indispensable. The want of funds called for the use of many expedients, and gave rise to transactions of a commercial nature, which render the accounts of the United States more intricate and complex than they would otherwise have been."

It is especially difficult to tell how commerce ought to be classified, according to the use that was made of it for public interests during the Revolution. It was used as an engine of war, also for profit; as a resource for the treasury, and for direct exchange as a means of getting things otherwise unobtainable.

The first use which the colonies made of commerce in connection with the disputes with the mother country was as an engine of coercion. According to the ideas of the time, Great Britain made great profits out of the colonies in the way of trade. The colonies had always, in words at least, recognized this and acquiesced in it. In fact, they had always resisted and evaded it, so far as it was true; that is, so far as their trade was confined to England against their interests. So far as their trade with England was consistent with their interests, the notion that England won any profit from them by holding them in a colonial relation fell to the ground. This was distinctly proved after the war, when the trade of America almost all returned to England, because that trade offered greater profits and advantages than any other.

The notion of the times, however, was that trade was a thing; that it could be appropriated and made a property; that "the trade of the colonies" was a concrete entity which could be disposed of in one way or another, — for instance, taken from England and given to France, or conquered by one nation from another. The colonists themselves had been brought up in this view, and always affirmed it in public discussions and literature; but privately and individually they acted entirely upon the assumption that the trade of the colonies was only an aggregate name for a group of relations, each one of which was a relation between a buyer and seller, who made an exchange with each other simply and solely for the mutual advantage of the individuals concerned.

If, now, the trade of the colonies was a thing of value, which could be conquered, sold, transferred, or given away, the colonists most naturally thought that they could dispose of it themselves as a consideration, by means of which to obtain political and other good things which they wanted; or that by withholding it from the mother country, they could coerce her. This was the philosophy of the association for non-importation, non-exportation, and non-consumption; in short, of commercial war. Any man or any party, however, must have a very exceptional position in the industrial organization if, by withdrawing from it, he can inflict on others an injury at all comparable with that which he must suffer himself. If A traded with B for the sake of any advantage which was to accrue to B, it is true that by refusing to exchange he could deprive B of that advantage; but A trades with B, in all normal and ordinary cases, for the sake of an advantage to accrue to A. If an advantage likewise accrues to B, A may consent to it, even with pleasure; but that is not his motive. Therefore if he withdraws from the transaction he must sacrifice the advantage to himself. This reduces commercial war to an effort to spite another by an injury done to one's self, except in those rare and most extraordinary cases in which one is really indispensable to one's neighbours.

John Adams says that the Continental Congress were astonished and delighted when he first broached to them the idea of the advantages to be won by France from dismembering the British Empire and winning American trade.[1] In December, 1775, Franklin wrote to Dumas that America wanted to find out whether any European state would enter into alliance with her for the sake of her commerce, which, before the war, amounted to seven millions sterling per annum.[2]

We shall see, however, that commerce as an engine of coercion and commerce for profit are as absolutely contradictory as negative and positive can be, and the colonists had no sooner established their system of commercial war than the exigencies of their situation drove them to carry on commerce for profit. Their system, therefore, turned into this, — that the government had forbidden all private individuals to trade, and then had undertaken to trade on

[1] Adams, ii. 506. [2] Dip. Corr. Rev. ix. 257.

its own account. As it had no apparatus for doing this, it could only accomplish its object by giving licenses to private individuals. Therefore, still again, the system took the shape of a general prohibition, with especial exceptions in favour of selected persons. Of course this led to charges of favouritism, to jealousies, and to genuine abuses. The operations were of two kinds, — the one first and most widely employed, both by Congress and by the States, was the purchase of cargoes of domestic commodities, which were exported to be exchanged on the best terms possible for the things which were of indispensable necessity. The other kind of operations, which came later, was real commerce with the hope of profit as a financial resource.

We are amazed at the recklessness with which the colonists plunged into the contest, when we realize their defenceless condition. When we find that they were obliged to collect muskets from house to house in order to obtain weapons; when we are forced to believe that the whole stock of powder in the thirteen colonies at the time of the battle of Lexington must have been reckoned in hundred weight, and that, as far as military resistance was concerned, General Gage might have marched from Boston to Savannah, because there was not powder enough in the thirteen colonies to keep up a week's military resistance; when we see that they were forced to make house-to-house collections of clothes, stockings, and shoes for the army, on a plan less efficient than that by which cast-off clothing is nowadays collected for charitable objects; when we see the desperate straits to which they were reduced for the lack of salt, lead, and iron, — it is hard to understand under what ideas or with what intention they took up arms in 1775.

The Committee of Safety of New York wrote to the

delegates at Philadelphia, July 15, 1775: "We have no arms, we have no powder, we have no blankets. For God's sake, send us money, send us arms, send us ammunition." The enlisted men are uneasy for want of money, which prevents the enlistment of others. Schuyler had just written down that an attack by Carleton was expected. To him they answered: "Our troops can be of no service to you, — they have no arms, clothes, blankets, or ammunition; the officers no commissions, our treasury no money, ourselves in debt. It is in vain to complain. We will remove difficulties as fast as we can, and send you soldiers whenever the men we have raised are entitled to that name."[1] The eastern provinces were sending despairing appeals to each other for powder. No one had any stock of it. As for the arms which were to be found in the colonies, astonishment was expressed that they were so bad. Washington accounted for it by the fact that these were the arms which the inspectors in the old English army in America had not thought worth retaining. The Governor of Rhode Island said that that province had no arms because it was surrounded and protected by Connecticut and Massachusetts.[2]

In form the Americans made the war offensive, for it was they who undertook to drive Gage out of Boston. After the expedition to Concord, he would without doubt have remained quiet in Boston for an indefinite length of time, if he had been unmolested. If the colonists had intended to have recourse to arms, it seems that they might easily have won a year for adequate preparation. The expedition into Canada was also offensive in character. It was an enormous drain on their resources at the time. The point, however, for our present purpose is that com-

[1] N. Y. Journ. i. 79.
[2] R. I. Col. Rec. vii. 448, 501.

merce was indispensably necessary to provide the colonies with the means of carrying on war.

The idea of an "association" was not new at the time of the Revolution. An association was taken by immense numbers of people throughout the realm in consequence of the Act of Parliament of 1696, after the failure of the Papist plot to assassinate King William. It was an agreement to protect the person and throne of the King, and avenge his death, if he should be killed.[1] The chief importance of this and other more or less vague efforts at common action lies in the fact that they were preliminary struggles toward social organization and political union.

It is in this point of view that the Stamp Act Congress and the non-importation agreement of 1765 are most important. We cannot find traces of any common sentiment or sympathetic feeling between the colonies. On the contrary, local and provincial prejudices were exceedingly strong. It required a sentiment of common danger and of common interest against the same enemy to force them to common action and union. The non-importation agreement of 1765 seems to have had some effect. A later historian has written of it: "The Exchange of London was in dismay. Half the firms of Bristol and Liverpool were threatened with bankruptcy. In Manchester and Nottingham it was said that three artisans out of every ten had been turned adrift. Civil war seemed to be at hand."[2] This view of the effect is well sustained by the contemporary authorities.[3]

October 28, 1767, resolutions were adopted at Boston to encourage the manufactures of the province, lessen the use of superfluities, and refrain from purchasing a great number of imported articles. These resolutions made a great

---

[1] Va. Papers, i. 79.   [2] Macaulay's Chatham, 165.
[3] Walpole's George Third, 303.

uproar in England.[1] The Americans believed that they had found a weapon which would be very efficient against the mother country. Of course this faith was based upon faith in the colonial system. It assumed that the trade of the colonies was of great value to the mother country. It assumed that the colonies were being exploited by the mother country; that in times of peace and contentment they submitted to this on account of major considerations of politics or sentiment, but that they could, if they chose, refuse, and resist the exploitation by refusing to exchange their products for those of the mother country. This line of action was expected to be so injurious to the merchants and manufacturers of England that they would bring pressure to bear upon the government to force concessions to the colonies.

In the Hutchinson Letters we read: "It has been asserted here that it is in the power of the colonies at any time to raise a rebellion in England by refusing to send for their manufactures."[2]

A table is often quoted showing the imports into the colonies from England and Scotland from 1764 to 1766, classified by colonies, in order to show how the different ones kept the non-importation agreement. The decrease of these imports or the increase of them shows that New York and Pennsylvania observed the agreement to a considerable extent, New England less, North and South Carolina about the same as New England, while Maryland, Virginia, and Georgia did not observe it at all.[3] A similar table for the agreement of 1768, said to have been sent from London by Johnson, shows that the colonies observed that agreement very much in the same comparative

---

[1] Franklin, vii. 371, editor's note
[2] Hutchinson Letters, 24.
[3] Dawson; Sons of Liberty, 87.

degree, except that South Carolina must be put in the list of those which did not observe it at all.¹

The New York Committee published a set of resolutions, in 1770, against the merchants of Rhode Island for violating the non-importation, and declared them enemies to the liberties of North America. They threatened to have no dealings with them, and to hand them down to posterity in detestation and abhorrence, unless they complied with the agreement. This was adopted by the Committee of Vigilance; but the Committee of One Hundred disapproved, which led to some discord between them. The Committee of Vigilance seized some goods which had been brought in from the eastward, and then, fearing that the Committee of One Hundred would frustrate their action, burned these goods, for which they were publicly rebuked by the Committee of One Hundred. New York was falling away from the agreement, and was blamed, both by Philadelphia and the eastern colonies. On the 9th of July the Committee of One Hundred resolved to import, and to abrogate the league except as to tea. The Sons of Liberty protested. In Boston the letter announcing this was declared infamous. Then Philadelphia began to follow New York, and in October Boston resolved to resume importation of everything but tea.²

A wide social and political division runs through the pre-Revolutionary history of New York City. It is the division between the mechanics and the merchants. The merchants were striving against the navigation laws, and they fostered and favoured the agitation by the mechanics, as less prominent and responsible persons, against the restrictions on commerce. When the mechanics, however, favoured a non-importation agreement, the merchants dissented more or less openly, because it meant a suspen-

---

[1] Franklin, vii. 441, editor's note.   [2] Leake's Lamb, 65.

sion of their industries. In May, 1774, they regarded such an agreement as precipitate, and likely to cause the port of New York to be closed, as Boston had been.[1] The Committee of Fifty-one in New York referred to the non-importation of 1769 as having been only partially observed, which they said makes a non-importation harm· ful; and in a set of mock resolutions, published in July, one reads: "That a strict adherence to a non-importation and non-exportation agreement, which was so easily effected and so faithfully observed in the time of the Stamp Act, is the only certain way of coming at the naked truth." [2]

Massachusetts adopted a non-importation and non-consumption agreement by the spontaneous action of the people, before the Continental Congress recommended it.[3]

The Continental Congress recommended the merchants, on the 19th of September, 1774, to send no orders to Great Britain, and to suspend orders already sent until Congress could act. September 27, 1774, they resolved that after the 1st of December there should be no importations from Great Britain or Ireland, nor from any place of export of Great Britain or Ireland, and that no goods imported after the 1st of December should be used or purchased. On the 30th of September they voted that after the 10th of September, 1775, exportation to Great Britain, Ireland, and the West Indies ought to cease, unless the grievances of America were redressed before that time. October 6, the Committee to prepare the form of an association were directed to include this, — that, after December 1, no molasses, coffee, or pimento from the British plantations or Dominica, or wines from Madeira and the Western Islands, or foreign indigo, should be

[1] Van Schaack's Van Schaack, 16.
[2] Jones's New York, i. 460, 466.
[3] Mass. Journals, 40.

imported into these colonies. This seems to have been an attack on luxury.¹

The completed Articles of Association of October 20, 1774, provided that after December 1, 1774, there should be no importation from Great Britain or Ireland of anything, or from any other place of British goods, nor any East India tea from anywhere, nor molasses, syrup, paneles, coffee, or pimento from the British plantations or Dominica, nor wines from Madeira or the Western Islands, nor foreign indigo; that they would not import or purchase any slave imported after the same date, and after that would not engage in the slave trade, nor let vessels for it, nor deal with those concerned in it. Out of consideration for their fellow subjects of the British Empire, they suspended non-exportation until the 10th September, 1775. Rice to Europe was excepted from the non-exportation. They resolved to boycott any merchant who broke the non-importation. They would improve the breed of sheep, and if any one had too many, he should sell them cheaply to his poor neighbours. They would encourage frugality, and discourage all extravagance, horse-racing, plays, and other expensive diversions and entertainments, and use no mourning but a piece of black crape or ribbon. They expressed confidence that merchants would not take advantage of the scarcity of goods. Committees were to be raised in each town or county to enforce the association, and to boycott any one who should break it. All manufactures of this country were to be sold at reasonable prices.²

If the commercial war was rational at all, it could only be as an independent means of coercion, not as the introduction to a military war. As an introduction to a military war, it had only the effect of tying the hands of the

¹ Journ. Cong I. 21.   ² Ibid 32.

colonies in the most critical period of preparation. If they had been intending to go to war with Great Britain, they should have bought all they possibly could, especially clothing, shoes, hats, and, if possible, powder and arms. As the British manufactures of these goods were the best in the world, they were just the ones to buy.

I. A study of the association shows that, in the first place, it produced dissension here, when unity should have reigned.

It is true that this was offset, to a considerable degree, by the sentiment of common voluntary action, which, under the enthusiasm of the moment, was very powerful and important; but the attempt to unite the great exporting colonies of the south, which depended on trade with the mother country for their existence, and the northern colonies, which formed an almost independent group, subsisting by their exchanges with each other, really translated into a fact of experience the fallacy of one of the notions of the time, — that importation and exportation were independent of each other, and could be treated separately. The most important dissension, however, was produced by the exception in the association, allowing rice to be exported to Europe.

In March, 1775, the planters of the West Indies presented to the House of Commons a petition with respect to the interruption of trade. They asserted that, at a low calculation, one third of the total export trade of Great Britain was affected by the anti-trade regulations of North America, and argued that this put at jeopardy the whole material prosperity of Great Britain. Their agent expressed his fears that one quarter of the four hundred thousand blacks in the West Indies might perish. His argument was that the Americans were strong, and that their association was likely to be effective. Hence he inferred that concessions should be made to them. He used with considerable effect the bugbear of the previous hundred years, that the Americans would learn to manufacture. He took good care, however, to laud the Navigation Act, which he called "half divine."[1]

In February, 1775, Parliament passed an Act to prohibit the New England States from fishing on the Banks of Newfoundland, or exporting to any place but Great Britain or the British West Indies, or from importing, except directly from Great Britain. In March this Act was extended to all the colonies except New York, North Carolina, and Georgia, which as yet held back from the association. July 4, Congress resolved that commercial opposition ought to be extended against these two Acts of Parliament.[2] August 23, the King published a proclamation in which he declared the colonies in a state of rebellion and liable to be treated accordingly.[3] In November, Parliament extended the prohibition to all trade with the thirteen colonies during the rebellion. This Act went into effect Jan. 1, 1776.[4]

November 1, 1775, Congress resolved that no produce of the colonies should be exported before the 1st of March following, without permission of Congress; that New York, Delaware, North Carolina, and Georgia ought not to avail themselves of the exception in their favour in the late Act of Parliament restraining trade; that no rice ought to be exported, under the exception in the association, to any British possessions in Europe; and that no live-stock, except sea-supplies and horses, ought to be exported or carried by water, except in rivers, bays, and sounds.[5]

[1] Parliamentary Hist. xviii. 461, 473.
[2] Journ Cong. i 133.
[3] 4th Ser. Amer. Arch. iii 240.
[4] Parl. Hist. xviii. 992.
[5] Journ. Cong. i. 212.

The Continental Congress construed the prohibitory Act of England to mean "that the King had abdicated the thirteen colonies, put them out of his protection, declared the inhabitants rebels, proclaimed war against them, deprived them of courts of justice, and of the laws, liberties, and privileges of Englishmen."[1] Hence these Acts were regarded as a justification of independence, and they helped greatly to sharpen and define the issue.

February 16, 1776, Congress debated a proposition in Committee of the Whole, to remove the restrictions on trade, but took no action.[2] The debate on this proposition was continued until the 6th of April, when the restrictions were repealed. The debate is quite fully reported by Adams.[3]

April 30, 1776, Congress repealed the article of the association which fixed prices at the level which existed before the war, except as to green tea, because the old stocks of commodities were exhausted, and new ones could be obtained only at greater expense.[4]

South Carolina was divided between indigo-planters and rice-planters, — the former in the interior, the latter on the coast. The indigo-planters regarded the rice exception as most invidious against them, and demanded that both things should be forbidden or neither. January 11, 1775, a Provincial Committee met which resolved itself into a Provincial Congress. In this body, which needed above all things unity and concord, the rice exception produced a violent dispute. Drayton gives a very full account of it, which presents in clear light some of the dangers and mischiefs of the project.

Gadsden said that the rice exception had "wellnigh occa-

[1] Jones's New York, ii. 108. [2] Journ. Cong. ii. 64.
[3] Adams, ii. 485. [4] Journ. Cong. ii. 147.

sioned a division in Congress; and so ill was a proposition of that nature received that it had occasioned a cessation from business for several days in order to give our deputies time to recollect themselves; that when the association was completing, and the members of Congress were signing that instrument, all our deputies but himself withdrew." Carolina was on the point of being excluded from the association, but her deputies were summoned again, "they returned into Congress, yielding up the article of indigo; and that Congress, only for the sake of preserving the union of America, allowed the article rice to be added to the association; that this, however, was illy received by the other colonies, who had thence become jealous of the rice colonies, and therefore it was his opinion that for the common good, as well as our own honour, we ought to remove this as soon as possible by having the words 'except rice to Europe' struck out of the fourth article of the association." [It seems from this that an attempt was made in the Continental Congress to get both indigo and rice excepted, but that it failed in respect to indigo. The fact that they got rice excepted, and not indigo, enraged the upland planters of South Carolina, and the fact that they got rice excepted enraged the other colonies.]

John Rutledge undertook the defence of himself and his three associates. A non-exportation, he said, would more surely effect the end, by retaining the commodities formerly shipped to Great Britain and Ireland, and not exporting them from America at all; but the northern colonies sent very little to England directly. They sent their fish and flour to other parts of Europe, and paid their debts in England circuitously, so that the association not to export to England would affect them very little. For instance, Philadelphia exported £700,000 sterling, of which hardly fifty went to the mother country. Those countries were less intent on annoying the mother country than on preserving their trade; while South Carolina sent nearly all of her indigo and two thirds of her rice to England. "Upon the whole," he said, "the affair seemed rather like a commercial scheme among the flour colonies, to find a better vent for their flour through the British channel, by preventing, if possible, any rice from being sent to those markets; and that, for his part, he should never consent to our becoming dupes to the people of the North, or in the least to yield to their unreasonable expectations. That as, by the association, the rice-planters preserved their property, so it had been the idea of the delegates at the Congress that they should make compensation to the indigo-planters who could not send their crops to the mother country. Such a plan was just and practicable, and it ought to be the subject of our debate, rather than expunging the means of exporting a great part of our annual crop, and therewith supplying ourselves with those necessaries we might require. The subject thus increased by this new matter of compensation brought into view, the debate became more general, and several members took part in the same." One party contended that compensation was impracticable; that, if given to the indigo-planter, it must be given to those interested in hemp, lumber, corn, pork, and butter. "As we were all one people, we should all suffer alike." "Union among ourselves was a *sine qua non*, and this odious distinction had cruelly convulsed the colony, besides which, our northern brethren beheld us with a jealous eye, and we ought to induce them to look upon us more favourably; for if blood were to be spilt in the American cause, theirs would be first shed, while ours would be running only in the usual channels." Others contended that compensation was prac-

ticable, and would remove opposition to the association.
Dislike to members of Congress ought to be avoided, and a
disposition to maintain union should be shown. At evening they appointed a committee to form a plan of compensation. The committee sat until midnight, and reported
at eleven o'clock the next day. Part of the report recommended that committees be organized who should permit
or forbid suits for debt. This they immediately agreed on,
but threw aside the rest of the report and recommenced
debate. "Great heat prevailed, and the members were on
the point of falling into downright uproar and confusion.
At length, all parties being wearied out, the question was
put by candle-light, and by mere accident, at the desire of
one among the indigo party, it was put in a manner that
lost it" [that is, the motion that the delegates to the Congress of 1775 should use their utmost endeavours to cause
the words "except rice to Europe" to be expunged from
the association]. Next day a committee was appointed to
adjust some mode of compensation, since the rice exception had not been expunged. The indigo-planters therefore wanted some sort of compensation; "and the other
party, sensible the same would never be executed, as
either there would not be any occasion for it, or the hostile
situation of affairs would render the compensation a dead
letter, very readily agreed to indulge them in the most
feasible manner."[1]

"By the arrangement which had taken place respecting the compensation, rice-planters were to make one
third of the crop of rice, or money arising from it
was to be exchanged for one third the crop of indigo,
hemp, corn, flour, lumber, pork, and butter respectively.
Thus each rice-planter was to deliver one third of his
crop to particular committees, and to receive for it an

[1] Drayton, i. 169.

equal value in any of the other commodities in turn, as they should have been deposited for such a purpose. Intricate as such a course of exchange would be, the mode was adopted, and no one reflected that a third of the crop of rice was scarcely equal to a third of the crop of indigo alone, and that, of consequence, the various other articles would not have any fund for exchange or compensation. One point of considerable consequence at that crisis was, however, gained by the measure, in quieting the minds of the members and restoring them to harmony and good-will to each other, having, as they thought, applied the greatest possible relief to the mischiefs which had presented themselves. This was a consummation of the last necessity, when promptness of action and union of sentiment were absolutely necessary for the public service."[1]

II. Secondly, it must be noticed that the association never was kept, and that the English merchants and manufacturers, as well as other persons interested in the question, had ceased to be frightened by it, because they did not believe that it ever could be kept.

Dr. Berkeley wrote to Johnson, August, 1774: "It is almost universally supposed here that your resolutions[2] against importing our manufactures will be violated by a great majority of the subscribers." Dr. Cooper declared that, under previous non-importation agreements, as soon as the stores in the houses were used up, great distress occurred, and complaints were made. Non-importation would soon have incited insurrection. He argued that non-commerce would be disastrous to the colonies themselves.[3]

[1] Drayton, i. 175.
[2] Beardsley's Johnson, 108.
[3] Friendly Address, 38.

In a poem of the period it is written: —

> "That foolish bugbear, your non-importation;
> For men do so hunger and so thirst after pelf
> That when thousands are starved, 't will blow up of itself." [1]

Adam Smith says that in anticipation of the non-importation, the colonies had drained Great Britain of the commodities fit for their market.[2] Charles Biddle says that on the day that the non-exportation went into effect (September 10, 1775) the river at Philadelphia was crowded with ships, many of which had been unloaded and loaded within two or three days.[3] If that was the case, then the suspension of that trade the next day must have been harmful to the Americans. The best evidence, however, that the non-importation was broken, and that it was injurious, lies in the violence which was necessary to enforce it.

At Charleston some people tried to trade; but they attracted the attention of the Committee of Inspection. "Broad hints of the public opinion were given by exposing in the street effigies of nonconformists to the general will, and in process of time reprehensions and punishments of novel natures were introduced against those who censured the popular measures, or who contravened regulations formed for the public safety."[4]

Two agents were sent to Georgia from South Carolina, who reported that illicit practices had come to their notice relative to the exportation of indigo from Georgia.[5]

The Council of Safety of Charleston wrote, on the 1st of January, 1776, to the Council of Safety of Georgia, reproving them for breach of the association in shipping indigo to England after the 10th September. While admitting that rice might have been shipped, they strongly

---

[1] Dialogue between a Southern Delegate and his Spouse, 1774.
[2] Rogers's Smith, ii. 188.
[3] Biddle, 75.
[4] Drayton, i. 187.
[5] Ibid. ii. 86.

urge that Georgia ought to have refrained from doing it until the sense of Congress should have been declared. They point to the boycott proposed in the resolutions of Congress as the proper punishment for offenders, and they offer to give help in enforcing the association. March 2, the Congress of South Carolina sent an armed force into Georgia with orders to help the whigs of Georgia to enforce the association, by unrigging the ships and taking off their rudders; also to arrest tories and imprison them. The Council of Safety of Georgia, on March 1, forbade any exportation of the products of the colony, except to procure means of defence, and ordered that the ships in the harbour should be dismantled. The South Carolina colonel commanding at Savannah reports that he had executed his orders, having sent two of his men, not in uniform but in common clothing, to mix among the common people and see it done; that is, it was done by a mob, lest the tories should say that the Carolinians had taken possession of Georgia.[1]

III. It was also vexatious to the Americans, and caused them to waste their efforts in the attempt to enforce it, when they needed all their strength for other purposes.

November 7, 1774, James Duane proposed to the New York Committee of Correspondence that eight persons should be chosen in each ward to observe the conduct of all persons touching the association, and to publish the names of those who violated it, in order that they might be boycotted. Such a committee was appointed. They wrote to the counties, proposing that similar committees should be appointed.[2]

December 5, 1774, the Massachusetts Congress resolved that, inasmuch as it would be difficult to distinguish goods imported after the 1st of December from those imported

[1] Drayton, ii. 223.   [2] Dawson's Westchester Co. 37.

before, no forbidden goods should be sold or purchased in the colony after the 10th of October next, although they may have been imported before December 1, 1774. They recommended the people not to sell or purchase them, and to prevent them from being exposed for sale. The Committee of Inspection in each town was recommended to enforce the association, and to take a full inventory of all goods in the hands of traders, whether imported before or after December 1. They were to require the traders to offer no more for sale; and if they did not obey, the committees were to take possession of the goods and store them at the risk of the owners.[1]

The trade restrictions produced a special distress to the people on the islands along the coast of Maine, who, in their petitions to the Massachusetts Congress, declared that they were starving for lack of provisions, and were also without powder and ball, because they could not dispose of their wood and lumber.[2] Nantucket was in a similar case.[3]

At Charleston, South Carolina, a riot was caused by the attempt of a family returning from England to bring in their furniture and horses, in March, 1775. The Committee voted that this was not forbidden; but a mob forced a reconsideration. "Edward Rutledge, who had been one of the most active in the affair, now commenced censuring the people in thus questioning the vote which had been given; but he was received with a clamour. The General Committee now began to think their authority insulted. Some members accordingly departed in anger, others became vociferous and raged, and for a few minutes all was in confusion. At length tranquillity prevailed; the consideration of the subject was postponed until a

---

[1] Mass. Journ. 57.   [2] Ibid. 244, 405, 411.
[3] Journ. Cong. i. 270.

more full committee could be procured, and the third day after was appointed for a final decision. To procure the presence of all the members of the Committee within reach was now an object of importance, and great exertions for that purpose were made by both parties. . . . The town was thrown into universal commotion. . . . The people declared if the horses were landed, they would put them to death. . . . Mr. Gadsden moved to reverse the former determination relative to landing the horses. He urged that the vote had been carried in a thin committee; that it was contrary to the association; that it would alarm the northern colonies in a most lively manner; and that our people were highly dissatisfied with it; and he contended that this last, of itself, was a cogent reason to reverse such a determination." Others contended that to reverse the judgment would bring the Committee into contempt, and that the spirit, not the letter, of the association ought to rule them. W. H. Drayton contended that the fact that an error had been committed was no reason why it should be continued; "that the people thought an error had been committed, and it was our duty to satisfy our constituents, as we were only servants of the public." The union of the people was the most important thing, and the interest of an individual could not weigh against it. " Landing the horses hazarded our union, for the people were in commotion against it. Upon all public and general questions, the people ever are in the right." It was decided by only one majority against the landing of the horses.[1] Nobody in this debate, so far as Drayton reports it, made the point that these horses were private property for private use.

On the other hand, the New York Provincial Congress voted, October 5, 1775, that " Ralph Izard, who desires to

[1] Drayton, i. 182.

come and live in this colony, may without violating the association bring in his coach, furniture, plate, books, and other effects for the use of himself and family." [1]

IV. The attempt to cut off trade exercised no coercion on Great Britain.

Chalmers says that the commercial war frightened Englishmen somewhat, "yet never did an event which threatened such devastation in its course pass away with so little mischief and so much silence, because its effects were unfelt.[2] He says that the Americans smuggled British manufactures from Holland during the war. Adam Smith states five reasons why the non-importation agreement had little effect on Great Britain. She found other markets in different parts of Europe, on account of political and commercial changes there.[3]

V. The Americans themselves could not sustain the policy, because it had the absurdity in it of making them violate their own interests.

In June, 1775, Robert and John Murray, who had attempted to import goods at New York, were compelled to submit. They printed a handbill, expressing contrition, and asking to be restored to commercial privileges. They landed the goods from their ship and delivered them over to the Committee of Elizabethtown, New Jersey, who were to hold them until trade should be reopened. July 4, the State agent of New York was authorized to buy some of these goods. August 2, he was authorized to buy some more, and to give the Murrays their price for them. The Committee of Elizabethtown were asked to give them up.[4]

In July, 1775, the New York Congress wrote to their delegates at Philadelphia that the merchants could not

[1] N. Y. Journ. i. 167.
[2] Effects of Independence, 125.
[3] Rogers's Smith, ii. 188.
[4] N. Y. Journ. i. 38, 65, 97, 99.

import Dutch goods which they might obtain, in spite of the Dutch prohibition, because their capital was invested in tea, which they are not allowed to sell. The Congress proposed that the sale of tea be allowed at a fixed price, subject to a tax of a shilling a pound. In this way " we might raise a considerable sum from the obstinate consumers of this article." At present tea is sold contrary to law. Still they protest that they do not mean to encourage the future introduction of tea.[1]

In the debate in Congress, in October, 1775, the members spoke of the non-exportation part of the association as if it had been a threat, — something which they did not want to do, and never intended to do. At the moment of putting it in operation, they shrank from it, and showed the division that had been introduced among them by the exception of certain colonies from the restraining act of Great Britain. Some members argued that the excepted colonies should voluntarily renounce their privilege, while others argued that it would be a good thing that some might prosper, although others could not. In the course of the debate, the absurdity of the association was very distinctly brought out, and also the radical contradiction between commerce as an engine of coercion, which meant the renunciation of commerce, and commerce as a means of obtaining supplies, which meant the prosecution of commerce. Robert Livingston expressed this sharply. " We are between hawk and buzzard. We puzzle ourselves between the commercial and warlike opposition."[2]

October 6, 1775, the committee to import gunpowder was authorized to make exportations, conformably with the continental association, in order to purchase arms and ammunition. On the 8th of November the Secret Committee were authorized to export to the West Indies any-

[1] N. Y. Journ. i. 92. [2] Adams, ii. 452–469.

thing but horned cattle, sheep, hogs, and poultry, for the purchase of arms and ammunition.¹ October 26, Congress recommended the authorities of the separate colonies to export in like manner and for the same purpose. November 22, they allowed a limited trade to Bermuda for salt, arms, and ammunition, and apportioned the supply of that island between the colonies, stating what each one might export thither. December 6, they allowed a specified person to export lumber and naval stores from North Carolina, under bonds not to take them to any British possession, and to bring back to North Carolina muskets and gunpowder of equal value, to be delivered to the continental army. Other similar cases of special license follow.

January 3, 1776, Congress voted that the Secret Committee should import as soon as possible specified quantities of blankets, cloth, needles, sail-cloth, duck, arms, lead, flint, tin, medicine, surgeon's instruments, and copper.²

It is evident that these articles were of prime necessity at that moment; and although great care was taken never to recognize in words the fact that the goods came from England through Holland and the West Indies, nevertheless we cannot doubt that such was the case, for English goods of these classes filled all markets. They were the best and the cheapest, and the necessity of Congress to get the goods was so great that they must close their eyes to a fact which they, however, really regarded as very important.

April 13, 1776, Congress resolved that tea might be sold, because many friends of the American cause who had imported it were embarrassed by inability to sell it. Inasmuch as the price of tea might be advanced on account of

[1] Sec. Journ. i. 30.   [2] Journ. Cong. ii. 8.

scarcity, and it "owes its worth to a habit in many respects pernicious to the inhabitants of these colonies," they fixed the price of it, and resolved that anybody who charged or gave more should be deemed an enemy to the American cause.[1]

September 25, 1776, Congress tried to organize a committee of one for each State, to obtain from all the States blankets and woollens and clothing, drawing upon the President of Congress for the payment.

October 1, 1776, as the necessity of salt threatened the public peace, the Governor and Council of Connecticut determined to send vessels under convoy, at public expense, to procure salt. They issued a warrant for the impressment of the vessels.[2] In October, 1777, the Assembly of Connecticut voted that blankets and woollens to the value of £20,000 sterling, for the supply of the continental army, should be imported as soon as possible.[3] Similar action was taken in Rhode Island.[4]

The States acted upon the recommendations of Congress, and exported for the purchase of the needed supplies. The records of the Committee of Safety of New York were read over for approval by the Provincial Congress in October, 1775. They came upon the appointment of a committee, to whom £4,000 had been intrusted with which to purchase and import supplies. They asked an account of the money, and were informed that the cargoes were sent out on account and risk of the Provincial Congress, which was to have the profit. If the ship was captured, the owner was to have £300 sterling for it; and he was allowed to put goods on board for his own account, if the goods of the charterers did not fill the ship. The Congress approved of this contract.[5] It is a good specimen of

[1] Journ. Cong. ii. 126.   [2] Hinman, 390.   [3] Ibid. 291.
[4] R. I. Col. Rec. vii. 496; viii. 18, 270.   [5] N. Y. Journ. i. 183.

a large class of contracts which were made by Congress and the States at this time. December 9, 1775, the Provincial Congress of New York appointed a committee to plan voyages on account of the colony, in order to procure arms and ammunition. December 19, this Committee reported that wheat ought to be exported to some ports in Europe; that the return goods should be transshipped at St. Eustatius and brought to the continent in different vessels. They enumerated the goods which were needed. They are always the same goods,—textile fabrics, clothing, and arms. Their proposal was approved, and they were guaranteed against loss on the bonds which they might have to give at the custom-house.

January 4, 1776, they asked leave to send ships to Europe. Flaxseed was the only thing which they could export, and the market for this was in Ireland; but the resolutions of Congress did not allow that trade. Thus it appears that the very things which were most strictly forbidden were just the ones which it was most necessary to do.[1]

The New York delegates declined to ask Congress to suspend the prohibition against the exportation of flaxseed, because they were sure that they would meet with a humiliating refusal. However, in March we hear of a ship loaded with flaxseed to go to Ireland with the consent of Congress.[2]

January 6, 1777, the Exportation Committee were ordered to send out an order for medicine. January 19, Comfort Sands was ordered to fit out a vessel with flour for Curaçoa, in order to bring back gunpowder and tent cloth. March 22, two persons were allowed to export produce in part payment for military stores imported from Amsterdam, so that trade with Europe (no doubt for Eng-

[1] N. Y. Journ. i. 212, 225, 236. [2] Ibid. 250, 353.

lish goods) was really going on. Many other permits to trade were granted by the New York Congress.

April 1, Simeon Deane applied to the New York Congress for leave to export flour to Connecticut, in order to re-export it from thence, under a permit from the Continental Congress, authorizing him and his brothers to ship goods to the West Indies and Europe.[1]

The Price Convention at Yorktown in March, 1777, had before them a resolution to recommend that *encouragement* be given to commerce with foreign parts, " to encourage by premiums and otherwise for a limited time the importation of medicines, both woollen and linen cloths, coarse hosiery, felt hats, raw hides, tanned leather, men's common shoes, salt and wool, cotton and tow cord," but to discourage the importation of luxuries. As the Convention was equally divided, no resolution was adopted.[2]

An interesting letter of Carter Braxton, which was intercepted in January, 1779, contains a statement of the way in which this matter appeared to a merchant at that time. He complained of the low price of tobacco, and wanted to open trade with Holland, so as to raise it, or to open trade for English goods through Antigua and St. Eustatius. "British goods would command on the first cost much more than any other, and they are so much to be preferred that America now winks at every importation of their goods. If they are not brought in this way, they will in some other; and the only difference is that in this way we shall get them cheap, while in another we pay an immense advance."[3] It should be said that this letter was regarded as disloyal. It ran counter to one of the things which at the time everybody had agreed to say, but it undoubtedly told the truth. The money which was expended

[1] N. Y. Journ. i. 396.   [2] N. J. Corr. 42.
[3] Penn. Packet, March 18, 1779.

by John Laurens, or his agent, in Holland, in 1781, was spent for English goods, — a fact upon which Lord Sheffield based a part of his argument, in 1785, that the United States must trade with Great Britain, whether they had a commercial treaty or not.[1]

We see clearly, then, that the Commercial War was an entire mistake. It pledged the colonists to abstain from doing just what it was their greatest interest to do, and they no sooner began to put their resolution in practice than they were forced to act in direct contradiction to it.

VI. The attempt to carry out this policy resulted in immense frauds and losses.

In January, 1776, the Committee of New York City complained that great dissatisfaction was produced, and that there were great abuses connected with the loading of the ships at night, which were going out under commissions from Congress.[2] In April, Comfort Sands asked for £1,150, in payment for two vessels which had been freighted out on colony account and had been captured. The sea was said to be full of cruisers.[3] In May, the Committee of Safety investigated a charge of fraud against a person who had purchased cloth on commission for the Continental Congress, and had charged fifty per cent more than it cost. It was asserted that persons who had sent cargoes to sea had made contracts with Congress that, if they were lost, Congress should pay, but if they arrived, Congress should give a hundred per cent advance on the cargo.[4] During the summer of 1776 the claims for losses incurred become frequent, and the arrangement disappears from the record, apparently because these losses became so great that it could no longer be used.

July 24, Washington wrote to the New York Convention

[1] Sheffield, 10.
[2] N. Y Journ. i. 264.
[3] Ibid. 409.
[4] Ibid. 428.

that a ship fitted out by Congress had been purposely thrown by its commander in the way of the British, that it might be captured, with a cargo of provisions.[1]

In his report of 1785, Morris said that a government should never undertake mercantile operations on its own account, that is, by its officers. He excused the government of the Revolution for undertaking mercantile transactions by the peculiar position of the United States at the time. His comment on these transactions shows distinctly that the commercial profit of the undertaking was the only resource aimed at by them for the United States.

[1] N. Y. Journ. i. 546.

CHAPTER VI.

EMBARGOES.

THE Americans did not invent embargoes. They were supposed to be strictly and legitimately useful in certain exigencies. There were so-called embargoes in the periods of war, which were simply applications of the notion of the time, that of course trade with an enemy in time of war must be suspended.

In April, 1775, the Assembly of Connecticut laid an embargo on all grain and meat, except ship stores, if transported by water. In May they continued it until August. Under date of July, 1775, it is said that the embargo caused vessels to decay at the wharves and provisions to be sold at low prices.[1]

February 10, 1776, the New York Committee of Safety ordered that no barrelled beef or pork should be exported from Westchester County out of the colony of New York, the idea being to secure provisions for the coming campaign; and a few days later the Provincial Congress approved of an embargo on provisions which had been laid by the towns at the eastern end of Long Island. In March they laid an embargo on salt. In April the Committee of Safety authorized the Committee of the city to allow the exportation of flour and iron to the neighbouring colonies. In June, on the application of the Commissary, in the

[1] Hinman, 163, 173, 547.

name of Washington, an embargo was laid on salt beef and pork for fourteen days.[1]

June 14, the Continental Congress prohibited the exportation of salt beef and pork. July 24, Washington asked the Convention of New York whether it would not be expedient to put an embargo on provisions, in order to keep them from the enemy, who captured them either outright or by collusion of the owners.[2]

In October, the King of England proclaimed an embargo on provisions from England until further orders.[3]

The different colonies laid embargoes on provisions and supplies which acted against each other in a disastrous way, breaking up the interdependence of the colonies which had previously existed. The eastern colonies had depended on the middle colonies for grain. Hence the great importance of the Hudson River as a dividing line, if the English could have won and maintained control of it. Hence also the mischief of the embargoes, so far as they produced the same result. The struggle of each colony to take care of itself, and to let the others do the best they could, was disintegrating, and very disadvantageous to the common cause. The Provincial Congress of Massachusetts addressed a memorial to the government of Connecticut,[4] asking them to take their embargo off grain and provisions, on behalf of the people of Maine, who were starving.[5]

A peculiar application of the embargo is presented by a letter of General Lee to the Governor of Rhode Island, November 27, 1776. He says that the rage for privateering hinders recruiting, and he proposes "a temporary embargo on privateering until the regiments of each State

---

[1] N. Y. Journ. i. 289, 322, 343, 401, 489.
[2] Ibid. 545.
[3] Almon, 1776, pt. iii. 148.
[4] Mass. Journ. 435.
[5] See page 122.

are completed."[1] Rhode Island acted on this recommendation, but the only effect of it was that the men went to Massachusetts to enlist on the privateers. April 20, 1777, we find the Governor of Rhode Island writing to the Governor of Massachusetts, proposing joint action to make this regulation effective.[2] Connecticut laid an embargo on privateers and all other vessels in December, 1776.[3] In April, 1779, Pennsylvania laid an embargo on all ships for fifteen days, in order to obtain men to man the State ships.[4]

Connecticut applied the device of the embargo with especial pertinacity, and it will be instructive to connect the history of her enactments with the effects of the same on Rhode Island.

In May, 1776, the Assembly of Connecticut, having been informed that persons were engrossing West India products, in order to export them, prohibited the exportation of such articles by land or water, until the 1st of November. In June an embargo was laid on grain, meat, vegetables, butter, cheese, and flour by water, and no pork was to be exported by land or water. This embargo was to last until the end of the October session. In October it was extended, and salt and cloth were added to it. In November the Governor was authorized to prohibit from time to time the exportation by land or water of such articles as he should think necessary, and a further embargo by land or water was laid on all West India goods. Any one who should violate it was to forfeit double the value of the goods.[5]

In October, 1776, the Rhode Island Assembly repealed an Act of the previous year, by which the people of Nan-

---
[1] R. I. Col. Rec. viii. 55.   [2] Ibid. 217.
[3] Hinman, 262.   [4] Penn. Col. Rec. xi. 761, 763.
[5] Hinman, 210, 221, 233, 245, 248.

tucket had been allowed to buy provisions in Rhode Island. In November, the committee who were to attend the price Convention were directed to propose that an embargo should be laid by all the States represented, until the continental forces were raised and the continental ships were manned.[1]

In December, 1776, Connecticut laid an embargo on all ships, unless they were permitted by the Governor to sail in order to import medicine and other necessary things. This embargo was to continue until May, and the exportation of leather, by land or water, was forbidden. At the same session a law was enacted, "that no person in a seaport town should, under any pretence, depart from any port, harbour, bay, creek, river, or other place in the State, in any boat, skiff, canoe, etc., without a written license from one of the selectmen of the town from which he should depart." All small craft were to be drawn up and secured under the control of the Selectmen. The penalty for a breach of the law was not to exceed forty shillings.[2] This was one of the laws which were cited in 1807 as precedents to justify the laws which were passed to enforce the embargo.

March 14, 1777, the Governor of Rhode Island remonstrated to the Governor of Connecticut against the embargo which the latter State had laid upon provisions. Rhode Island never produced her own supplies in time of peace; now she was reduced to distress. In May, Rhode Island laid an embargo on rum, sugar, molasses, raw cotton, coffee, leather, wool, and unshorn sheep. In June the embargo was repealed, but the exportation of enumerated articles was made subject to the permission of the Assembly. In August the prohibitions were entirely repealed.[3]

[1] R. I. Col. Rec. viii. 8, 53.   [2] Hinman, 253, 262.
[3] R. I. Col. Rec. viii. 242, 257, 269, 289.

In October, 1777, an Act was passed by the Assembly of Connecticut, that no person should transport goods through the State without a license from an Assistant or Justice of the Peace, proof being given that such goods were procured in some other State, and that the applicant was friendly to the liberty of America. If any person desired permission to export his products for the purchase of salt, for which purpose only it would be allowed, he must apply to an Assistant or Justice of the Peace, who, with two or more Selectmen of the town, might determine what quantity might be exported and grant a permit for it. If the permit was to export by water, bond must be given, to three times the value of the goods, that they would not be sold to the enemy. In no case could sheep's wool or clothing be exported.[1]

In February, 1778, it was alleged that the demand for transportation was employing so many oxen that the raising of grain and provisions was interfered with. Therefore the Assembly enacted that no private property should be transported from place to place in this State, or through it, on any vehicle for which more than one pair of oxen was used, on penalty of forfeiting all the goods and all the oxen more than one pair. If any officer in the public service used a team drawn by more than one pair, he must furnish the driver with a written permit. Selectmen were to inspect and scrutinize all teams.[2]

In June, 1778, the Assembly of Rhode Island enacted an embargo like that laid by Congress on the 8th of June. October 31, the Governor of Rhode Island wrote to the Assembly of Connecticut that the crop was short; the State had been harassed by the enemy, the men had been kept under arms, the ports had been blockaded, and the neighbouring States had laid embargoes

---

[1] Hinman, 290.   [2] Ibid. 314.

on provisions. Rhode Island was in great distress. He begged Connecticut to allow free-trade in provisions. This appeal having produced no result, he wrote in January, 1779, to the Rhode Island delegates in Congress, asking them to lay the matter before Congress, in order that the embargoes of New York and Connecticut might be repealed. He wrote to the Governor of New York, saying that Rhode Island had always imported bread-corn from the Middle States, and was now in distress. January 21, he wrote to the General Assembly of Connecticut, repeating his appeal, and saying that in the previous July half the fencible men in the State were under arms for over a month in the harvest time. In October an embargo was laid on all goods whatsoever, both by land and water, perhaps in the hope that retaliation might have some effect; but Rhode Island was in great distress for salt, on account of the embargo of the neighbouring States. In December, the delegate of Rhode Island to the proposed price Convention at Philadelphia was instructed to urge the repeal of all inland embargoes.[1]

In the mean time other States had adopted the same device.

In February, 1777, Massachusetts transmitted to the other States a copy of an embargo which she had been forced to adopt, because the sister States had not adopted price tariffs, so that the Massachusetts goods were drawn away by the high prices elsewhere.[2]

June 8, 1778, Congress laid an embargo on grain, rice, and provisions, for the whole United States, from the 10th of June to the 15th of November, except for ship stores, in order to supply the American army easily, and to prevent the supply of the enemy by the capture of such provisions if exported.[3] August 1, the Council of Penn-

[1] R. I. Col. Rec. viii. 430, 479, 498, 599, 615, 634.
[2] N. J. Corr. 28.   [3] Journ. Cong. iv. 240.

sylvania laid an embargo for thirty days, but they solemnly protested against the embargo laid by Congress as an invasion of State rights.[1]

February 1, 1779, Massachusetts appealed to Pennsylvania to raise the embargo on grain, declaring that bread was very scarce in the former State. The Council deferred action until Congress should act.[2]

February 26, Congress, considering that Massachusetts and Rhode Island were suffering for want of bread, recommended the executive authorities of Maryland, Virginia, North Carolina, and South Carolina to allow the executive authorities of the former States to purchase grain and flour.[3] The appeal of Massachusetts to Pennsylvania produced no result. There was a surplus in Pennsylvania, but it was thought that it would be wanted for the army.[4]

Among the other eager discussions of the summer of 1779, the embargo also received a great deal of attention. August 7, an anonymous writer in the "Packet" gave seven reasons for repealing the embargo. The chief one was that a supply would thus be brought to market. September 16, in the same paper, a "citizen of Pennsylvania" protests against the renewal of the embargo, and strives to show how it stops production; but September 25, "Embargo" defends the embargo, and maintains that without it Pennsylvania would not raise flour enough for herself. The sum of the controversy, as far as it was carried, was this: The opponents of the embargo argued that it made things scarce, because it restricted production, or caused producers to send their goods to some market where the embargo was not in effect. The other party replied that things were already scarce, and that if the embargo was taken off, they would be exported, which must make them

---

[1] Penn. Col. Rec. xi. 545. [2] Ibid. 682.
[3] Journ. Cong. v. 57. [4] Reed's Reed, ii. 83.

still scarcer. This might be taken as a type of the form to which such popular discussions of economic questions generally bring the controversy. There is a sharp definition of the issue, and an absolute contradiction in the position. Everything depends upon a criterion by which it may be known which position is true.

August 21, 1779, Congress recommended the States which had embargoes to continue them, until January 1, on breadstuffs and provisions, and that those which had no such embargoes should lay them. September 8, an attempt was made to reconsider and limit the embargoes to October, instead of January; but it failed.[1] May 22, 1780, Congress resolved that there should be a general embargo on provisions, and requested Delaware to renew the embargo. It appears that she had repealed it, and that Pennsylvania had complained.[2]

February 28, 1781, the President of Pennsylvania informed the Assembly that the law requiring an exporter of flour to offer one third of it to the Commissary of Purchases hurt trade and inconvenienced the State. Trade was driven to Delaware, and Pennsylvania was forced to pay an advance of twelve per cent over the market-price on flour so received.[3]

In August, 1781, the Governor of North Carolina wrote to the Governor of Virginia: "Some ill-judged acts of government in this State have, contrary to all good policy, rendered the imported property of the merchants precarious, and thereby so depressed the spirit of commerce that we now feel great distress from want of her supplies, and it will require peculiar attention and encouragement to revive it to any degree of enterprise equal to our necessities." Hence he intends to break over some regulations

[1] Journ. Cong. v. 243.   [2] Ibid. vi. 51.
[3] Minutes House Rep. of Penn. i. 579.

of Congress prohibiting exportation, in order to obtain salt and military requisites.[1] Nevertheless, in the following month we find that the Governor of Virginia laid an embargo on provisions.[2] We shall see that it was not an embargo that was required in Virginia, in the month before Cornwallis's surrender, in order to keep the army from starving.[3]

[1] Va. Papers, ii. 334. [2] Ibid. 395. [3] See page 241.

CHAPTER VII.

IMPRESSMENT.

IF all regular financial organization for bringing the resources of the country into use for the accomplishment of public purposes was wanting, how were the resources obtained? It was by impressment, which was employed through the whole war and throughout the whole United States. Impressment took the place of finance.

Transportation was the greatest industrial difficulty of the period. The development of North America in the eighteenth century was conditioned in the very first degree by the fact of the great navigable rivers which flow down from the Alleghanies to the ocean, and by the sounds, bays, and gulfs along the coast. These made water transportation possible. Land transportation was exceedingly difficult, slow, and expensive. In the Rhode Island tariff of prices in 1776, it does not seem to be contemplated that there will be any horse-teams. The price set for a man with a cart or wagon drawn by one yoke of oxen and one horse, or by two yoke of oxen, is thirteen shillings ($2.16) per day. The price set in Pennsylvania, in April, 1776, for a man, wagon, and horses per day, was fifteen shillings ($2).[1] Transportation for the army was rated in the Rhode Island tariff at four shillings per ton-mile for the first mile, and for every mile thereafter at one shilling and

[1] Votes and Proc. 704.

sixpence.¹ We may justly believe that it would have been impossible to subsist an army of ten thousand men at a distance of twenty miles from tide water. In all the records of the Committees of Safety, we find that the question of transportation is of constant recurrence. The system on which it was obtained was that of impressment at a tariff rate, like that which has just been quoted. This was not a new thing. We find instances of it in the earlier colonial history. It probably was employed so rarely that it was of very little importance. The system of impressment for transportation, however, from the ancient empires down to modern Russia, has been one of the most oppressive burdens and most vexatious abuses under which people have suffered.

September 16, 1775, the New York Committee of Safety, inasmuch as all efforts to hire or purchase arms in sufficient numbers for the continental troops in New York had failed, ordered that all suitable arms which were found in the hands of any person who had not signed the association should be impressed. Such arms were to be appraised by a committee, and a certificate of value was to be given to the owner. Bodies of militia were assigned to execute this order in Queens and Westchester, where the tories were most numerous.²

November 4, 1775, Congress recommended the New England legislatures to empower the generals to impress vehicles, horses, and vessels, at a reasonable rate, for the transportation of goods for the army.

In April, 1776, it was reported to the New York Committee of Safety that the gunsmiths employed by the State did not work satisfactorily. The State agent was directed to report any of them who refused to despatch the public work.³

---

[1] R. I. Col. Rec. viii. 89.   [2] N. Y. Journ. i. 149.   [3] Ibid. 412.

In 1776, when the New York Congress sent a committee to General Woodhull on Long Island, they ordered them to impress boats and other necessaries for their journey.[1]

The people of Long Island were greatly annoyed by the impressment of their wagons by the English after they occupied it. It appears from the statements that the English did not pay even as well as the Americans.[2] In December Congress took up with great indignation the case of some contractors in Massachusetts, who had contracted with the "Clothier General" for a large quantity of clothing, at enormous prices, which, nevertheless, they would not deliver until they got the cash, "thereby adding to extortion the crime of wounding the public credit as far as in them lay, and manifesting a disposition callous to the feelings of humanity, and untouched by the severe sufferings of their countrymen, exposed to a winter campaign in defence of the common liberties of their country." They order the officer to pay only for what he has actually taken, and urge Massachusetts to seize the rest, which shall be paid for only according to a resolution of theirs of December 20, which urged the States to seize all clothing in the possession of the inhabitants and give certificates expressing the quantity and quality, and to inflict any penalty they think best on persons who try to evade; and that these goods so taken be assessed at the prices fixed by the Committees of the several States. They further ordered that the President should write to the Council of Massachusetts expressing their pain that these persons should raise their price and refuse to sell on credit. "This irrefragable evidence of the depravity of morals in so many of the citizens of these States is a most alarming circumstance; and if the several governments do not speedily exert their authority, effect-

[1] N. Y. Journ. i. 528.
[2] Onderdonk's Queens County, 209, Jones's New York.

ually to suppress such unheard of extortion, it will unquestionably issue, and at no very distant period, in the destruction of the liberties of this continent."[1]

In October, 1776, it was enacted in Connecticut that if any person should refuse to contribute supplies or transportation when it was called for, a Justice of the Peace should issue an impress warrant, authorizing the military officer to take the same upon payment of a reasonable price.[2] The Commissary of prisoners was also authorized to impress buildings or vessels in which to lodge prisoners of war.[3]

In May, 1777, the Assembly of Rhode Island apportioned a requisition of two hundred and fifty barrels of flour, five hundred blankets, and eighty hundred-weight of iron between the towns of the State. In October they apportioned a thousand pairs of stockings in like manner, and in December two thousand pairs. They were to be collected by the tax collectors; and the power of impressment was added, at reasonable prices, in case any person should refuse to contribute.[4] In May, 1777, a committee was authorized to impress blankets from any person who had more than he needed for his own family, but would not give them up. At the same session the officers of the ship "Warren" were authorized to impress, under the direction of a Justice of the Peace, any transient and foreign seamen, not inhabitants of the United States, for a cruise which the ship was about to make. Later the officers of the ship "Providence" received the same authorization.[5]

In October, 1777, the Quartermaster of Rhode Island informed the Assembly that supplies could not be obtained at the tariff, except by impressment, upon which he had lately been forced to rely. In February, 1778,

[1] Journ. Cong. iii. 466.   [2] Hinman, 237.   [3] Ibid. 295
[4] R. I. Col. Rec. viii. 253, 314, 332.   [5] Ibid. 230, 245.

he was authorized to impress transportation for firewood required in camp, and the tenants of adjacent wood-lands were ordered to assess themselves and to contribute the necessary wood by shares. It appears that these acts of impressment produced such results that the Assembly were forced to adopt an Act, in December, to regulate impressment. If the Quartermaster applied to any person for what he needed, and that person refused to part with it, or demanded an exorbitant price, the officer was to apply to the Governor or other magistrate. The delinquent was then to be summoned; and if it should appear that he could spare the goods, an impress warrant was to be issued to the military officer. January 5, 1779, General Sullivan protested against this law. It had evidently protected the citizen, but defeated the military necessities. He showed that it would produce delays and altercations at the most critical moment in military operations.[1]

November 8, 1776, the Council of Safety of Pennsylvania authorized Colonel Grubb to impress teams to transport cannon made by him to Philadelphia, and an officer was authorized to impress vessels to weigh the *chevaux de frise*.[2] In the same month a committee was appointed to collect blankets and stockings, with the usual power of impressment.[3]

During the years 1777 and 1778 the system of impressment was employed with great rigour in Pennsylvania. In November, 1777, the Council of Safety allotted the requisition for wagons on the counties, on repeated occasions.[4] At the end of the month it was necessary to promise that no wagons which brought wood or provisions to Lancaster should be seized, and in December

[1] R. I Col. Rec. viii. 311, 357, 522.
[2] Penn. Col. Rec. x. 781.
[3] Ibid. xi. 18.
[4] Ibid. xi. 303, 343.

a wagon-master was appointed for that county. Wagons were to be listed and requisitions were to be systematized under the direction of that officer. In one case a wagon was rescued from the wagon-master; but the guilty persons were sent to jail. December 24, the Council represented to the Assembly that the impressment system was mischievous, and proposed that the pay should be increased. Complaints, however, continued. January 9, 1778, an organization was adopted with a wagon-master for the State and a subordinate in each county.[1] January 30, two hundred and eighty wagons were called for and apportioned among the counties. A little later, a charge was made that some wagons thus impressed had been sent to Boston on private business. In April the Executive Council reported that great difficulty was experienced with the wagon law. Teamsters ought to be free of militia duty while engaged as teamsters.[2]

In September, 1778, the Quartermaster-general demanded eight hundred wagons, and in October he demanded eight hundred more. The Executive Council remonstrated to Congress against the excessive burden.[3]

January 18, 1779, the wagon-master of Chester County complained to the Executive Council that wagons which had been impressed in his district had been sent to Egg Harbor on private business. Upon investigation, this abuse of impressment was traced up to General Arnold. It constituted one of the most important charges against him at Philadelphia. He left before the hearing took place by the Executive Council, which body addressed a complaint to Congress.[4]

In October, 1777, provisions for a factory were impressed in Pennsylvania.[5]

---

[1] Penn. Col. Rec. xi. 350, 398.   [2] Ibid. xi. 409, 453, 467.
[3] Ibid. 588.   [4] Ibid. 672, 722.   [5] Ibid. xi. 339.

In April, 1779, the Pennsylvania Assembly passed an Act, in the preamble of which it is recited that wagons belonging to Pennsylvanians, and drawn out for public service, "have been, through the peculation and fraud of dishonest men, misapplied and perverted to the purposes of conveying and transporting private property." It is said that the federal Quartermaster-general has abused the power given him by a previous Act to demand wagons. Such demands hereafter are to be complied with by the wagon-master only under the orders of the Council of the State.[1]

April 2, 1779, Vice-President Bryan of Pennsylvania informed the House of Representatives that, by an abuse of replevin, an officer of the State impressing provisions for the army in Bedford County had been sued and saddled with damages. A bill was pending to prevent the abuse of replevin.[2]

In October, 1779, the claim of certain woollen manufacturers in Pennsylvania for woollen cloth impressed from them by General Washington was allowed by Congress and ordered paid. It was worth about $8,500.[3]

In New Jersey, in February and March, 1778, we find numerous orders for impressment, especially for the transportation of provisions.[4] We note that a month later the Governor advertises that farmers may bring in provisions to Trenton, without fear of impressment of wagons, horses, or cattle.[5] A fortnight later, however, it is ordered that teams be impressed for not more than six days to remove cannon and stores belonging to the navy board of Pennsylvania.[6]

In January, 1780, Luzerne wrote that provisions in the

---

[1] Penn. Packet, April 1 and April 15, 1779.
[2] Penn. Journ. i. 356.   [3] Journ. Cong. v. 287.
[4] N. J. Council of Safety, 205, 209.   [5] Ibid. 213.   [6] Ibid. 217.

American Army were so scanty that the French had been obliged to lend them some, and that at last the Americans had been obliged to pillage the country [New Jersey].[1] In August of that year Washington wrote to Governor Livingston that the army was in great distress for want of provisions. After a vigorous exaction from the surrounding country, he had obtained only two or three days' supplies, consisting of milch cows, and calves of one or two years. This method, however, is ruinous to the discipline of the army, and distressing to individuals. His foraging parties have committed great distresses: they are as bad as British troops, and assume the odious character of plunderers.[2] Timothy Pickering also wrote to the Legislature of New Jersey that he was entirely out of forage and must take it by force. It would be better that this should be done by the civil authority, if it must be done.[3]

In June, 1780, President Reed wrote to Washington that the number of wagons in Pennsylvania had amazingly diminished. The county of Lancaster, which formerly returned sixteen hundred and twenty, now had but three hundred and seventy, and other counties have fallen off in the same proportion. The cause is poor pay under impressment.[4] Marshall, in his Diary, notes the impressment of horses in this summer under martial law. They were taken first from those who had not taken the test of loyalty. He inveighs against the impressment of teams in harvest time. There was a horse race, at which he says horses might have been impressed with advantage.[5] In September General Wayne wrote to Reed that the farmers of Pennsylvania would have little objection to submit to England. The same is true in the neighbour-

---

[1] Durand, 217. [2] N. J. Corr. 256.
[3] Ibid. 264. [4] Reed's Reed, ii. 215.
[5] Marshall's Diary, 244, 255.

hood of the camp, on account of the impressment of rations and wagons.[1] In 1781 there was very great difficulty to get wagons in Pennsylvania.[2]

By far the best opportunity to study the effect of impressments is afforded by the Virginia Papers in connection with the Yorktown campaign. The second volume is full of the difficulties experienced in the summer of 1781 in obtaining wagons and supplies, showing the difficulties of impressment, the inadequacy of it to the public service, and the cruel injustice of it to the people. In January a case is mentioned where teams were impressed; but as there were no guards to detain them, the drivers went off with them. A plan was formed by which the Commissary of Provisions was to register wagons and vessels by counties, in brigades of ten wagons each, and vessels in some convenient way, with a master of each brigade. When impressment was necessary, the vehicles were to be taken in rotation, and not otherwise, and they were to be appraised. A wagon, team, and driver was to be paid for at fifty pounds of tobacco per day and found. Those who did not register were not to be treated with consideration in impressment, and an owner who failed to respond was to do double duty.[3]

In March Colonel Davies, who was at the head of the State war-office, reported to the Governor the great need of wagons. All there were were in use. Stores which were scattered about must be collected; cannon must be moved and set up. He wanted to impress all things necessary to do it.[4] Great complaint arose that the policy of impressment was very costly. Horses cost far more than their value.[5] In May, after very great difficulty, wagons were obtained to bring on from Philadelphia arms for

[1] Reed's Reed, ii. 284.   [2] Penn. Archives, ix 420.
[3] Va. Papers, i. 447, 449.   [4] Ibid. 604.   [5] Ibid. 529.

Baron Steuben. The drivers were ordered, after delivering the arms, to take a load of hemp, which they were to carry back to Philadelphia. We find mention of these wagons several times afterward, on account of delays and counter-orders, showing a great deal of vexation and loss to which the owners must have been exposed.[1] They were by contradictory orders detained sixteen days, so that three of them were captured by Tarleton, and lost their wagons and teams. They begged redress from the Assembly. In May the State agent reported that there were plenty of wagons on the other side of the mountains, which seems to imply that they had been withdrawn thither to avoid impress. In June, Major Claiborne reported that there were numbers of horses with teams to be had at Stanton, but he had no money to induce them to turn out. The people had refused to conform to the plan for brigading the wagons.[2] In the same month a surgeon reported that he had seventy patients in hospital "entirely destitute of every article, except a few pounds of rice, that can render them comfortable or hasten their recovery. I have wrote repeatedly to Philadelphia for cash or stores and assistance, but have had the mortification to see my applications and the department neglected." He encloses a requisition for the things absolutely necessary, or for a sum of money. With the latter he could purchase all the things which are absolutely necessary. He has provided the regimental surgeon with some bandages, lint, and tow. "These I procured from the inhabitants by begging, borrowing, stealing, or rather forcibly taking. However, I am quite tired of such practices, and am determined, for my own reputation, rather to want them than practise or countenance such methods any more. Should an action take place, I am confident the wounded must suffer beyond conception."[3]

[1] Va. Papers, ii. 111, 172.   [2] Ibid. 165.   [3] Ibid. 186.

The following, taken from the second volume of Virginia Papers, all belong to the period between July and October, 1781, the time of the siege of Yorktown. Major Pryor writes: "If it was to save life, wagons could not be procured within a week. I am sick of the whole world." Another writes that the people are greatly incensed at the impressment of their horses without pay; another, that "the people entertain so detestable an opinion of the army that they cannot be prevailed on to serve in it, with property so liable to be lost and destroyed" as teams and wagons. The Governor informed the war-office that Lafayette wanted cannon mounted on carriages. Artificers, tools, and everything else must be impressed.[1]

As time goes on a struggle develops between the military officers and the wagon owners. One of the former reports that scarcely a wagon can be seen on any plantation but what either wants a wheel or gear. It is useless to impress them. Another says that the people take their wagons to pieces, and that if he impresses a horse he brings a fight on his hands. The Commissary complains that Colonel Davies and Major Claiborne do not furnish wagons; he resigns as Commissary-general. "There are at this time large quantities of bacon and spirits the south side of James River in a perishable condition, — the bacon belonging to the State, and the spirits to the Continent; both of which the army is suffering for want of, and no probability of getting it. If the quartermasters would have the provision brought to the army, if it was double the number it is at present, they might be fed with the greatest ease. Hitherto they have been fed on Indian meal, which is a great saving to the State, and still might

[1] In January, 1781, Colonel Davies asked the Governor for authority to impress a shop and tools (Va. Papers, i. 428).

have been, but the mills are nearly all dry, and there is no further depending on them."

The Governor of North Carolina wrote to the Governor of Virginia that some people in the former State were sending their horses into the latter, in order to avoid impressment. He proposes that they co-operate to stop this. A little later, however, he writes that he has revived the good will and activity of the merchants by promising that there shall be no impressment, but that they shall be paid. In spite of all this, Colonel Davies reported to the Governor that there was not a single magazine for provisions on James River; that some counties had not had their grain called for; that six hundred barrels of flour were stored within thirty miles of the Commissary, and he did not know it, so that it was found by a kind of accident. The next day the Governor, who certainly was in no enviable position, received notice from Colonel Carrington: The French army has now been several days on land, and cannot move for want of wagons to transport the baggage. He proposes to impress them in the neighbouring counties. There is also great need of horses for the French artillery and field officers. Lafayette is in alarming distress for provisions. He has had to borrow bread from the French since they landed. It is said that there are two hundred barrels of flour at Winchester, and boats sufficient to bring them down; also five hundred barrels at Fredericksburg, private property.

The Governor gave authority to impress teams and wagons and negroes to forward food. He wrote to Colonel Hendricks at Alexandria, asking him to forward flour from that place. "We have been much embarrassed for want of wagons. As your part of the country abounds in them, I must also give you the trouble of impressing as many as you can." An agent, however, who had been doing this in Loudoun County, reported: "I have been much perplexed, for after having impressed them, the owners of some, by themselves or others, have taken, in the night-time, a wheel or something to render them useless; and I don't recollect any law to punish them, if it could be proved." This was just at the time that Washington arrived in camp before Yorktown. At the same time the man in charge of the mills reported that they could turn out fifty to a hundred barrels of flour a day, but that teams could not be obtained to transport it. The siege having now commenced, warrants were issued for the impressment of spades, axes, shovels, and hoes. The Quartermaster, in despair, begs the war-office: "Let me entreat, sir, that something may be done to draw the people with their means of transportation into the service willingly. I find them so opposed to every measure that is oppressive that it is almost impossible to effect anything of consequence that way. Many of the teamsters upon the late occasion have deserted with their wagons after throwing their loads out at improper places; others with their wagons were sent for loads, and others with their teams, leaving the wagons exposed. Certain it is there is no way to remedy this evil but by inducing them by some way or means to serve willingly." Another says: "Neither the necessity of the case nor anything he can urge for their own or the public good has any influence with the people." And another: "Some rascals have run away with their wagons and teams and hid them." A Commissary reports from Buckingham County that the people are suffering from want of salt to cure bacon. "Many are reduced to want; others of the most respectable families have bread and milk or chickens. They deem it a great hardship that they cannot use their wagons to procure salt, for fear of impressment."

In January, 1782, Virginia passed a law to subject any one to imprisonment who should exercise a right of impressing under any other authority than an Act of the State legislature. After this the people absolutely refused to furnish food or forage, and we find an officer reporting that, without a special order to impress, he could not fulfil his orders.[1]

In July the Assembly authorized the Governor to issue warrants of impressment, to provide for the French army marching through Virginia.[2]

News of the peace arrived at Charleston April 16, 1783. On the 22d there was a general illumination. "On that day and for several before it, the army had no bread,—not even rice to eat. . . . Never did peace come more opportunely to the relief of a country, an army, and its commander. The army had now become very unpopular, the people regarded them as little else than the last enemy to get rid of." The army was still supported by impressment, at least for forage for the horses. "It is not easy to conceive how it would have been possible for the southern commander, perhaps for the United States, to have maintained another campaign. The people were utterly worn out and disgusted with this system of impressment and specific contribution."[3]

Enumerating the woes of the war, Pelatiah Webster mentioned the impressment of goods, wagons, stock, grain, cattle, etc. "These things may have been necessary, but they were a heavy tax."[4]

This is but a small part of the evidence which might be adduced that the policy of impressment was vexatious and burdensome to the population in the last degree, while it was unproductive of results to the public service; and

[1] Va. Papers, iii. 8.
[2] Ibid 203.
[3] Johnson's Greene, ii. 391.
[4] Webster, 93.

it may be taken to demonstrate that the lack of a competent administration inflicted the maximum hardship on the people with a minimum result as to the cause they were fighting for.

Many instances could be collected to show what fate, in all probability, awaited the man who allowed himself to be carried away by zeal for the public service, to engage his personal responsibility in his efforts to obtain supplies, or to forward recruiting.

Another chapter could be made of proofs that where a reasonable willingness to furnish supplies, etc., existed, — for it did exist to a certain extent, upon payment, — this disposition was turned into dread and detestation of public business and duty by the system of impressment.

The only case we have found in the Virginia Papers in which a man is said to have voluntarily given something for the use of the army is that of a man who gave his wagon and team, but was himself pressed into service as a soldier for six months, contrary to law. The result of this was that he declared that he would sell the horses and lay the wagon by, and hire a substitute for himself. Major Claiborne writes: "All the arguments I can make use of cannot drive the notion out of his head but that the court-martial has treated him ill."[1]

[1] Va Papers, ii. 466.

CHAPTER VIII.

SUPPLIES FROM EUROPE ; HISTORY OF THE MISSIONS THERE UNTIL 1781.

IF France was drawn into an unfair position, and unduly used by the American colonies in obtaining their independence, she had herself chiefly to blame for it.

In 1764 Choiseul, the French minister, sent M. de Pontleroy to America to report on the disposition of the colonies toward the mother country; that is to say, France had no sooner lost Canada than her statesmen began to reckon upon a counter blow to England by depriving the latter of her colonies. This agent reported that the feeling in the colonies was greatly affected by their relief from fear on the side of Canada.[1] Choiseul in fact made it a part of his policy to watch the disaffection in America, and to stimulate it as opportunity offered. From 1766 on, he was collecting documents about the English colonies in America. In 1768 he sent Kalb to America to see whether the Americans needed engineers, artillerists, and supplies of the munitions of war.[2]

Before Franklin came home in the spring of 1775, he had opened negotiations with a class of merchants in England, Holland, and France, for sending munitions of war to America.[3]

When hostilities actually broke out in 1775, the French government began to put to use the information it had obtained, and began to put in operation the plans it had

---

[1] Bancroft, vi. 25, 67.   [2] Kalb, 45.   [3] Doniol, l. 133.

formed. Bonvouloir was sent out from London to America in September, 1775. December 28, he made a report from Philadelphia, in which he stated that the Americans had already sent a shipload of flour to Nantes to be exchanged for munitions of war. "Everybody here is a soldier; the troops are well dressed, well paid, and well commanded. They have fifty thousand men under pay and a large number of volunteers who desire no pay. . . . They are stronger than people think. It surpasses one's imagination, and you would be surprised at it. Nothing frightens them. Take your measures accordingly."[1] It is difficult to understand upon what facts he based this report; for no evidence can be found elsewhere that any such state of things existed. If the French government accepted his report as fact, it would account for some of the delusions into which they were led immediately afterward.

No sooner did the troubles in America begin than European adventurers of every description — real soldiers, soldiers of fortune, speculators, renegades, smugglers, bankrupt merchants, etc. — began to seek their opportunities. Dr. Dubourg, who had an acquaintance with Franklin through common interest in natural science, took up the American cause with considerable zeal, and also with an evident disposition to make gain out of it. He united himself with some merchants named Pliarne, and they drew in a partner named Penet, an Alsatian. Penet and one of the Pliarnes went to Philadelphia at the end of 1775, where they made considerable sensation, and affirmed that they had the support of the French ministry, causing some trouble.[2] Dubourg and Penet made contracts with the Secret Committee of Congress in the winter of 1775 and 1776, by which it is said that fifteen thousand guns from the arsenals of Lyons were provided.[3] These persons do not appear ever to have

[1] Doniol, i. 287.   [2] Ibid. 377.   [3] Ibid. 505, 508.

had any capital. The disposition of the French government to stimulate the revolt and to lend secret aid to it gave opportunity for the speculators, who hoped to obtain rejected weapons from the arsenals and sell them to the colonies.

In April, 1776, Beaumarchais was in London, ostensibly on an errand to collect Spanish dollars for remittance to the colonies.[1] He sought out Arthur Lee, and arranged with him a plan for sending supplies and money, by way of the West Indies, under the firm of Hortales & Company. Lee informed Congress of this arrangement, through Story.

On the 2d of May, 1776, Vergennes addressed a memorial to the King, in which he proposed to send for Montaudoin, one of the merchants with whom Franklin had negotiated, under a pretence of calling him to account for dealings with the Americans, but really in order to provide him with help to be sent to the Americans. Dr. Dubourg's operations are referred to, and the tone of the document is that these somewhat ludicrous adventures of incompetent persons had been tolerated because no suitable merchants had yet been found for carrying on the necessary operations in the proper way.[2]

On the 3d of May, 1776, Vergennes wrote to Grimaldi, the Spanish minister, that France intended to advance a million livres for aid to the English colonies. "The government will not appear in the matter at all. All will be done in the name of a commercial firm, directed by a merchant in one of our seaports, who will take security in truth of no very heavy obligation; but he will give to his zeal the colour of a motive, plausible enough on the part of a merchant, namely, the desire to draw to himself most of the commissions from America, when the commerce of the colonies will become free by the declaration of their independence."[3]

---

[1] Lomenie, ii. 107. [2] Doniol, i. 372. [3] Ibid. 375.

June 10, 1776, Dubourg reported to Franklin that Penet had arrived from Philadelphia, but had left his papers in Holland for fear of capture. Dubourg constitutes himself American agent, and will risk everything to serve America. The ministers receive and help him. He has obtained fifteen thousand muskets from the arsenal. France is overwhelmed by debt and lacks bread. Hence the ministers do not dare to seize upon the chance of getting American commerce away from England. He has made engagements with some officers to go to America. He mentions Du Coudray, who is mixed in many quarrels. He has a copy of the contract of the Secret Committee with Penet, Pliarne, & Co. He has presented Penet to Vergennes, and has arranged with the Farmers-general that they shall obtain tobacco from the colonies directly, instead of through England as formerly. He has planned general commercial operations between France and the United States. Du Coudray has credit in the war department. He and Dubourg are planning to get cannon. The latter has also opened communications with Arthur Lee.[1]

According to Silas Deane's address of 1784, in January, 1776, he contracted with the Commercial Committee of Congress to go to France and purchase goods for £40,000 sterling. They engaged to furnish the money to pay for them, and allow him five per cent. At the same time the Secret Committee appointed him commercial and political agent for the United States in Europe, and ordered him to purchase one hundred cannon, arms and clothing for twenty-five thousand men, and ammunition, and to engage ships to transport them, and agreed to allow him five per cent. He left Philadelphia in March, 1776, in a ship in ballast. She was obliged to put back, and he sailed in

[1] 4th Ser. Amer. Archives, vi. 771.

another, which had a cargo. He then states in detail what resources he took with him. They amounted to £3,377 sterling. Livingston, Lewis, Alsop, and Morris sent out goods to Delap, with orders to hold the proceeds at Deane's orders; but they never sent him any money. He also borrowed of Beaumarchais, and obtained funds from a shipment to Soulier to the amount of 148,045 livres. Morris, in 1781, did not remember such a contract with Deane.

"I arrived at Paris," wrote Deane, "early in the month of July, a stranger to the language as well as to the manners and customs of the nation." The bills he relied upon were protested. He had neither money nor credit, nor friends at court; and Dr. Bancroft told him that the war was not unpopular in England. No remittances came to him, and the merchants would sell him nothing unless some banking-house would indorse his bills. Here Beaumarchais came forward; was bold and eager, and had political relations with the Prime Minister.[1]

Beaumarchais seems to have come to Deane, in the midst of his weakness and distress, like a good fairy. We leave aside here all the long controversy about the rights and wrongs of Beaumarchais, which have never been completely and satisfactorily solved, but it appears that a large part of the misunderstanding between him and Deane and Arthur Lee is attributable to a change of plan between April and July, 1776. Beaumarchais's scheme of operation, when he saw Lee in London, was to expend money which should, at least in pretence and form, be obtained from the voluntary contributions of wealthy Frenchmen in aid of the American cause; but in July, when he saw Deane, that scheme had been dropped, and the project was that he should appear as a merchant. We have seen

[1] Deane's Narrative, 20.

that, in May, there was a plan on the part of the French government to employ a real merchant; now the plan was to employ a comedy merchant. This was exactly the *rôle* which Beaumarchais was qualified to fill, and he proceeded to establish and open a large house, with all the accessories of a house of business, as the same are understood and represented on the stage. At that time it was believed that the colonists had plenty of exportable products which they could and would contribute for the purpose of arms and ammunition. It was thought that their main difficulty would be to find any market in which they could purchase contraband of war. The chief assistance, therefore, which they would need from France would be secret permission to make this exchange in France. Beaumarchais's commercial operations would be real commercial operations, and at worst could only issue in some expenses and losses, on the balance of account, which the French government might have to make good. Beaumarchais approached Deane with all the forms and reality of a commercial proposition, and Deane assured him that he should have some returns in six months, and full pay for everything which he supplied in a year.[1] Two days later they made a contract by which Congress was to pay the current price of the goods in America when they should arrive, or take them at the cost price, with insurance, charges, and commission " proportional to the trouble and care, which cannot now be fixed."

Dubourg criticised Beaumarchais as a man of pleasure; and Deane says: " I saw that he [Dubourg] was so far from sounding the views of his superior [Vergennes] in this manœuvre that he was, with the best intentions in the world, in danger of counteracting his own wishes." The French had recently changed their arms, and seventy or eighty

[1] Lomenie, ii. 128, July 20, 1776.

thousand lay useless in the arsenals. "I apprehended it no way impossible to come at a supply from hence, through the agency of some merchant, without the ministry being concerned in the matter. In such case the merchant would be accountable to the ministry, and the colonies to the merchant, by which means a greater time of payment might be given, and more allowance in case of our being disappointed." Gerard, first Secretary of Foreign Affairs, told Deane, August 18, that he might rely on whatever Beaumarchais "should engage in the commercial way of supplies."

Deane wrote: Chaumont, "a very wealthy person, and intendant for providing clothes, etc., for the army, has offered me credit on account of the colonies to the amount of one million of livres. I was directed to apply for arms and clothes for twenty-five thousand men, and for a hundred field-pieces, with ammunition and stores in proportion. This I wished to get of the ministry direct; but they evaded it, and I am now in treaty for procuring them through the agency of M. Chaumont and M. Beaumarchais, on a credit of eight months from the time of their delivery. If I effect this, as I undoubtedly shall, I must rely on the remittances being made this fall and winter without fail, or the credit of the colonies must suffer."

All the above is in a despatch of August 18, 1776. In a sort of diary appended to this, under date of August 15, he says: "I find M. Beaumarchais, as I before hinted, possessing the entire confidence of the ministry. He is a man of wit and genius, and a considerable writer on comic and political subjects. All my supplies are to come through his hands; which at first greatly discouraged my friends, knowing him to be a person of no interest with the merchants; but had I been as doubtful as they, I could not have stepped aside from the path so cordially marked out for me by those I depended on. . . . Everything he [Beaumarchais] says, writes, or does, is in reality the action of the ministry; for that a man should but a few months since confine himself from his creditors, and now on this occasion be able to advance half a million, is so extraordinary that it ceases to be a mystery. . . . Considering the importance of having two hundred pieces of brass cannon, with every necessary article for twenty-five thousand men, provided with an able and experienced general at the head of it, warranted by the minister of this court to be an able and faithful man, with a number of fine and spirited young officers in his train, and all without advancing one shilling, is too tempting an object for me to hesitate about, though I own there is a silence in my instructions. I therefore honestly declare I am at your mercy in this case."[1]

August 18, Beaumarchais writes to the Committee of Secret Correspondence that, led by esteem for a people struggling for liberty, he has established an extensive commercial house, solely for the purpose of supplying them with all things useful, even gold for the payment of troops; and that without waiting for their consent he has already procured two hundred cannons, two hundred thousand pounds of powder, twenty thousand guns, with balls, lead, clothing, etc. He wants the cargoes consigned to him in return, and promises that he has great power to use any consignments whatsoever; but he wants especially tobacco. He signs this letter Roderique Hortales & Co.[2]

September 23, 1776, Robert Morris wrote to Jay, detailing the arrangements which had been made with Deane on behalf of the Committee of Secret Correspondence, for a correspondence with invisible ink.[3] This element of dime-novel conspiracy fits very well into the rest of the scheme

[1] Dip. Corr. Rev. i. 13 fg.   [2] Ibid. 35.
[3] Johnston's Jay, i. 85.

for freeing the colonies, as it stood at that moment; but the English ambassador, by means of his spies, had immediate knowledge of the arrival of Deane and of all his proceedings.

As soon as the Declaration of Independence was adopted, an alliance with France presented itself as the most obvious political measure by which independence could be maintained. The previous intrigues and suggestions of France had already assured the leading public men of the colonies of her willingness to aid.

September 26, 1776, Franklin, Deane, and Jefferson were elected Commissioners to France. The Secret Committee were ordered to export produce or remit bills of exchange until they should lodge in France £10,000 sterling to the order of the Commissioners. The plan therefore at this moment was a perfectly legitimate and straightforward one to produce means of payment from America with which to buy what was wanted. The pay of the Commissioners was not fixed; but it was voted to give them "a handsome allowance," besides their expenses. October 22, Jefferson declined the appointment, on account of family circumstances, and Arthur Lee was appointed. December 23, the Commissioners were authorized to borrow, on the faith of the thirteen United States, a sum not exceeding two million pounds sterling, for not less than ten years.[1]

In the mean time Deane and Beaumarchais were working away with the greatest energy to obtain and forward supplies; and doubtless Deane imagined that he was discharging with the greatest success the commission on which he had been sent abroad. A million livres were advanced by Spain to Beaumarchais, August 11, 1776,[2] and the Farmers-general of France advanced a million livres,

[1] Secret Journ. ii. 31 and fg.   [2] Durand, 89.

but took advantage of the distress of the Americans to stipulate that it should be paid for in tobacco at half its then current price.¹ Beaumarchais also advanced money to Deane for his personal expenses;² and it has never been doubted that he exerted himself with the utmost energy, if not always with the greatest prudence, to expedite the shipment of the goods.³ Of the three ships which he despatched at the end of the year, two were captured by the English; but the one which arrived was of the greatest possible value to the cause.⁴

In October Deane was alarmed that he did not receive news. He wrote to the Committee of Secret Correspondence, "I once more put pen to paper, not to attempt what is absolutely beyond the power of language to paint, my distressed situation here, totally destitute of intelligence or instructions from you since I left America, except Mr. Morris's letters of the 4th and 5th of June last, covering duplicates of my first instructions; nor will I complain for myself, but must plainly inform you that the cause of the united colonies or United States has for some time suffered at this court for want of positive orders to me, or some other person." ⁵

On the 6th of November Deane wrote to the Committee complaining still more bitterly that he had had no news for five months, although many ships had arrived from America in France. He says that his anxiety is so great that his life is a burden. "Two hundred pieces of brass cannon, and arms, tents, and accoutrements for thirty thousand men, with ammunition in proportion, and between twenty and thirty brass mortars, have been granted to my request; but the unaccountable silence on your part has delayed

---

[1] Deane's Address of 1784, 14. [2] Lomenie, ii. 148. [3] Ibid. 137.
[4] The Amphitrite; list of her cargo; Stevens, 240.
[5] Dip. Corr. Rev. i. 53.

the embarkation some weeks already. I yesterday got them again in motion, and a part are already at Havre de Grace and Nantes, and the rest on their way thither; but I am hourly trembling for fear of counter orders. Had I received proper powers in season, this supply would before this have been in America, and that under the convoy of a strong fleet." [1]

On the 1st of December, referring again to the cannon and stores, he says it amounts to nearly half a million sterling, "not ostensibly by the court, but by a private company." He says that everybody else demanded security or an indorsement.[2]

December 3, he wrote to Jay: "Without intelligence, without orders, and without remittances, yet boldly plunging into contracts, engagements, and negotiations, hourly hoping that something will arrive from America. . . . M. Beaumarchais has been my minister in effect, as this court is extremely cautious, and I now advise you to attend carefully to the articles sent you. I could not examine them here. I was promised they should be good, and at the lowest prices, and that from persons in such station that, had I hesitated, it might have ruined my affairs." [3]

Franklin arrived at Nantes, December 8, 1776, and reported to the President of Congress that he heard that an underhanded supply of guns and ammunition had been obtained from the government, and that he found several vessels at Nantes laden with military stores for America.

When Arthur Lee received his appointment as Commissioner to France and entered upon the discharge of his duties, he found that the promises made to him by Beaumarchais and reported through Story had not been kept. He reported to the Committee of Secret Correspondence that a change in the mode of sending had been

[1] Dip. Corr. Rev. i. 61.   [2] Ibid. 85.   [3] Ibid. 91.

settled between Deane and Hortales. He never freed his mind from the suspicion that this had been a corrupt arrangement between them, to the detriment of the United States.[1]

January 17, 1777, the Commissioners wrote home that they had made a bargain to supply the Farmers-general with a large quantity of tobacco in exchange for stores and supplies, and also that there were wealthy people who were prepared to make very large advances to the United States. They therefore suggest that Congress may draw bills on them for a sufficient amount to pay the interest on loans contracted. In the postscript they said that they already had five hundred thousand livres in hand.

It will be noticed that two plans are here combined, — one of shipments with which to buy, the other of subsidies or loans. The effect of Story's report, that subsidies were to be obtained, seems to have been to cause zeal for the plan of shipments to flag.

As early as January, 1777, we find that the plan of shipping American products to France to exchange for supplies, and to support the envoys, encountered serious obstacles. Morris wrote on behalf of the Secret Committee that it was hoped that France would grant loans, because it was very difficult to get the products out. Congress was forced to adjourn to York in September following, on account of the occupation of Philadelphia. The winter of 1777-78 was spent in an almost entire interruption of all operations. In May, 1778, the Secret Committee wrote to the Commissioners that the cruisers were so numerous that they could not make the exportations.[2] It appears, therefore, that in the course of the year 1777 this plan was abandoned. The plan of depending on loans and subsidies from the French government took the

[1] Lee's A. Lee, i. 61. [2] Ibid. 295.

place of it. According to the banker's account, three million livres were placed in his hands to the credit of the envoys during that year. During the year 1778 he received the same amount in four instalments.[1]

At the beginning of 1777 Congress enlarged their scheme of agents in Europe, apparently under a belief that all the important nations in Europe stood ready to lend them money or grant them subsidies. January 1, 1777, Franklin was elected Commissioner to Spain. May 7, Ralph Izard was elected Commissioner to Tuscany; May 9, William Lee to Vienna and Berlin. May 31, the Committee for Foreign Affairs brought in a draft for a commission to Arthur Lee to be Commissioner to Spain. In fact, the Commissioners at Paris had already agreed to separate; Lee to go to Spain, because Franklin declared that he was too old to undertake that journey, and either Franklin or Deane to go to Holland. The Commissioners to Berlin and Tuscany were instructed by Congress to urge the advantages of free-trade with the United States. It may be added that, February 4, 1778, the Commissioner to Tuscany was instructed to try to borrow a sum not exceeding a million sterling.[2] The Commissioners to France and Spain were to offer to Spain a treaty like that offered to France for commerce, and to offer to help Spain to capture Pensacola, provided that the United States might have the navigation of the Mississippi and the use of the harbour of Pensacola; and to promise further, if it was true that the King of Portugal had expelled or confiscated American vessels, that the United States would declare war against him, provided that France and Spain would agree to this and support it.

February 5, 1777, the Commissioners in France were directed to use their utmost endeavours to send forty thou-

[1] Rep. of 1785.   [2] Secret Journ. ii. 41 and fg.

sand suits of clothes, and trimmings for forty thousand more, one hundred thousand pairs of stockings, eighty thousand blankets, one million flints, and two hundred tons of lead; and Congress pledged the faith of the United States to fulfil any contracts which they should make.[1]

March 12, the Commissioners reported to the Committee of Secret Correspondence that Lee had received assurances of good-will from Spain; that powder and stores had been deposited at New Orleans for the Americans; that merchants at Bilboa were ready to ship goods; that Americans were to have admission into Havana and a credit in Holland.[2] They were in great distress because they had received no intelligence or remittances since November. "We are left in a situation easier to be conceived than described. . . . We are really unable to account for this silence." They say that all the news in Europe about America comes through the enemy. The Committee of Congress had indeed written, explaining that they had not neglected to write, but that their letters had either been captured or destroyed to prevent capture. Since Franklin went over, they had not written, because the Delaware was blockaded.[3]

It seems very clear that the removal of Congress to Baltimore had been a great interruption of its business. We shall see that nearly all the activity of the federal government at that juncture was being carried on by Robert Morris at Philadelphia, and the fact that no letters were written to the Commissioners in France during that winter manifests extraordinary neglect on the part of the

[1] Secret Journ. ii. 478.
[2] Dip. Corr. Rev. i 275. Gerard, in a despatch of July 25, 1778, mentions that Spain had some time before granted secret favours to the United States; amongst the rest, had sent five ships with powder to New Orleans (Doniol, iii. 293).
[3] Ibid. 268.

Committee of Correspondence. An energetic administration would certainly have succeeded in sending a communication from some part of the coast to the agents in Europe, on whom they placed their chief reliance, in spite of the blockade of the Delaware.

March 13, 1777, the Committee of Secret Correspondence were directed to instruct the agents abroad to send no more gentlemen to America unless they knew the language.[1] This had reference to the great number of military men who had come over, under contracts with Deane to teach the Americans the art of war.

March 12, the Commissioners at Paris wrote to the Committee of Secret Correspondence that the French ministers were careful to maintain appearances. "Though it was at that time no secret that two hundred field-pieces of brass and thirty thousand fusils, with other munitions of war in great abundance, had been taken out of the king's magazines for the purpose of exportation to America, the minister in our presence affected to know nothing of that operation, and claimed no merit to his court on that account." Public orders were given forbidding the departure of ships with military stores and of officers, and it was forbidden to bring prizes into French ports, at the same time that assurances were given to the Commissioners that France was not yet ready for war, and therefore must do these things, but that they might be assured of her good-will to them. The gift of two million livres from the crown is here represented as an offset to the contract with the Farmers-general, which had fallen through. No acknowledgment was asked of them, but they were told to keep it secret.[2] "We are continually charged to keep the aids that are or may be afforded us a dead secret, even from the Congress, where they suppose England has some

---

[1] Secret Journ. ii. 479.   [2] Dip. Corr. Rev. i. 271.

intelligence, and they wish she may have no certain proof to produce against them, with the other powers of Europe." The Commissioners feel forced to break this prohibition as to Congress, but entreat that the secret may not transpire, nor the assurances that America will never be required to pay for either the money or the stores received.[1]

April 1, 1777, Morris, writing to Jay, mentions the arrival at Portsmouth, New Hampshire, Philadelphia, and Maryland, of clothing, arms, and ammunition from France.[2] A fruitful source of subsequent trouble to all concerned lay in the fact that there were no regular invoices or receipts of these cargoes.

John Laurens, writing to his father in November, 1777, mentions the report of a big consignment for thirty thousand men, which was said to have arrived by the " Amphitrite " (Beaumarchais's first ship), and which he said seemed to have been monopolized by one State in New England, having been landed at Portsmouth, New Hampshire. His reason for saying this is that a regiment has just arrived from New England which is very finely fitted out, compared with the others in the army.[3]

A committee of Congress, in 1780, found that Beaumarchais had sent, in May, 1777, a large quantity of clothing for the United States to Cap François and San Domingo, part of which had been shipped to the United States in small vessels, " most of which, it is said, have safely arrived in North and South Carolina." The agent at Cap François, however, still held large quantities of these goods in 1780, which he could not ship for want of vessels. Congress ordered a frigate to be sent there to get the goods.[4] The Secret Committee had issued a form

---

[1] Dip. Corr. Rev. i. 333. [2] Johnston's Jay, i. 125.
[3] Laurens Cor. 69. The "Amphitrite" brought no cloth or clothing.
[4] Secret Journ. i. 171.

of commission to be used in calling for supplies left at Martinique for the United States, at the beginning of these operations. It was signed by Franklin and Morris.[1]

In 1779 Franklin wrote to the President of Congress that he had just learned that the equipment for two frigates, which were sent to Congress from France two years before, was still lying in warehouse at Cap François. He said that there was only one case, out of all the goods that they had shipped to America, in which they had received a receipt.[2]

From time to time, during 1778 and 1779, Robert Morris sent notice to the Council of Pennsylvania that one of his ships had brought a few guns or other supplies belonging to the State from the West Indies.[3]

May 30, 1777, the Committee of Foreign Affairs wrote to the Commissioners that they wanted another loan. "We conceive the credit of America to be as well founded, at least, as any in the world, having neither debt nor taxes when she began the war; yet she is like a man who, with a large capital all in property, is unable to make any new purchases till he can either convert some of it into specie or borrow in the mean time."[4]

It is evident that the credit of America in 1775 and 1776 was extremely high; that is to say, that the leading continental nations of Europe believed that the colonies were sure to win their independence. It was also universally believed that the Americans had great resources, and could and would enjoy great prosperity. It was also believed that they would engage their future power of production in order to win their independence, and would keep their engagements. The most extraordinary fact, however, in regard to the behaviour of the Americans is that, while

[1] Hist. Mag., Nov., 1869.
[2] Dip. Corr. Rev. iii. 116.
[3] Penn. Col. Rec. xi. 552, 653, 771.
[4] Dip. Corr. Rev. i. 301.

they talked about their credit, and entered upon promises, they really took no practical steps whatever to fulfil their promises, or to bring their resources to bear upon the enterprise which they had in hand. They constantly "pledged the faith of the continent;" but this pledge could mean nothing except that, if any one would lend them what they needed at the moment, they would immediately set about the necessary measures to meet and discharge the obligations which they had undertaken. This step, however, was exactly the one which they omitted. Consequently they lost their credit.

Deane speaks of the last of the supplies sent off under his arrangement with Beaumarchais as those in the "Flammand," Captain Landais, which were despatched secretly and at great risk in September, 1777. They were landed at Portsmouth.[1]

October 7, 1777, the Commissioners complained that they received no remittances, and were in imminent danger of bankruptcy on the contracts they had made.[2]

October 17, 1777, Congress ordered bills drawn on the Commissioners in Paris for a total amount of $37,592.[3] December 3, they resolved that loans should be obtained in Europe, to be a fund for reducing the paper money;[4] and the same day they recited that the operation of taxes was very slow, and that the payment of interest by bills on France did not fill the loan offices as fast as was necessary. They urged the Commissioners in France to borrow two millions sterling.[5]

November 30, the Commissioners still write to the same effect: "We are scarce allowed to know that they give us any aids at all, but are left to imagine, if we please,

---

[1] Deane's Narrative, 37.   [2] Dip. Corr. Rev. i. 333.
[3] Journ. Cong. iii. 348.   [4] Secret Journ. ii. 55.
[5] Journ. Cong. iii. 431.

that the cannon, arms, etc., which we have received and sent are the effect of private benevolence and generosity. We have nevertheless the strongest reasons to confide that the same generosity will continue."[1] In November, 1777, the "Amphitrite" returned with some rice and indigo. The "Mercure" also brought some lumber and spars. These were, up to this time, the only returns which had been made to Beaumarchais for his shipments.[2] The Commissioners endeavoured to take possession of these, and it was only by very energetic action that Beaumarchais succeeded in obtaining them for himself. Arthur Lee always held the attitude of suspicion that Deane and Beaumarchais were in a conspiracy to levy contributions for themselves on the free gifts of France to the United States. Franklin always affected to ignore the dealings with Beaumarchais, and to treat them as exclusively in the hands of Deane; while Congress always showed themselves very careful not to pay for anything which possibly was intended as a gift. Therefore Deane and Beaumarchais were left for years to claim and protest that there had been genuine mercantile contracts which had not been fulfilled, and they could scarcely obtain attention.

The stores which were sent were of exceedingly poor quality. In December, 1776, Kalb wrote to Deane that the guns and artillery wagons obtained by Du Coudray were not worth the freight.[3] William Lee wrote to Nicholas, August 9, 1777: "Powder has been sent that was hardly sufficient to burst an elder gun, and guns not fit to shoot snow-birds; cannons made also of a factious metal, composed of improper iron with small quantities of lead and some pewter mixed, which have been tried in Europe and found to be useless."[4] He also said that

[1] Dip. Corr. Rev. i. 345.
[2] Deane's Narrative, 51.
[3] Doniol, ii. 354.
[4] Ford's W. Lee, 210.

the arms furnished by Penet under a contract with Virginia were very poor.[1]

Deane said that he had heard that the supplies were not good, but that he could not go to examine them, because it would show that they were intended for America, which fact must be kept secret.[2] It would seem that Arthur Lee might have been more careful in his animadversions upon others, in view of the fact that he was cheated in some guns which he bought at Berlin of the King's contractor.[3] Morris said that many of the goods were " not only base, but despicable." [4]

It is safe to infer that all sorts of inferior supplies and arms were palmed off upon the colonies, at extravagant prices, under the circumstances of the case.

September 8, 1777, Congress voted that Deane had no authority to make contracts with persons to come to America. November 21, they voted to recall him. Undoubtedly the vexation which Deane had caused them by sending over a great number of persons to serve in the army, under contracts which enabled them to demand large pay and high rank, was the chief cause of irritation against him; but Arthur Lee had also been poisoning the mind of his brother, and through him, of the whole Lee-Adams faction in Congress, with suspicions of Deane's honesty. Deane had found himself transferred, within a period of two or three years, from an utterly obscure existence at Wethersfield, Connecticut, to the position of a quasi-ambassador at the court of France. He adopted a large and expensive style of living, and kept open house for the Americans at Paris.[5]

It is very reasonable to suppose that this large expendi-

[1] Va. Papers, i. 329. [2] Deane's Narrative, 36.
[3] Dip. Corr. Rev. ii. 196. [4] Secret Journ. iii. 254.
[5] Stevens, 248.

ture on his part was one of the chief grounds of belief that he was making great gain out of his position.¹ The whole group of persons at Paris, at the time, who were busying themselves with the American struggle, consisted of bankrupts, English spies, stock gamblers, renegade Americans, illicit traders, and other more or less disreputable persons. They were all trying to win pecuniary gain. They flattered and cajoled the Commissioners in order to obtain information, and there was no one of the Commissioners who was not victimized by them.

The one of these persons who had the most marked and important success was Hynson. He had won Deane's entire confidence. He was a ship-captain and an American. Deane relied on him for the most confidential service in carrying despatches. Hynson succeeded, after the despatches were in his hands, in transferring the duty to another; but while he held the papers, which were not sealed, he abstracted them from the cover, and put blank paper in their place. The package was then sealed and forwarded. Deane soon afterward learned of his treachery, and wrote him a letter, which at least shows that he was not privy to the outrage.²

John Adams says of Deane that he was voluble and ostentatious; that he was not esteemed in Connecticut, and was left out of Congress in October, 1775. He says that he had no solid judgment or information.³ Later he added that Deane lived expensively and lacked order; "but he was active, diligent, subtle, and successful, having accomplished the great purpose of his mission to advantage." ⁴

One of the English agents, comparing Franklin and Deane, probably in 1777, wrote: "The latter appears to

---
¹ Ford's W. Lee; W. L. to R. H. L., March 25, 1779.
² Stevens, 203, 205, 208, 275.   ³ Adams, iii. 4.   ⁴ Ibid. 138.

be the more active and efficient man, but less circumspect and secret; his discretion not being always proof against the natural warmth of his temper, and being weakened also by his own ideas of the importance of his present employment."[1] The spies often say that his temper was hot and that he was not polite.

Doniol speaks very highly of Deane, especially of his zeal and judgment, and thinks that he showed great aptitude for diplomacy.[2] He thinks, however, and there is much to support the opinion, that Franklin was tired of Deane, and was glad to see him recalled.[3] Arthur Lee throws the blame of Conyngham's extravagant proceedings on Deane, who, he says, wrote to Morris to apologize for them.[4]

The affair of Silas Deane has importance far beyond the merits or the fate of that individual. The quarrel over him and his rights and wrongs, as will presently be seen, entered into the hottest party contests in Congress during the next two or three years, and it comes up again often subsequently. It has even been asserted that the intimacy into which John Adams was thrown with the Lees, in this connection, was what made him President of the United States, by winning him votes from Virginia in 1796.[5]

January 1, 1778, Beaumarchais, having heard that money had been given to the Americans through Grand, the banker, writes to Vergennes: "So I have lost the fruit of the most noble and incredible labour by those very exertions which conduct others to glory." It had now come to his turn to be sacrificed to the advance of the Revolution, as Dubourg had been sacrificed before. On the 22d he wrote that he had heard of the arrival of two of his

[1] Stevens, 248.   [2] Doniol, i. 495, 644.   [3] Ibid. ii. 336.
[4] Lee's A. Lee, ii. 117.   [5] Hamilton's Works, vi. 402.

ships at Charleston. The goods are there; but how is he to get his money? He is in terror of bankruptcy.[1] Inasmuch as a treaty of alliance between France and the United States was now made, matters had entered upon a new stage. Beaumarchais, with his fictitious firm of Hortales, was no longer necessary or useful. The French government dealt directly with the American envoys in granting supplies and subsidies. April 7, Congress made a contract with Hortales that they should pay, for all the cargoes already shipped and those to be shipped, the first cost, charges, and freight, in France. The contract between Beaumarchais and Deane is recognized. Hortales is to pay bills drawn every two months at double usance for twenty-four million livres annually. This article, however, is subject to ratification by the house in Paris and the American Commissioners at Paris. American produce is to be exported and consigned to this house. Interest is to be paid on all sums due, with a commission of two and a half per cent.[2]

From this time Beaumarchais falls out of sight as an agent of aid and supplies to the American cause, and becomes a claimant, who considers that he has been treated with injustice and ingratitude by the United States. January 15, 1779, Jay, as President of Congress, wrote to him a letter of compliments and thanks. This was the first answer which Beaumarchais had received from America.[3] June 5, 1779, Francey, as agent for Beaumarchais, submitted a statement of account showing Congress indebted to his principal for the sum of £200,000 sterling. He proposed that bills should be drawn for £100,000 sterling, payable at the end of three years, and that produce should be shipped to meet those bills. Congress agreed to this.[4]

[1] Doniol, ii. 686.
[2] Journ. Cong. iv. 140.
[3] Lomenie, ii. 175.
[4] Journ. Cong. v. 184.

On the 18th of June it was voted to draw bills in favour of Beaumarchais for 2,400,000 livres, payable the 15th of June, 1782. Of these bills we shall hear again.[1]

In June, 1781, Franklin wrote to the agent of the French treasury, referring to Beaumarchais's accounts: "Hitherto there seems to have been no regular method adopted for our proceedings." He describes the changes of method and the confusion. The letter shows that he knew nothing about the matter. "At present all that transaction is in darkness, and we know not whether the whole, or a part, or no part, of the supplies he [Beaumarchais] furnished, were at the expense of government, the reports we have had being so inconsistent and contradictory; nor, if we are in debt for them or any part of them, whether it is the King or M. Beaumarchais that is our creditor." He proposes a complete statement of account, covering all the advances by whomsoever made. He cannot change the receipts given by the Joint Commission, "for that would subject me to the same censure from my enemies as Mr. Deane has experienced."[2]

In November, 1782, Congress ordered the Superintendent of Finance to have the Beaumarchais accounts adjusted, and to make no further remittances on any previous order of Congress. On the 5th of December, 1782, he reported a draft of instructions for the commissioner to settle the account. In it he says, "As I have reason to believe that whatever may have been the characters of the persons concerned, either for abilities or integrity, the business which has passed through their hands has not been well done, I must desire that these accounts undergo the strictest scrutiny." He orders him to scrutinize particularly commission and brokerage, and to consider the original prices.[3]

---

[1] See vol. ii. p. 6. [2] Franklin in France, i. 52. [3] Secret Journ. iii. 254.

Beaumarchais had also an account with the State of Virginia for supplies furnished. It was liquidated in 1785, by the State authorities, at 973,023 pounds of tobacco.[1] It was still pending, however, in 1801, on a question of depreciation. It was then decided that Beaumarchais was bound by the State scale.[2]

Arthur Lee wrote to his brother, January 9, 1778: "Things are going on worse and worse every day among ourselves, and my situation is more painful. I see in every department neglect, dissipation, and private schemes."[3] The day before that, Deane had written: "Mr. A. L. must be shaved and bled, or he will be actually mad for life."[4] Lee mentioned two ships in which Deane and Williams were partners, which he was satisfied were fitted out with public money.[5] In the year 1778, as soon as the treaty of alliance was made and Deane was recalled, Lee began to quarrel with Franklin, and during that summer the strife and discord between the envoys at Paris became notorious and caused a great public scandal.

April 1, 1778, Franklin answered Lee: "There is a style in some of your letters — I observe it particularly in the last — whereby superior merit is assumed to yourself in point of care and attention to business, and blame is insinuated on your colleague, without making yourself accountable by a direct charge of negligence or unfaithfulness, which has the appearance of being as artful as it is unkind." April 4, he wrote a long letter, in answer to Lee's complaint that he had not been informed of Gerard's mission. He says that he will tell him the reason some time, but at present it is not proper. He says that Lee's letter is made to sound as if he were the only honest man on the commission, and the other two had some knavish reasons

---

[1] Va. Papers, iii. 3. [2] Call's Rep. iii. 107. [3] Lee's A. Lee, ii. 127.
[4] Stevens, 490. [5] Lee's A. Lee, ii. 147.

for keeping the accounts in the dark. He resents Lee's inquiry why he acts inconsistently with his duty to the public. He admits that he has not answered all Lee's letters, "particularly your angry ones, in which you, with a very magisterial air, schooled and documented me as if I had been one of your domestics. I saw in the strongest light the importance of our living in decent civility toward each other while our great affairs were depending here. I saw your jealous, suspicious, malignant, and quarrelsome temper, which was daily manifesting itself against Mr. Deane, and almost any other person you had any concern with. I therefore passed your affronts in silence, did not answer, but burnt your angry letters, and received you when I next saw you with the same civility as if you had never wrote them." [1]

The strife among the envoys was much intensified by certain questions of money. Franklin considered that Arthur Lee had secured to himself the custody of 185,000 livres, and his brother William that of 48,000 livres, by a deception on the commission.[2] In May he wrote that Lee and Izard were very angry with him for not honouring their draft, saying that he had disobeyed an order of Congress. They had drawn 5,500 guineas in nine months, when he was in the greatest straits for money, and either of them could draw money of his own from England.[3] John Adams, having been sent out in the place of Deane, arrived in Paris in that month. He wrote back: "Prodigious sums of money have been expended, and large sums are yet due; but there are no books of account, nor any documents from whence I have been able to learn what the United States have received as an equivalent." There are three Commissioners, each living at an expense of about £3,000 sterling, one of them at an expense of £5,000 or

---

[1] Franklin, viii. 256. [2] Ibid. 272. [3] Ibid. 358.

£6,000. Ten months later he wrote that this statement was somewhat exaggerated, and was written by him when he was not well informed; but it no doubt had a great effect on Congress, and influenced them in the action which they took about Deane and the other Commissioners in the autumn of 1778.[1] May 14, 1778, Adams wrote: "A fatal misunderstanding between some characters of importance has given rise to reflections upon each other's conduct that must have hurt the reputation of our country. . . . I wish there was no ground for any of these reflections, but one thing I know, that an immense sum of money is gone, that a great sum of money is still due; and another thing I know, that I am at a loss to discover what America has received as an equivalent for all these sums and debts."[2]

May 24, he wrote to the Commercial Committee that American affairs were in great confusion in Paris, as they were in America, and probably from the same causes,— "the novelty of the scene, the inexperience of the actors, and the rapidity with which great events have succeeded each other. Our resources are very inadequate to the demands made upon them, which are perhaps unnecessarily increased by several irregularities of proceeding."[3] He said that there were no account or letter books at Passy.[4]

In July Franklin wrote to ask whether Congress thought it necessary to keep three Commissioners at Paris. "We have indeed four, with the gentleman intended for Tuscany, who continues here, and is very angry that he was not consulted in making the treaty, which he could have mended in several particulars; and perhaps he is angry with some reason, if the instructions to him do, as he says they do, require us to consult him. We shall soon have a fifth, for

[1] Dip. Corr. Rev. iv. 245, 293.
[2] Franklin in France, i. 233.
[3] Dip. Corr. Rev. iv. 248.
[4] Adams, iii. 131.

the envoy to Vienna, not being received there, is, I hear, returning hither. The necessary expense of maintaining us all is, I assure you, enormously great. I wish that the utility may equal it. I imagine every one of us spends nearly as much as Lord Stormont did." He adds that Stormont was considered miserly.[1]

At about the same time the Committee received a letter from Lee, in which he declared that Ross had had more than 400,000 francs, and Jonathan Williams more than a million of public money, for which they could account only by saying that they had shipped goods. If then the ships are lost, the whole may be charged to the public account. Five million francs have been spent, yet everything is to be paid for. Hodge spent £100,000 for which there is no account. Chaumont has also been favoured, apparently because he is a friend of Franklin. June 9, he wrote that Williams had given in his account. The ships of war which had been fitted out by the Commissioners had been an enormous expense. Hardly one of them had cost less than 100,000 francs, and the prizes bring in nothing to the commission.[2] In commenting on one of these letters, Deane quoted a letter of Izard, of June 28, in which he said about Franklin: " His abilities are rare and his reputation high. Removed as he is to so considerable a distance from the observation of his constituents, if he is not guided by principles of virtue and honour, those abilities and that reputation may produce the most mischievous effect. In my conscience I declare to you that I believe him under no such internal restraint, and God knows that I speak the real unprejudiced sentiment of my heart."[3] This letter of Izard is repeated;[4] but the last sentence, beginning " In my conscience," is wanting there.

[1] Dip. Corr. Rev. iii. 55.
[2] Lee's A. Lee, ii. 50-58.
[3] Dip. Corr. Rev. i. 149.
[4] Ibid. ii. 418.

The Americans who sailed on D'Estaing's fleet put goods on board for commercial speculation until the admiral stopped them. This includes Deane and the pilots who were on board.[1] It was allowed at the time, at least in the American service, that an agent might put a trunk or two on board a public ship. Deane says that he had great chances to make profits in this way. "I never lost a moment on the subject."[2]

In October Adams proposed to Lee that the Commissioners should have a common meeting-place, or all three live together. "It would remove the reproach we lie under, of which I confess myself very much ashamed, of not being able to agree together; and would make the commission more respectable, if not in itself, yet in the estimation of the English, the French, and the American nations; and I am sure, if we judge by the letters we receive, it wants to be made more respectable, at least in the eyes of many persons of this country."[3]

Congress had, however, already taken action to reorganize the commission. October 21, 1778, credentials were adopted for Franklin as sole minister to France, and he was instructed to lay before France the deranged state of America's finances. They also sent to him a plan for the reduction of Canada, and perhaps also of Quebec and Halifax, in which France was asked to join.[4]

In the spring of 1779 the quarrels about money between the envoys became still more bitter. As already stated, the Lees and Izard had in the previous year obtained large credits and then drawn the whole in cash. January 4, 1779, Franklin replied to a new demand by Izard: "It is not a year since you received from us the sum of two thousand guineas, which you thought necessary on ac-

---

[1] Doniol. iii. 181. [2] Deane's Narrative, 69.
[3] Franklin, viii. 262. [4] Secret Journ. ii. 103.

count of your being to set out immediately for Florence. You have not incurred the expense of that journey; you are a gentleman of fortune; you did not come to France with any dependence on being maintained here with your family at the expense of the United States in the time of their distress, and without rendering them the equivalent service they expected."[1]

Izard complained to the Committee on Foreign Affairs, January 28, 1779. He said that he drew a bill for five hundred louis d'or for his expenses, which Franklin would not accept. "He said the two thousand louis d'or which I had already had was so extravagant a sum that he was sure I could not have spent it, and if I had, he saw no reason why Congress should support my family." Franklin told him that the law of Congress to which he referred directed that the Commissioners at the other courts should draw, but that "as I was not at Florence, he would not pay me." Franklin promised to give the reasons in writing, but did not do it. Lee and Adams accepted the bill.[2]

August 11, 1780, Izard presented a claim for 52,113 livres, balance due him. Congress ordered it paid by Henry Laurens out of what he intended to borrow in Holland.[3]

March 13, 1779, Franklin quoted Lee as saying that he was satisfied that Williams had in his hands over one hundred thousand livres which had not been employed in the public use. Franklin calls on him for the evidence, saying that he intends to have an investigation made immediately, by indifferent persons, to see if that is true.[4]

Doniol thinks that Lee must have been in English pay. The faults of his character are not enough to account for

[1] Secret Journ. ii. 309. This is a draft of a letter which perhaps never was sent.
[2] Dip. Corr. Rev. ii. 442. [3] Journ. Cong. vi. 3.
[4] Franklin in France, i. 282.

his misbehaviour.[1] John Laurens made a very clever parody of Izard's letters, in which that gentleman was made to avow explicitly what might be assumed to be his vain, personal, and selfish motives; that is, that he wanted to be minister to France until the peace, and then minister to England. Arthur Lee is mentioned as if the writer understood him correctly.[2]

In April, 1779, a committee of Congress reported on the foreign agents: "In the course of their examination and inquiry they find many complaints against the said Commissioners and the political and commercial agency of Mr. Deane; which complaints, with the evidence in support thereof, are herewith delivered." They reported resolutions: "That suspicions and animosities have arisen among the said Commissioners which may be highly prejudicial to the honour and interests of these United States; that the appointments of the said Commissioners be vacated, and that new appointments be made; that there be but one Plenipotentiary, Minister, or Commissioner for these United States at a foreign court;" that persons be appointed to settle Deane's account, and those of the other agents.[3]

April 20, Congress censured all the foreign ministers, except John Adams, for animosities. Motions were tried for recalling each of those in France. On the motion to recall Franklin, only Virginia and South Carolina voted in the affirmative. May 3, the question was taken on A. Lee. The States were equally divided. June 8, Izard was recalled.[4] John Adams was thrown out by the reorganization of the mission. He embarked for America, June 17, 1779, with Luzerne and Marbois. He went back in November, and reached Paris, February 10, 1780. He had a commission to treat with Great Britain for peace.[5]

[1] Doniol, iii. 170.   [2] Laurens Corresp. 86.   [3] Journ. Cong. v. 112.
[4] Secret Journ. ii. 540 and fg.   [5] Adams, iii. 210 fg.

December 15, 1780, Luzerne wrote that Congress was full of intrigues to recall Franklin. Massachusetts led in them. Franklin had no one to support him. He was retained because each party feared to see a member of the other in his place. Izard and Lee denounce him for negligence and for concession to France.[1]

October 4, 1779, Congress fixed the salary of foreign ministers at £2,500 sterling.[2] In May, 1782, on a proposition of Livingston, who reported that living at Paris was twenty per cent cheaper than at Philadelphia, at Amsterdam ten per cent cheaper, and at Madrid a little dearer, the salary was reduced to £2,000.[3] Franklin, however, informed Barclay, agent for adjusting the accounts in 1785, that he had continued to draw £2,500, not supposing that the reduction applied to pre-existing arrangements.[4]

[1] Durand, 239.
[2] Secret Journ. ii. 272.
[3] Ibid. iii. 129.
[4] Dip. Corr. U. S. ii. 49.

CHAPTER IX.

1775-77: MORRIS IN THE COUNCIL OF SAFETY, THE PENNSYLVANIA ASSEMBLY, AND THE CONTINENTAL CONGRESS.

IT is noteworthy that John Adams, who mentions a great number of prominent people of Philadelphia whom he met in 1774 and 1775, does not mention Robert Morris, unless he is the "Mr. Morris" who was present at a dinner company, September 7, 1774.[1] We must infer that Morris was, at this time, a lukewarm whig. After June, 1775, however, we find him extraordinarily active in public affairs. In June he was appointed on the Council of Safety; in October he was elected a member of the Provincial Assembly, the last one under the old charter; in November, 1775, the Assembly appointed him one of the delegates to the Continental Congress; in October, 1776, he was elected a member of the first Assembly under the new Constitution.

June 30, 1775, the Pennsylvania Assembly approved of the Association, and recommended the associators to arm themselves. They also appointed a Council of Safety for the State. Robert Morris and Thomas Willing were members of it. A treasurer was also appointed, and the Council of Safety were authorized to draw on him.[2]

During the last six months of 1775 Robert Morris was very active in the business of this committee. He was placed on a committee which was the most important one

[1] Adams, ii. 369.   [2] Penn. Col. Rec. x. 279.

under the Council of Safety, under the existing circumstances, — to procure powder and arms, as described in Chapter V., by the exportation of products to ports where arms and ammunition could be obtained. He was also charged to apply to the provincial treasurer for an advance until the bills of credit were ready to be emitted, and a little later we find him charged to borrow money of the Port Wardens, also to import medicines, and to obtain guns for the armed vessels which were being constructed. He also acted as the banker of the committee, for in many cases they paid their expenses by drafts upon him. In the absence of Franklin, who was President, he presided over the Council, and in that capacity he signed the warrant for the commitment of Dr. Kearsley.

October 20, the Assembly appointed a new Council of Safety for the ensuing year, of which Morris was one. The Council was organized on the same day by the election of Franklin as President and Robert Morris as Vice-President. December 11, the Council of Safety instructed Willing and Morris to load a ship with the produce of Pennsylvania, in order to import arms and ammunition of equivalent value. On the 26th of January, 1776, Morris applied to the Council for leave to export commodities equal in value to that of powder imported by him and sold to the Council. On the 8th of March he applied for payment for goods exported on account of the Council. In May he produced an account of the sale of two cargoes in the West Indies, and the Council promised to pay the excess value of powder returned; but in July the vessel which was bringing the return cargo was shipwrecked, and Morris was ordered to adjust the loss.

Morris was appointed a member of the Continental Congress in November, 1775,[1] and during the winter his attend-

[1] Votes and Proc. 644.

ance at the Council of Safety was very irregular; but in April, 1776, when a list of the committees of the Council was made up, he appears at the head of the committee to export products for arms and ammunition, and he no doubt continued to act in that business even when not attending the meetings of the Council. The last day when he was present was June 22, 1776.

June 20, 1776, he informed the Continental Congress that the Pennsylvania Assembly had adjourned without raising the troops which Congress had called for. The demand for them had been addressed to the Assembly, and not to the Council of Safety. Lest some blame might be thrown on the Council of Safety for not acting, he called on Congress to say whether they demanded that the Council should act. They took no action. He therefore drew up a formal statement of this fact, and obtained the attestation of two of his fellow-members to its correctness. His name appears several times as the agent through whom Congress communicated with the authorities of Pennsylvania.

August 6, 1776, the Council of Safety elected a new President and Vice-President, and therewith his services in that body may be said to have closed.[1]

In October, 1775, he was chosen one of the representatives of the county of Philadelphia in the Provincial Assembly.[2] The government of the State was revolutionized in the summer of 1776, when the old charter and the Assembly under it were thrust aside by a mass meeting and a revolutionary committee.[3] From the 8th of June

[1] Penn. Col. Rec. x. 279-672.
[2] Marshall's Diary, 44.
[3] In June, 1776, the Pennsylvania Assembly rescinded the instructions to their delegates in Congress, and prepared new ones, through a committee of which Dickinson, Morris, Reed, and others were members. The new instructions did not refer to independence. On the 1st of July, in Congress, of the

on, the old Assembly never could get a quorum.[1] Its last meeting was September 26. On the 5th of November following, Morris was elected one of the State Assembly-men. Out of six, he stood third in number of votes.[2] On the 8th a mass meeting was held to instruct the delegates from the city to obtain amendments to the recently made Constitution, which became a source of bitter party conflict from the moment of its adoption.[3] The minority of the Assembly, being the party with which Morris always acted, disliked the Constitution so much that they almost refused to act under it, until Congress sent them word in December, when the enemy were expected, that if they did not act as an Assembly, Congress would take the government of Pennsylvania into their own hands.[4]

In the Assembly, during the winter of 1775-76 Morris served on the Committee of Correspondence and on committees to audit loan office accounts, to report on the state of taxes, to report on the manufacture of saltpetre, to prepare rules for the military organization of the associators and for taxes on non-associators, to regulate fines on those who harboured deserters, and to draft instructions to the delegates in Congress. The instructions of 1775 had been most explicit against independence. The new

seven Pennsylvania delegates, three voted for independence and four against it, in committee of the whole. On the 4th, two of those who voted against independence being absent, of whom Morris was one, the vote of Pennsylvania was thrown for it. On the 14th of June the people chose delegates to a Provincial Conference, which organized a Convention. The Convention made a Constitution, which was proclaimed on the 28th of September, and on the 28th of November, 1776, the new State government was organized. The old Assembly held its last meeting on the 26th of September, when twenty-three members denounced the Convention and its proceedings (Reed's Reed, i. 187).

[1] Stillé's Dickinson, 180. [2] Marshall's Diary, 102.
[3] 5th Series Am. Archives, iii. 598. [4] Stillé's Dickinson, 208.

ones, adopted June 5, 1776, gave the delegates authority to declare independence if it seemed advisable. Morris does not appear to have been very active in the Assembly. His name does not appear in the last lists of yeas and nays.

July 20, 1776, the Convention of Pennsylvania reappointed him delegate to Congress.[1] This was the very crisis of the Revolution in Pennsylvania, when the old charter and the old Assembly were being thrust aside. Morris had just before voted against independence.

In November he was elected to the first Assembly under the new Constitution. Very little was done during the winter by that body, and no trace of any activity of Morris in its proceedings appears.

February 5, 1777, the Assembly elected him delegate to Congress. On the 6th a letter from him was read: "Although his private business suffers exceedingly by giving up his time and attention to the public, yet as he means to serve his country to the extent of his abilities in the present struggle for liberty, the honourable House of Assembly may depend on his exertions in the station they have thought proper to assign him." [2]

February 25, another member of the Assembly was elected in his stead.

September 18, 1775, Congress appointed a Secret Committee to contract for the importation of arms and ammunition. Apparently Willing and Morris were the first persons with whom such a contract was made. In the same month great excitement was produced in Congress by information that a contract had been made with them by which they stood to win £12,000. The dispute was as to whether they were guaranteed against loss or guaranteed a profit.[3] Willing was then in Congress. Morris was not.

[1] Penn. Journ. 53.   [2] Ibid. 108.   [3] Adams, ii. 448.

Finances of the American Revolution. 193

The latter made the contract. This incident seems to have first given them a reputation for seeking their own profit in the public necessity.

Morris took his seat in Congress November 3, 1775.

On the 16th of November he was appointed to provide two swift vessels, and also on a committee to devise ways and means of using these vessels, the most important of which was to carry despatches.[1] On the 29th of November he was added to the Secret Committee,[2] taking the place of Mr. Willing, and on the 14th of December he was put on the Committee for raising a naval armament.[3] From these appointments, it is plain that they made use of him at once as an expert in the management of commerce and ships. We shall see immediately that they also made use of him as a banker, his firm being at the time one of the largest dealers in bills of exchange in the colonies.

January 30, 1776, Morris was added to the Committee of Secret Correspondence,[4] and in the same month the Secret Committee were ordered to import as soon as possible large quantities of blankets, cloth, needles, sail-cloth, arms, metals, medicine, and surgeon's instruments.[5] In February we find Morris writing to Charles Lee that more than one man's share of public business falls to his lot. He asserts that America does not want the aid of France, but only protection for commerce; and that if America becomes independent, all will be eager for her trade.[6] He had in mind the preparations that were being made to send out Deane, whose instructions were completed by the Secret Committee, March 3.[7] In March he was put upon com-

[1] Adams, ii. 232.
[2] Secret Journ. i. 36.
[3] Journ. Cong. i. 273.
[4] Ibid. ii. 45.
[5] Ibid. 8.
[6] Lee Papers, i. 303.
[7] 4th Series Am. Archives, v. 48.

mittees to devise ways and means other than bills of credit, and to fortify one or more ports on the coast.¹ In April he was ordered to buy bills of exchange for £3,000 sterling and deliver to Mr. Price for the service of the Continent in Canada, and he was guaranteed against loss.² In that month John Adams wrote to Gates: "You ask me what you are to think of Robert Morris. I will tell you what I think of him. I think he has a masterly understanding, an open temper, and an honest heart; and if he does not always vote for what you and I would think proper, it is because he thinks that a large body of people remain who are not yet of his mind. He has vast designs in the mercantile way, and no doubt pursues mercantile ends, which are always gain; but he is an excellent member of our body."³ In May the Committee on Ways and Means, of which he was a member, made a report. What it was we do not know, but an issue of five million more bills of credit was voted.⁴

Morris was one of those who were slow to come to the determination of independence, like Jay, Duane, Edward Rutledge, Henry Laurens, William Livingston, Dickinson, and others. It may have been that, like Dickinson,⁵ he was restrained by his wife, who, as we shall see below, did not consent to independence till nearly a year later. During the winter of 1775–76, Morris was corresponding with Charles Lee, who was opposed to independence in December, but reached the point of favouring it in January.⁶ In April Morris wrote to Gates with some irritation that

---

[1] Journ. Cong. ii. 87, 104.
[2] Ibid. 130, 139.
[3] 4th Series Am. Archives, v. 1019.
[4] Journ. Cong. ii. 153.
[5] Adams, ii. 408; Thomson Papers, 269.
[6] Lee Papers, i. 233, 255, 266.

the expected commissioners of peace (the Howes) did not appear.[1] He wanted it settled whether liberty could be won by reconciliation or by independence. He therefore opposed the Declaration of Independence. His position on this matter is very fully stated in the following letter to Reed, of July 20, 1776: —

"I am sorry to say there are some amongst us that cannot bear the thought of reconciliation on any terms. To these men all propositions of the kind sound like high treason against the State, and I really believe they would sooner punish a man for this crime than for bearing arms against us. I cannot help condemning this disposition, as it must be founded on keen resentment or on interested views; whereas we ought to have the interest of our country and the good of mankind to act as the mainspring in all our public conduct. I think with you that if the Commissioners have any propositions to make, they ought to be heard. Should they disclose powers different from what we imagine them to be vested with, and an inclination to employ those powers favourably to America, it is our duty to attend to such offers, weigh well the consequences of every determination we come to, and in short to lay aside all prejudices, resentments, and sanguine notions of our own strength, in order that reason may influence and wisdom guide our councils. If the Admiral and General are really desirous of a conference, I think and hope they will address our General properly. This may be expected if they have powers beyond granting pardon; if they have not, it is idle for them to solicit any intercourse, as no good can possibly arise to them or their cause from it. But on our part, I think that good policy requires that we should hear all they have to say. I am not for making any sacrifice of dignity, but still I would hear them if pos-

[1] Lee Papers, i. 388.

sible, because, if they can offer peace on admissible terms, I believe the great majority of America would still be for accepting it. If they can only offer pardon, and that is fully ascertained, it will firmly unite all America in their exertions to support the independency they have declared; and it must be obvious to everybody that our united efforts will be absolutely necessary. This being the case, why should we fear to treat of peace, or to hear the Commissioners on that subject? . . . I have uniformly voted against and opposed the Declaration of Independence, because in my poor opinion it was an improper time, and will neither promote the interests, nor redound to the honor of America; for it has caused division when we wanted union, and will be ascribed to very different principles than those which ought to give rise to such an important measure. I did expect my conduct on this great question would have procured my dismission from the great council, but find myself disappointed; for the Convention has thought proper to return me in the new delegation, and although my interest and inclination prompt me to decline the service, yet I cannot depart from one point, which first induced me to enter the public line. I mean an opinion that it is the duty of every individual to act his part in whatever station his country may call him to in times of difficulty, danger, and distress. Whilst I think this a duty, I must submit, although the councils of America have taken a different course from my judgment and wishes. I think that the individual who declines the service of his country because its councils are not conformable to his ideas makes but a bad subject. A good one will follow if he cannot lead." [1]

The Declaration of Independence, having been engrossed, was signed by the members on the 2d of August,[2]

[1] Reed's Reed, I. 199.   [2] Secret Journ. Cong. ii. 49.

when Morris signed it with the rest, and, having thus adopted a determination, he was dissatisfied with the conflicts and bickerings which arose in Pennsylvania over the new Constitution, and desired that the military operations should absorb all the energy of the country.[1]

In 1776 Morris was charged with certain negotiations with General Charles Lee. In January, 1775, Lee acknowledged a letter of credit which he had received from Morris, which shows that Morris was at that time engaged in this class of business.[2] In July Lee wrote that he was glad that Pennsylvania affairs were in Morris's hands.[3] Lee's military reputation was very high, perhaps higher than that of any other man in America; but he was an English half-pay officer, and would suffer pecuniary loss if he took the American side. He stipulated for an indemnity from Congress for this loss, and it was arranged that an estate in Virginia should be purchased for him through Robert Morris. September 7, 1775, Lee wrote to Morris that he was glad that the latter was to arrange the purchase, and, December 9, he thanked him for having completed it.[4] January 3, 1776, he wrote asking Morris to explain to Congress the state of his Virginia purchase, and that his estate in England had no doubt been confiscated; and January 30, he put his case before Congress in Morris's hands. In July, 1776, he wrote that the half of his estate which was paid for was more properly Morris's than his own. He wanted Congress to pay off the encumbrances, and give him a capital with which to manage it. He did not know certainly that his English property was confiscated.[5] The estate in Virginia had been bought for £5,000 or £6,000, and the money to pay for it had been borrowed of Morris. The bills which Lee drew on England in order to pay for

[1] Letter to Gates, 5th Series Am. Archives, ii. 1262. [2] Lee Papers, i. 168.
[3] Ibid. 199.   [4] Ibid. 205, 220.   [5] Ibid. ii. 118.

it were returned protested.¹ October 7, 1776, Congress ordered $30,000 to be advanced to General Lee upon his bond to take such steps in conjunction with Robert Morris as would secure the transfer of his interests in England to reimburse Congress for the advance now made to him. Two days later this bond was reported to and approved by Congress.² In 1781 we find Lee complaining that Morris does not honour his drafts,³ and in 1782 it appears that Morris furnished the means to deliver Lee from a bad bargain he had made to sell some land.⁴ In 1784 Congress authorized Morris to discharge the estate of General Lee from all liens for the $30,000 advanced to him, upon the payment of the balance due to the United States.

As the year 1776 went on, the functions of the committees of which Morris was a member became more and important. In August and September the Secret Committee charged him to buy up tobacco for export on account of the United States.⁵ Here began an affair which, as we shall see, pursued him with great trouble all his life.

October 1, 1776, Thomas Story, an agent whom the Secret Committee had sent to London, came home and reported that Arthur Lee had charged him to say that the Count de Vergennes had sent an agent to Lee to say that the French could not think of going to war with England, but would send from Holland to the West Indies £200,000 sterling worth of arms and ammunition, which could be obtained by inquiring there for M. Hortales. This was told only to Franklin and Morris, who kept it secret, because everything that was made known in Congress speedily leaked out, and also because Morris belonged to all the committees which could properly be employed in

¹ Moore's Treason of Lee, 33.   ² Journ. Cong. ii. 378.
³ Lee Papers, iii. 459.   ⁴ Ibid. 476.
⁵ State Dep. MSS., Reports Committees, iv. 273.

receiving and forwarding these goods from the West Indies.¹

Morris was also on the committee to devise means of regulating the post-office and to establish advice boats between Philadelphia and the southern colonies;² and on that to determine the rank and pay of naval officers.³ December 12, he was empowered to borrow a sum not exceeding $10,000 for the Marine Committee, with the promise that Congress would indemnify him. On the 20th, Congress, having removed to Baltimore, requested him to send one hundred half johannes⁴ to General Washington for the use of General Lee, who had just been captured and taken to New York. On the 21st they appointed Morris, Clymer, and Walton a committee to execute continental business at Philadelphia during the absence of Congress, and approved of a plan of Morris to fit out the continental frigates at Philadelphia for sea as quickly as possible.⁵

This flight of Congress from Philadelphia in December, 1776, was much blamed by some ardent whigs. John Cadwallader wrote to Robert Morris: "For God's sake, why did you remove from Philadelphia? You have given an invitation to the enemy; you have discovered a timidity that encourages our enemy and discourages our friends; you have given a stab to your credit, and if you pay off your present army, I believe you cannot find money to raise a new one. The city cannot be taken by surprise. You should have left the city when our troops retreated through it."⁶ The people fled from Philadelphia in great alarm.⁷ Wilkinson said that the city was as silent as a

---

¹ Dip. Corr. Rev. ii. 16. ² Journ. Cong. ii. 315. ³ Ibid. 410.
⁴ A Portuguese gold coin worth four dollars of that day.
⁵ Ibid. 466. ⁶ 5th Ser. Amer. Arch. iii. 1231.
⁷ Marshall's Diary, 105.

wilderness of houses.[1] Morris, however, remained there,[2] charged with the duties of the committee above mentioned, and he appears to have been the representative of "the Continent," while Congress was at Baltimore and Washington was executing the manœuvre by which he fell upon the English at Trenton and Princeton. The moment was one which may be fairly called the real crisis of the Revolution.

We have a great number of long and important letters written by Morris during these weeks of midwinter, 1776–77, to the Commissioners in France, to Congress, and to Washington. December 21, he wrote to the Commissioners: "This city was for ten days the greatest scene of distress that you can conceive. Everybody but Quakers were removing their families and effects, and now it looks dismal and melancholy. The Quakers and their families pretty generally remain; the other inhabitants are principally sick soldiers,— some few effective ones under General Putnam, who has come here to throw up lines and prepare for the defence of the place, if General Washington should be forced to retreat hither. You may be sure I have my full share of trouble on this occasion; but having got my family and books removed to a place of safety, my mind is more at ease, and my time is now given up to the public, although I have many thousand pounds' worth of effects here, without any prospect of saving them."

He describes the depreciation of the currency and its immediate effects, and urges the Commissioners to get aid from France. "If the court of France open their eyes to their own interests, and think the commerce of North America will compensate them for the expense and evil

[1] Wilkinson, i. 127.
[2] Mrs. Morris went to Baltimore on a visit to her sister, and remained until March (Penn. Mag. ii. 158).

of a war with Britain, they may readily create a diversion and afford us succours that will change the face of affairs; but they must do it soon. Our situation is critical, and does not admit of delay. I do not mean by this that instant submission must ensue if they do not directly afford us relief, but there is a great difference between the benefit they will derive from a commercial connection with this country in full health and vigour, and what they can possibly expect after it is exhausted by repeated efforts during the precarious process of a tedious war, during which its cities will be destroyed, the country ravaged, the inhabitants reduced in numbers, plundered of their property, and unable to reap the luxuriant produce of the finest soil in the world. Neither can they, after a tedious result in negotiations, expect that vigorous assistance from us in prosecuting the war that they may be assured of if they join us in its infancy. If they join us generously in the day of our distress, without attempting undue advantages because we are so, they will find a grateful people to promote their future glory and interest with unabating zeal. And from my knowledge of the commerce of this country with Europe, I dare assert that whatever European power possesses the pre-emption of it must of consequence become the richest and most potent in Europe. But should time be lost in tedious negotiations and succours be withheld, America must sue for peace from her oppressors. Our people knew not the hardships and calamities of war when they so boldly dared Britain to arms. Every man was then a bold patriot, felt himself equal to the contest, and seemed to wish for an opportunity of evincing his prowess. But now when we are fairly engaged, when death and ruin stare us in the face, and when nothing but the most intrepid courage can rescue us from contempt and disgrace, sorry am I to say it, many of those who were foremost in noise shrink cowardlike from the danger, and are begging pardon without striking a blow. This, however, is not general; but dejection of spirit is an epidemical disease, and unless some fortunate event or other gives a turn to the disorder, in time it may prevail throughout the community. No event would give that turn so soon as a declaration of war on the part of France with Great Britain, and I am sure if they lose this golden opportunity they will never have such another. . . . In short, nothing but the most arduous exertions and virtuous conduct in the leaders, seconded by a spirited behaviour in the army, and a patient endurance of hardships by the people in general, can long support the contest. Therefore the court of France should strike at once, as they will reap an immediate harvest. . . . I will not enter into any detail of our conduct in Congress; but you may depend on this, that so long as that respectable body persist in the attempt to execute as well as to deliberate on their business, it never will be done at all, and this has been urged many and many a time by myself and others. But some of them do not like to part with power, or to pay others for doing what they cannot do themselves." He admits the justice of the complaints about want of intelligence, and throws the blame on his colleagues. "You know well I was not put on that committee to carry on the correspondence, but to find out the conveyances. However, I have been obliged to write all the letters that have been written for some time past. . . . Some of us are of very sanguine complexion, and are too apt to flatter ourselves that things are not so bad as they appear to be, or that they will soon mend, etc. Now, my notion is that you, gentlemen Commissioners, should be fairly and fully informed of the true state of affairs, that you may make a proper use of that knowledge, — keeping secret what ought to be so, and promulgating what should be known." [1]

Two days later he wrote to Washington bewailing the situation, which he attributed to short enlistments adopted by the influence of New England. He gave lists of goods which had arrived, in order that Washington might order from them what he needed, and he sent bills of exchange for General Lee.[2] He also transmitted the news he had received from Deane, that an outfit for thirty thousand men would be sent out, and, on account of the public papers in his hands, asked Washington to tell him when to leave Philadelphia. December 13, he wrote to the President of Congress that he was sending away the public ships, lest Howe should cross the Delaware, and was paying the debts of the Marine Committee.[3] He reported to Congress the news received from Deane, especially Deane's complaint that he had been so long left in ignorance and unprovided with remittances. He urged that competent executive officers should be constituted and appointed, even as a measure of economy, and made a prediction which was fully justified in the following years, that more would be lost if this step were not taken than "would have paid all the salaries Paine ever did or ever will grumble at." He also stated that the continental currency continued to depreciate, and that the mills would not work for the Commissary, either through disaffection or opposition to the currency. These letters from him to Congress in December and January are very numerous; and they show that he received and forwarded supplies, borrowed money, repaired and fitted out ships, sent them out to obtain information, and sent salt out of the city that it might be saved from capture;

---
[1] Dip. Corr. Rev. i 237.
[2] R. I. Col. Rec. vii. 167 and viii. 165.
[3] 5th Ser. Amer Arch. iii. 1198.

also that the extent of the duty which he thus undertook led him to fear that Congress might not approve.[1]

In answer to an appeal from Washington for £150 in hard money for secret service, without which information could not be obtained, Morris undertook to supply it, borrowing silver and promising to repay in gold, which he must obtain as he could. "I had long since parted with very considerable sums of hard money to Congress, therefore must collect from others; and as matters now stand, it is no easy matter."[2] Washington made another appeal immediately after for money with which to pay a bounty to his soldiers, in order to keep them in the service; for at this moment his army had almost entirely disappeared. Morris replied: "It gives me great pleasure that you have engaged the troops to continue; and if further occasional supplies of money are necessary, you may depend on my exertions, either in a public or private capacity."[3]

It should not be inferred that Morris advanced any sums otherwise than as a small and temporary loan, especially of hard money. He was a debtor to Congress on the commercial account, and was secured for all advances. The transaction between silver and gold, by which he proposed to induce holders of silver to lend it to the public, could all the more easily be executed for himself by himself.

We have already seen what the case was when he acted as a merchant. We here see what it was when he acted as a banker. It has been mentioned above that Congress ordered him to send a sum in coin to General Lee. They gave this order because they supposed it impossible to send bills, or because they had forbidden the negotiation of bills with the English. He found an opportunity to send bills indorsed by himself, which he thought could be negotiated

---

[1] State Dep. MSS. 137, App. 16 and fg.
[2] Letters to Washington, i. 315.   [3] Ibid. 317.

in New York. In such a transaction he was banker, broker, and buyer all in one.[1]

It will be found that Morris's life was embittered by both large and small attacks upon him as having made gain for himself out of his services to the public, and we have seen that he was in a false position. The public sought his services in the position of a statesman, not because he was a statesman, but because he was a merchant and banker, and they wanted the professional services of a merchant and banker. What his high-principled critics demanded was that in his public capacity he should be both public man and private man, but that in his private capacity he should abstain from any knowledge or opportunity of the public man. In the present case, for instance, how could a *statesman* plan to borrow silver and pay gold in order to obtain money for public use? Morris was not in any financial office; he was a volunteer, to whom everybody turned in a moment of crisis and who was anything or everything for the service of the cause. He employed for the public all the knowledge or opportunities which he possessed. Every man in the Revolutionary period who acted with disinterested zeal and energy exposed himself to abuse, misrepresentation, and trouble. The reason was because, when no business methods were duly observed, such men acted without obtaining proper records; but when they came to the accounting, the strictest record might be demanded of them. It was impossible and unreasonable to demand that a public man should buy and sell goods, gold, and bills of exchange as if he had been a broker, and that a private banker and merchant should be a public man without buying and selling goods, gold, and bills of exchange. Yet this was the false position in which Morris was placed. The transactions which were to be

[1] R. I. Col. Rec. viii. 167; Lee Papers, ii. 356, 366.

made between paper and metal, between gold and silver, between the currency and bills of exchange, offered him great chances of gain; and if he put his hand in his own pocket upon occasion, the repayment involved an inevitable transaction affecting his own interest. There is no reason to doubt that he profited largely as an individual by all his connection with the public service. If we were to enter upon an inquiry how far this was right and proper, we should find it a very delicate question, which would require far more minute information than we possess about the facts; but Thomas Paine and others insisted that it was wrong for him to gain at all.

After April, 1777, the Committee of Secret Correspondence was called the Committee of Foreign Affairs, and in July it was reconstituted and called the Committee of Commerce, the Secret Committee being ordered to close its accounts and transfer balances to this Committee.[1] Morris continued a member of it through all its changes. In a letter written by his wife in April, it is stated that he had been offered the presidency of Congress, but had refused on account of his private business. She says that she begins to be reconciled to independence.[2]

There are many entries in the Journal of Congress in 1777 which show that Morris acted as the banker of the Secret Committee. Its agents drew on him, or on Willing and Morris, and Congress paid by drafts on the loan offices.[3]

We also find many traces of the activity of Morris as a merchant on behalf of Congress, and on behalf of the various committees of which he was a member.

In May, 1776, on behalf of the Marine Committee, he issued orders to Captain Hopkins to bring cannon from

---

[1] Journ. Cong. iii 221. [2] Penn. Mag. ii. 160.
[3] Journ. Cong. iii. 168; cf. Bland Papers, i. 50, 62, and 65.

Providence to New York.¹ In February, 1777, he wrote to the Council of Safety of Pennsylvania, enclosing a report that the enemy intended to make an attack on the salt-works at Tom's River. He proposed to send the armed boat "Delaware," belonging to the State, to defend the works.² In April he wrote for the Marine Committee to the Council of War of Rhode Island, asking them to fit out frigates there and send them to Boston. They were to be manned with men drafted from the militia.³

In November, 1776, Paul Wentworth reported to Lord Suffolk that Deane had made a contract on behalf of Willing and Morris with persons in France, England, and Holland, to form a company for trading between France and America in clothing, sail-cloth, shoes, blankets, and drugs. The capital was to be £400,000, and the cargoes were to be represented as French property and placed on French ships, but with American passes. No military stores were to be shipped. The French ambassador promised to avoid war with England, in order not to jeopardize this property.⁴ In June, 1777, one of the English spies sent word that a ship was coming from the Mississippi with forty thousand dollars for account of Willing and Morris, and proposed that a ship should be sent to cruise and intercept this vessel. He also mentioned a privateer, the "Tartar," which was going into the Mediterranean, and was owned by Conyngham, Nesbitt, Willing and Morris, and S. Deane, the captain of which had a credit from Thomas Morris on Marseilles.⁵

Some of these adventures were evidently independent enterprises, planned with a view to selling, either to Congress or in the open market, commodities which were selling at the time at greatly advanced prices. The profits

[1] Penn. Col. Rec. x. 565.   [2] Ibid. xi. 126.
[3] R. I. Col. Rec. viii. 214.   [4] Stevens, 131.   [5] Ibid. 168.

must have been very great, if the vessels escaped capture.

June 26, Morris signed the oath of allegiance to the State of Pennsylvania under an Act of the Assembly requiring all white persons to do so.[1]

As indicating the position in public affairs which was generally attributed to Morris, we may note the following: In March, 1777, Lewis Morris, being charged with important business on behalf of the State of New York with Congress, wrote to the State Congress that he was very sanguine of success, since he had secured the assistance of Robert Morris, whose abilities and influence were rated very high.[2] In a paper by Paul Wentworth, in October, it is said that Congress is ruled by R. H. Lee, S. Adams, J. Adams, and Morris. "The highest degree of political profligacy already prevails."[3] In a more elaborate paper by the same person on men and parties in America, written probably in 1778, the statement about Robert Morris is: "Active, zealous, a great and the most useful partisan on the continent, bold and enterprising, of great mercantile knowledge, fertile in expedients and an able financier, very popular in and out of Congress, grown extremely rich, was the first promoter of privateering and the commerce to France and the West India Islands, is much confided in by all the cabals."[4]

[1] 2d Ser. Penn. Archives, iii. 9.
[2] N. Y. Journ. ii. 404.
[3] Stevens, 277.
[4] Ibid. 487.

CHAPTER X.

1777–81: MORRIS IN THE PENNSYLVANIA ASSEMBLY; THOMAS MORRIS; SILAS DEANE AND PARTIES IN CONGRESS; THE SHIP "FARMER;" THE COMMITTEE OF PHILADELPHIA; THE FORT WILSON RIOT; THE TENDER LAWS OF PENNSYLVANIA.

AFTER the capture of Philadelphia and the removal of Congress to York, Morris obtained from the State Council, November 11, 1777, leave of absence from Congress for six months. He said that the firm of Willing and Morris was about to dissolve; and he proposed to take the books of the Committee of Commerce to his house at Manheim and adjust the public accounts.[1]

November 29, he was appointed on a committee of Congress to visit the camp and urge Washington to make a winter campaign against the English in Philadelphia.[2] It did not lie with Washington to assume the offensive. The astonishment of all the onlookers was that Howe did not attack Valley Forge. Duportail did not see what would become of the Americans if he should do so, and Stedman's book seems to have been written in order to express his indignation at the supineness of the English commanders.[3]

Morris appears to have been at the time under a fit of dissatisfaction with the course of things. He wrote to General Gates in October: "We are disputing about

[1] Penn. Archives, v. 759. See p 223 fg. [2] Journ. Cong. iii. 424.
[3] Stedman, 1. 308.

liberties, privileges, posts, and places, at the very time we ought to have nothing in view but the securing of those objects and placing them on such a footing as to make them worth contending for among ourselves hereafter. But instead of that, the vigour of this and several other States is lost in intestine divisions; and unless this spirit of contention is checked by some other means, I fear it will have a baneful influence on the measures of America."[1]

Indeed, there was sufficient ground for anxiety and distress of mind. Duponceau, who visited York with Steuben, in February, 1778, wrote: "The Congress of the United States were not at that time the illustrious body whose eloquence and wisdom, whose stern virtues and unflinching patriotism, had astonished the world. Their number was reduced to about one half of what it was when independence was declared. All but a few of the men of superior minds had disappeared from it. Their measures were feeble and vacillating, and their party feuds seemed to forebode some impending calamity. . . . Such was the state of things when we arrived at York. Parties were then at their height; but as Congress sat with closed doors, the country at large was not agitated as it would otherwise have been. There were not wanting out of doors disaffected persons who railed at 'King Cong.,' and a bunch of 'kings.' Such was the slang of the day among the tories. But the great mass of the people was still in favour of the Revolution, and the Press did not dare to utter a sentiment inimical to it."[2]

Duportail thought the Americans unenthusiastic, fond of ease, and destitute of fortitude. "There is a hundred

---

[1] Quoted in Sparks's Morris, i. 231, note.
[2] Steuben, 100; cf. R. I. Col. Rec. viii. 370.

Finances of the American Revolution. 211

times more enthusiasm for this Revolution in the first café you choose to name at Paris than there is in all the United States together."[1]

Morris's estate of Manheim, which has just been mentioned, was about ten miles north of the city of Lancaster. It was laid out by a German named Stiegel in 1762, who built a large square house of imported brick, having a "meeting room" in the second story, where he preached to his servants and the employés of a glass factory which he had established. He became bankrupt, and the house was sold in 1777. Morris's name is not among the list of taxables in 1780, and this estate is not mentioned among his property at a later time.[2] Baron Steuben and his party were at Manheim, February 4, 1778.[3]

Immediately after Morris obtained his leave of absence and went to Manheim, John Brown of Philadelphia came from Thomas Willing to Morris with a message that General Howe had proposed to some members of Congress that if they would rescind the Declaration of Independence, he would withdraw his fleet and army, restore the status of 1763, and establish the paper currency.[4] The Council of Safety, which was sitting at Lancaster, committed Brown to jail. Morris gave assurances of Brown's innocent intentions, saying that he had been one of his own employés. He wanted Brown paroled to Manheim.[5] Brown seems to have lain in jail two months; but on the 25th of January, 1778, he was released on bail, under a parol not to go more than five miles from Manheim.[6] The Pennsylvania Council published a criticism of this

[1] Stedman, i. 387.
[2] Ellis & Evans, Lancaster Co. 607; Penn. Mag. ii. 161.
[3] Steuben, 99.   [4] Penn. Col. Rec. xi. 346.
[5] Penn. Archives, vi. 45.   [6] Penn. Col. Rec. xi. 406.

attempt at reconciliation, pointing out with much force its weak points, — a verbal message, by an obscure and unauthorized person, etc. The incident would have very little importance if it were not that it was often afterward brought up against both Willing and Morris.

It was during the winter of 1777-78 that Morris suffered great annoyance and chagrin from the misbehaviour of his half-brother, Thomas, for whom he had secured an appointment as commercial agent of the United States at Nantes. Robert had brought up and educated Thomas, but the young man had contracted dissipated habits, whereupon Robert sent him to Europe to separate him from his bad companions, and to give him an opportunity to learn French and Spanish.[1] He was made also commercial agent of Willing and Morris at Nantes, so that he had under his control both the prizes, and the cargoes shipped by that firm on government account.[2]

In July Ross wrote to Deane that they two must dispossess Thomas of his office, and protect the interests of Robert Morris, on account of the young man's bad habits.[3] Deane and Franklin tried to displace him and put Williams, Franklin's nephew, in his place. They wrote to Congress stating the facts about Thomas, and explaining what they had done. Robert Morris then asked Congress if the conduct of his brother in the discharge of his duty had not been satisfactory. There was no proof to the contrary. Thereupon Robert wrote to Thomas a letter which one of the English spies pretended to quote as follows: " 'T is not all the Commissioners in France that are able to remove his brother from his present office, in spite of all the nephews or relations they may have or

[1] Laurens Corresp. 71.
[2] Morris to Tilghman, June 10, 1784; Ford MSS.
[3] Laurens Corresp. 35.

wish to provide for."¹ Thomas, with this letter in his hands, defied and insulted the Commissioners. He also pasted it up at Nantes, so that it might be seen by all the merchants there.

Franklin considered himself "rapped over the knuckles" by Robert Morris, and left the further responsibility to him.² The English spy wrote that the affair had greatly humbled the Commissioners, and that they had promised to report nothing further about Thomas to Congress.³

From friend and foe alike, however, Robert now received information of the misdoings of his brother. William Lee wrote to his brother, and to Robert Morris directly, that Thomas's affairs were in hopeless confusion, but later he tried to make common cause with Thomas against the Commissioners.⁴ Izard, being ill, caused his wife to write that Thomas was a disgrace to America.⁵ Deane wrote deprecating Morris's anger, but saying that Thomas's behaviour was outrageous.⁶ He said that he bore no grudge against Robert Morris.⁷

Upon the receipt of these letters, Morris wrote to Peters begging him to come to Manheim for the holidays, saying that he had a sad Christmas on account of the misbehaviour of a worthless brother.⁸ He was busy at the time writing a long letter to the President of Congress in regard to the matter. "It adds very much," he wrote, "to the distress and unhappiness this unworthy young man has involved me in, to think I should have passed censures on Dr. Franklin and Mr. Deane which they did not deserve. I did it under a deception that most men

---

[1] Stevens, 199. [2] Ford's W. Lee, 259.
[3] Stevens, 204. [4] Ford's W. Lee, 240, 336.
[5] State Dep. MSS., Letters of Izard, etc. 89.
[6] Laurens Corresp. 117. [7] Stevens, 194, 199. See also 295.
[8] Peters MSS.

of feeling would have fallen into, and I shall as freely own it to them as I do to you, holding it more honourable to acknowledge an error and atone for any injuries produced by it than, with a vindictive spirit, to persist because you happen to have committed it. My distress is more than I can describe. To think that in the midst of the most arduous exertions I was capable of making to promote the interest and welfare of my country I should be the means of introducing a worthless wretch to disgrace and discredit it, is too much to bear."[1] A few days later he wrote: "I hope no time will be lost in transmitting Mr. Thomas Morris's dismission, that the Commissioners may be no longer plagued, nor the public injured, by his indiscretion."[2]

On the 28th of February, 1778, the Commissioners wrote that Thomas Morris was dead.[3] They obtained delivery of his papers to William Lee, by whom they were delivered sealed in a trunk to Franklin, who refused to separate the public and private papers.[4] A year later W. Lee wrote to R. H. Lee that he thought Morris had made use of his position on the Secret Committee to conceal Lee's letters until he got the order that Thomas Morris's papers should be delivered to him.[5] September 4, 1778, Congress ordered that these papers should be surrendered to Robert Morris, that he might proceed to a settlement of the accounts.[6] These papers and the accounts of Thomas Morris are mentioned over and over again in connection with the accounts of the Committee of Commerce, and seem to have added very much to the complication and difficulty of those affairs. Robert Morris promised to pay to the government anything which

[1] Laurens Corresp. 78.
[2] State Dep. MSS. No. 137, App. 201.
[3] Dip. Corr. Rev. i. 372.
[4] Lee's A. Lee, i. 392, 399.
[5] Ford's W. Lee, proof sheet.
[6] Journ Cong. iv. 370.

Thomas Morris owed; but the house at Nantes also had credits for money of Willing and Morris which had been spent for the account of Congress there. The unbusinesslike proceedings had been by no means all on one side.[1]

Simeon Deane, writing to Silas Deane, probably in the spring of 1778, says that the southern and eastern men in Congress are opposed to Morris, also that the President of Congress is opposed to him.[2]

March 5, Morris signed the Articles of Confederation on behalf of Pennsylvania. His name does not appear in the yeas and nays until July 15. It seems that he did not attend at York at all.

In the summer of 1778 his name was prominently connected with the Peace Commission, which was sent out from England. Johnston, one of the Commissioners, wrote to him in June:[3] "I believe the men who have conducted the affairs of America incapable of being influenced by improper motives; but in all such transactions there is risk, and I think that whoever ventures should be secure, at the same time that honour and emolument would naturally follow the fortunes of those who have steered the vessel in the storm and brought her safely to port. I think Washington and the President have a right to every favour that grateful nations can bestow, if they could once more unite our interests and spare the miseries and devastations of war."[4] On the 11th of August Congress adopted a declaration, in which they recited the above and other passages from letters to Morris and Joseph Reed, and resolved to have no intercourse with Johnston. The other

[1] Almon for 1778-79, 385.   [2] Deane Papers.
[3] The Editor of Reed's Reed says that there is among the Morris Papers a letter from Johnston to Morris, dated February 5, 1778, informing him of the conciliatory movement of the government, and begging him to try to prevent a connection with France (Reed's Reed, i. 379).
[4] Almon, 1778-79, 11.

Commissioners published a declaration that they knew nothing of these letters. Quite a literature grew out of the affair, but Morris was not actively interested in it.

August 27, 1778, Morris was made chairman of the Committee of Congress on Finance. His term in Congress ended November 1, 1778, according to the limitation in the Constitution of Pennsylvania, he having served two years since that Constitution was adopted. In the last month of his service he voted in favour of a motion, which was adopted, that "all limitations of prices of gold and silver be taken off;" in favour of resolutions discountenancing theatrical entertainments, horse-racing, gaming, and dissipation, and that army officers should repress profanity and vice; also with the minority against a resolution that officers of the army who frequented plays and play-houses should be dismissed. Throughout his career he voted for the sober and moderate view of things.

He continued to act, upon occasion, as the banker of Congress. In June, 1779, the Board of Treasury was authorized to borrow five hundred guineas, assuring the lenders of the repayment of principal and interest in hard money, "as soon as the Treasury shall be supplied with a sufficient sum."[1] Morris advanced this sum.[2] In February, 1780, Congress ordered the loan officer of Pennsylvania to draw on Jay at Madrid in payment of this advance. John Jay had nothing, but was, at just about the time that the bill drawn in pursuance of this order would have been presented to him, importuning the Spanish minister to grant him $333 with which to take up a bill.[3] Franklin described bills of this kind as "drawn on the pump at Aldgate."[4] We can only guess how much this bill was worth at Philadelphia when drawn, or how it was paid. If the banker of

---

[1] Secret Journ. i. 120.
[2] Ibid. 142.
[3] Franklin in France, i. 409.
[4] Ibid. 430.

Congress received large commissions, he took great risks. It was not in the temper of the times to take account of this.

Morris was elected a member of the Pennsylvania Assembly as soon as his term in Congress expired, and took his seat November 6, 1778. He was one of the members who, at the opening of that session, in taking the oath to the Constitution, reserved the right to agitate for the amendment of it.[1]

The party with which he acted immediately set about an attempt to secure a convention to revise it. It was voted to take the sense of the people whether such a convention should be called, but on a petition to rescind this vote it was done.[2] The bitterness of the struggle over the revision of this Constitution was so great that it had deep and lasting effects on the reputation and relations of all the public men of the State, and on the course of affairs, including the relation of Pennsylvania to the Confederation. Morris remained a member of the State Assembly until June, 1781, with the exception of the legislative year November, 1779, to November, 1780.

The most important affair of the winter of 1778–79, both for public interests and for the personal fortunes of Morris, was that of Silas Deane. Deane's chief offence had been, as we have seen, that he had put Congress to a great deal of annoyance by sending over a number of officers under contracts which it was inconvenient or impossible for Congress to fulfil. This had irritated them against him. The charges, however, which were formulated against him were that he had traded on his own account under cover of his public capacity; that he had misapplied public money, and had owned shares in privateers which were fitted out at public expense. Similar charges were also formulated

[1] Penn. Journ. i. 232.   [2] Ibid. 324.

against the other Commissioners, varied only to fit the case of each.[1]

The general opinion of students of this matter at the present time seems to be that Deane was a victim of circumstances and of imprudent zeal. The charge against him of trading on his own account was not without foundation.[2] In his address of 1784, he said that he engaged in two commercial ventures while in the service of Congress. Morris, as will presently appear, mentioned three enterprises in which he had been engaged with Deane. Deane also claimed that he was sent out to France with instructions to maintain the character of a merchant, and that he had a right to be a real one.

He came home in March, 1778. An account of the expenditures in Europe, especially of the transactions with Beaumarchais, was demanded of him, although he had not been told when he was recalled that this was what was desired, but rather had been given to understand that Congress wanted a full explanation of the diplomatic and political relations.[3] His proceedings and his interests became really the sport of parties in Congress. In general the party of union, which sustained Washington, was favourable to Deane, while the party against Washington and in favour of State rights was against Deane. Sectionally, the latter party was a combination of Virginia and Massachusetts,[4] with the Lees and the Adamses as the leaders of it. Arthur Lee had infused an element of base suspicion and calumny into the whole affair by his letters from Europe.[5]

[1] Deane Papers, 87.
[2] See Letter of Simeon Deane, and Carmichael's Examination in the Deane Papers; Lee's A. Lee, i. 351, 363, 410; ii. 134.
[3] Deane's Narrative, 57; Secret Journ. ii. 485.
[4] We meet with a suggestion, in a paper by Paul Wentworth, that the union of Virginia and Massachusetts rested on similar interests with regard to western land claims (Stevens, 200). [5] Franklin, viii. 446.

By bringing together the papers which remain, we can at the present time see that there was a veil of mystery over all the parties and their relations with each other. If Arthur Lee and Deane could have been confronted with each other in Philadelphia for an hour, it seems that much of the difficulty might have been cleared up, but they were never both on this side of the water at the same time.[1]

In May, 1779, Lee wrote: "There is, you may depend upon it, some deep design against our independence, at the bottom. Many of the faction are, I know, actuated by the desire of getting or retaining the public plunder; but besides this, Duane, Jay, Morris, and others, who were originally against our independence, have it certainly in view to bring us back to our former denomination. . . . The same men who have been tempted by avarice to plunder the public, have avarice, vanity, and ambition to tempt them to sell the public." Also from another letter, of August 3, 1779: "So effectually have the seeds sown by the father of corruption here prospered, both in Europe and America, that everything yields to it. Dumas has been at Passy some weeks, but is not permitted to come near me. Sayre tells me his object is to get the agency for a loan into the hands of a French house. If he offers good *private* reasons it will embarrass the good Doctor exceedingly, because the house of Grand, in whose hands it is at present, is in partnership with Deane, in which probably the Dr. may share; and therefore it will wound those honourable and friendly feelings which bind them together. As to the public, that is out of the question."[2]

In June, 1776, Arthur Lee had sent to Deane, who forwarded it to Morris, on account of the latter's position on the Committee of Correspondence, a letter concealed in the cover of a dictionary, which contained a warning

---

[1] Cf. Franklin, viii. 428.   [2] Ibid. 446; Ed. note.

against Joseph Reed, and also an assertion that members of Congress were in correspondence with persons at London, through whom information was given to the ministry. Morris did not know the secret of the dictionary, but laid it aside at his country seat, Manheim.[1] January 5, 1778, Morris sent to the President of Congress, from Manheim, all Deane's letters down to October 1, 1777. "The contents are mortifying to me; but as I am conscious that I do not deserve the reflections and insinuations made against me, so I hope the Congress will be convinced thereof by the letter I had the honour to write you on the occasion."[2] Deane was kept waiting by Congress in Philadelphia without a hearing until August, when it was voted that he should give a statement of all his transactions in France and of the state of the funds there;[3] but the hearing and investigation were not conducted to a conclusion.

There is a singular lack of straightforwardness about the whole affair. Congress did not pursue it as if they were bent on finding out the facts and disposing of the matter. On the other hand, Deane never made a really clear and satisfactory statement of facts on which his friends could rely. It was said that he refused to answer any questions which might incriminate himself.[4] He was justly blamed for not being in a position to explain affairs in Europe. The conclusion seems unavoidable that party spirit controlled the affair. Paine made a list of the votes on his own dismissal as showing the position of parties in the Deane affair. It is a close party vote as the parties then stood.[5]

There are many suggestions in connection with the

[1] 4th Ser. Amer. Arch. vi. 685; Reed's Reed, i. 397.
[2] State Dep. MSS. No 137. App. 201.   [3] Journ. Cong. iv. 336.
[4] Lovell to Lee; Lee's A. Lee, ii. 146.   [5] Penn. Packet, April 13, 1779.

Deane affair which would lead one to suppose that Carmichael was to blame for the disadvantageous opinions about Deane which were entertained by members of Congress.[1] Carmichael was examined September 28, 1778.[2] His evidence, however, is not at all of a character to account for the injurious opinions. He expressed his own suspicion that Deane had used money obtained from Beaumarchais to buy ships which were sent out for private interests. He thought that Franklin knew about the fitting out of these vessels; but Franklin said that Beaumarchais charged the expenses to Deane's private account. Carmichael showed very clearly that he had no ground whatever for his suspicions, but had taken them up as a bystander who had no information by which to understand what he saw going on.

When Deane was recalled, the French government apparently perceived that a fierce fight was to be made against him. In Gerard's instructions of April 22, 1778, he was told not to be drawn into this contest at all; he was to persuade Deane to stay in America, and was to show the Americans that France had entered into the war entirely on their account, and not from interested motives.[3]

Gerard thought that Deane's case illustrated the policy of the Americans to ostracize any man who, having become important, could be spared.[4]

Finally, Deane, his patience being exhausted, appealed to the public through the newspapers in an address to the " Free and Virtuous Citizens of America."[5] He said that "the ears of Congress were shut" against him. One party now declared that this proceeding on Deane's part was

[1] Journ. Cong. iv. 395.   [2] Deane Papers, 144.
[3] Doniol, iii. 280.   [4] Ibid. 295.
[5] Penn. Packet, Dec. 5, 1778.

entirely improper, while the other defended it. Laurens resigned the presidency of Congress. It seemed to him that Congress admitted the justice of Deane's complaint if they did not resent his publication.[1] It is certain that by this step Deane got attention to his case. John Adams was greatly outraged at his proceeding. He thought it "a dissolution of the Confederation" that Congress had not censured him.[2]

Thomas Paine took it upon himself to reply to Deane in a series of letters. Other letter writers took part in the controversy. As it went further, Paine widened the scope of his assertions. In the "Packet" of January 2, 1779, he said that Deane was supported by many persons for interested reasons; that there was a clique which wanted him to be minister to Holland,[3] and he asserted that the supplies were promised to the United States before Deane arrived in Paris, as he could show from the records in his office, he being clerk of the Committee of Foreign Affairs, if Congress would grant an order for him to do so. He had in mind the information sent from London by Arthur Lee. Congress now called on the editor to state who wrote this article.[4] He said that it was Paine. On the 7th of January Congress resolved that this publication on foreign affairs was premature and indiscreet; that Congress had never received military stores as a present from any European court; and that Paine should be dismissed under censure by the Committee on Foreign Affairs. They had been driven to this action by the remonstrance of the French minister,[5] whom they informed that they disavowed the publication; were convinced that the supplies were not a present; and that the King gave

---

[1] Almon, 1778-79, 381. [2] Adams, iii. 191.
[3] Cf. Penn. Packet, Dec. 21, 1778; "Plain Truth."
[4] Journ Cong. v. 9. [5] Dip. Corr. Rev. x. 258.

no supplies before the alliance. On the 16th they voted to demand all papers from Paine, but a motion to discharge him from his office was lost. He resigned.

Inasmuch as Morris left Congress in October, 1778, he was not called upon to take an active part in the Deane controversy; and we find no evidence that he voluntarily tried to take part in it, but it was well understood that he was on Deane's side. He had been the representative of Congress in their business with Deane when the latter first went out, and had been interested with Deane in commerce. He sympathized with him in his situation. It must be borne in mind that Congress sat with closed doors, and that the published journal of its proceedings was at this time two years in arrears.[1] The Deane-Paine affair led to a weekly publication of the proceedings,[2] which was ordered March 31, 1779.[3]

It was at the stage of the affair which had been reached in January, 1779, that Morris was drawn into it.

Paine, after his resignation, followed up his enterprise by further letters in the newspapers, especially the branch of it against the alleged supporters of Deane. He charged Deane with having stolen the lost despatches in order to sell them to the English. This was Arthur Lee's theory of the case.[4] Paine asked the States to investigate the mercantile operations of their members, beginning with Pennsylvania. This was plainly directed at Morris, who answered in a letter to the public, January 7. He said that he had had three ventures with Deane, which had been unsuccessful. He told about his proceedings in the winter of 1777-78, when he obtained leave of absence in order to settle the accounts of Willing and Morris and

---

[1] Penn. Packet, April 1, 1779. [2] Ibid. April 20.
[3] In September, 1782, the journals for 1779 were not yet published (Va. Papers, iii. 296). [4] Lee's A. Lee, ii. 42.

himself with Congress, having been intrusted with the books of the Secret Committee. There were complaints that he should have these books in his possession, but nevertheless Congress ordered him to keep them. He returned them in July, having done very little with them, on account of his mission to the army and other interruptions.[1] "Many gentlemen, from New Hampshire to Georgia, entered into contracts for procuring supplies, on which they received part of this money," which was distributed by the Secret Committee for commercial undertakings. He had twice settled Willing and Morris's accounts; the last time was in May, 1778, when there was a balance in their favour. Many accounts were still outstanding in Europe and the West Indies. He had urged Congress to employ accountants in order to settle these accounts.

Paine replied to this letter on the 11th, affirming in the broadest terms that Morris had no right to engage in commerce while he was a delegate, or Deane while he was an agent; and he affirmed again that Deane was supported only in order to cloak big mercantile speculations. The newspaper war between Paine, Deane, R. H. Lee, and the anonymous letter writers went on more and more vigorously, but it lies apart from our subject. On the 22d of January Mifflin wrote to Morris: "I do not remember to have been more surprised and provoked at any event than at the rascally and ill-managed attack against your character. The attention you have given the public business for the three last years, and the commercial sacrifices you have made to your country, I believe would have placed you out of the reach at least of the attempt of every censorious scoundrel; but I was deceived. Paine, like the enthusiastic madman of the East, was determined to run

[1] Those books are now lost, probably burned.

amuck. He sallied forth, stabbed three or four slightly, met with you, but missing his aim fell a victim to his own stroke, and, by attempting too much, will enjoy a most mortifying and general contempt."[1]

On the 9th of January, while this affair was at its height, Henry Laurens made some statements in Congress which implied fraudulent proceedings, to the detriment of the public, by Willing and Morris. He was ordered to submit his statement in writing.[2] February 10, a letter from Morris was read in Congress. He said that he had been traduced by an officer formerly in the service of Congress (Paine), "and being also informed that insinuations have been thrown out against me in the House respecting the books of the Secret Committee," he asked for a committee of investigation, "to examine the entries and settlement made by me in those books, and examine into the expenditure of public money intrusted to me, and to the late house of Willing, Morris, & Co., and to examine into the state of their and my present unsettled dependencies with the United States," that Congress and the public may be informed of the truth about them.[3]

A Committee of Investigation was accordingly appointed. When this Committee reported, Laurens himself said that their report had reminded him of facts which would contribute to clear up Morris's conduct, and he brought in a letter of the Secret Committee about the ship "Farmer," showing that it had been loaded on public account, and that the Secret Committee, on account of their confidence in Morris's integrity and commercial ability, had employed him to manage the affair, and to make the purchases under the name of his firm, in order to prevent that advance in prices which always took place when

[1] Letters to Morris, 441.   [2] Journ. Cong. v. 13.
[3] State Dep. MSS No. 137, App. 245.

purchases were made on public account; so that for the interests of the public, the colour of a private transaction was given to the affair. "Upon the whole, your Committee are of opinion," said the Committee of Investigation, "that the said Robert Morris has clearly and fully vindicated himself; and your Committee are further of opinion that the said Robert Morris, in the execution of the powers committed to him by the said Secret Committee, so far as his conduct has come to the knowledge of your Committee, has acted with fidelity and integrity and an honourable zeal for the happiness of his country."[1] In the manuscript of this report in the State Department, there are a great many changes and erasures in the last sentences, and the accompanying documents of evidence which were before the Committee seem to show beyond any doubt that Willing and Morris had a private shipment on board the ship.[2]

The matter attracted very wide attention, and was reported from New York by Andrew Elliott to Lord Carlisle. "In the course of his 'Common Sense' he [Paine], has touched on Mr. Robert Morris's public accounts, which has called him to answer. Mr. Morris has all along conducted the mercantile affairs of the Congress. A private connection in trade between him and Deane has given room for much jealousy. Morris declines declaring their present connection. B——y P——g has got an intercepted contract for establishing a house at Nantes with a French merchant, Silas Deane, Mr. Morris, Mr. Wilson, two Mr. Nesbitts, Mr. Bannister, and Mr. Duer. All but the Nesbitts are or were in Congress."[3] As Morris was out of Congress, and Deane had been recalled for more than a

---

[1] State Dep. MSS No. 137, App. 36.
[2] Ibid., Reports of Committees, IV. 195, 220, 221.
[3] Stevens, 115.

year, with little prospect of being employed again, Morris maintained that it was no one's business what their relations with each other might be at this time.

Jay, as President of Congress, wrote to Morris a formal letter of exculpation. "When characters rendered amiable by virtue and important by talent are exposed to suspicion, and become subjects of investigation, the sensibility of individuals, as well as the interests of the public, are concerned in the event of the inquiry. It gives me particular pleasure, therefore, to transmit to you an unanimous act of Congress of the eleventh instant, not only acquitting your conduct in the transaction it relates to of blame, but giving it that express approbation which patriotism in the public, and integrity in every walk of life, always merit, and seldom fail ultimately to receive."[1] Although it is nowhere explicitly so stated, it seems a reasonable interpretation that Congress did not find that the shipment by Willing and Morris was wrong.

Hardly had the excitement of this matter passed away when another began, in which we can see that the newspaper animadversions which have just been described had affected public opinion about Morris; for the political party to which he was opposed contained a large mass of people without property, or much knowledge of affairs, who were in favour of paper money, embargoes, price laws, etc., and who were quite ready to believe that he had used his public knowledge for private gain.[2]

On the 25th of May, 1779, a public mass meeting was held at Philadelphia, presided over by Mr. Robardeau.[3] He made a very inflammatory speech. "The way to make

[1] State Dep. MSS Letters Pres. Cong. No. 14, 49.
[2] In 1780 the French minister wrote that members of Congress generally used their information for private speculations (Durand, 220).
[3] See p 72.

our money good is to reduce the prices of goods and provisions. . . . The tax that has been laid on us by monopolizers and forestallers within these six months past, for it may justly be called a tax, amounts to more money than would carry the war on twelve months to come." The preamble of the resolutions adopted recited that there was an advance in prices beyond what the amount of money would justify, and that the public had a right to inquire into the causes, and continued: "Whereas, since the late importation of a cargo of goods, said to have been since purchased or consigned to the management of Mr. Robert Morris, merchant, or others, the prices of all kinds of dry goods have been greatly advanced, to the injury of the public and the great detriment of trade; Resolved, that this meeting justify their conduct on the necessity of the measure, and being deeply affected and injured by those increasing evils, will appoint a committee to inquire of Mr. Robert Morris or others what part he or they have acted respecting the said cargo, and to require from him or them their answers in writing to such questions as the Committee may find it necessary to put, and to report the same at the next general town meeting." They demanded that prices should be put back where they were May 1st, and appointed a committee to publish this tariff, also to put it into execution "throughout the United States." They go on to say that extraordinary rumours were afloat about persons who had been intrusted with public money; and they ordered the Committee to hear the complaints, and to inquire of the Pennsylvania delegates what Congress had done about it. Finally, they wanted all inimical persons to be banished. Thomas Paine was a member of the Committee to call on Robert Morris.[1]

July 2, the Committee published an order to detain

[1] Penn. Packet, May 27, 1779.

flour bought by Holker and Morris for the French fleet at a price above the tariff. In the "Packet" of July 3, in which that order was published, Robert Morris asked for a suspension of judgment. On the 8th of July he published a long letter to the public, saying that Congress, at his request, had recently appointed a committee on his accounts, but that both they and he had been so occupied with other things that it had been necessary to defer that business; also that goods were now coming in which belonged to the account between him and the Committee of Commerce, but which had been detained on the way. Then, as to the cargo which he was charged with monopolizing, he said that he sold it on commission, as agent for the owners. He denied that he sold bills on France for continental notes at a very low rate for the latter. The City Committee had invited him to appear before them on June 17, but he excused himself on account of sore eyes, and said that all the flour he had was bought for the French fleet. They asked for details of those transactions, and cited the current reports that he was purchasing flour above the tariff. Holker was the purchasing agent for the French fleet, and would not consent that Morris should give the information which was demanded of him. Morris therefore referred them to Holker. He goes on to say that women came to him with sacks for flour, saying that they had been sent by the Committee. The Committee declared that they had interfered in order to appreciate the currency and save the King of France from paying too much. When the Committee applied to Holker, he assumed the responsibility, but said that he would be responsible for his acts only to Congress. All this is rehearsed in Robert Morris's letter of July 8, to which he adds that the first effect of the price tariff was to produce a scarcity of flour; and he refers to his party position in opposition to the existing Constitution of Pennsylvania, as furnishing a motive to his opponents.

The Committee returned to the attack on the 24th of July. They say they thought that the ship whose cargo he was charged with monopolizing might have belonged to Deane, and that, although Morris may be within commercial rules, nevertheless he is "somewhat out of character" in view of the public station which he has filled. Hence they carried the doctrine one step further, and now held that, having been a public man, he ought not to be a merchant afterward. It must be noticed, in order to understand the degree of deference which Morris paid to this Committee and the politic evasions of his reply, that committees at this time exercised an irresponsible tyranny, so that their powers of harming a man were great and indefinite, and he had no competent protection against them.[1]

The Committee were not satisfied with the answer given them about the breach of the embargo by Holker. They agreed to deliver up a part of the flour if he would come before them and declare that it was for the French fleet. On the 29th an adjourned meeting of the citizens of Philadelphia was held, at which General Cadwallader tried to make a speech, but was prevented by a body of men armed with clubs. Therefore the conservative part of the meeting went to the college yard and organized with Robert Morris in the chair. They denounced the violation of free speech, resolved to help stop the depreciation of the paper currency, and also resolved that Robert Morris had acquitted himself of all charges against him.[2]

On the 2d of August, Congress declared their knowledge and approval of the proceedings of Holker to obtain flour for the French fleet, and on the 4th they declared that they did not believe that Holker had anything to do

[1] See Hamilton, Chap. VI. [2] Penn. Packet, July 29.

with the shipping of provisions on private account on board vessels despatched in the name of the King of France.[1] Chastellux's translator expresses the opinion, which was current, that Holker took advantage of his opportunities to export flour, in time of embargo, for his own account, on the French ships.[2]

On the 5th of August Morris published a letter to the public in answer to one of the Committee on the 24th of July. He had been so much touched by the evidences of approval which he received at the town meeting that he could not finish the speech which he tried to make there. He gave his word that neither he nor Holker had exported any flour contrary to the embargo, except for the French fleet and army. He denied that he had engrossed the cargo of the ship, which he defines like what we now call cornering. He is proud to be a merchant, and does not agree with the Committee that he is out of character as such in the stations he has held and the times in which he lives. The engrossing of "promises" with which they charged him would be poor business in these days. On the 10th the Committee voted to give up the flour claimed by Holker, being satisfied that there had been no breach of the embargo by him or under his connivance. On the 10th of September a number of merchants, of whom Morris was one, published a remonstrance against the price regulations and the proceedings of the Committee of May 25th. To this the Committee replied that the issue was whether any regulation was proper. They invoked the common good as the justification of interference with the rights of property; said that the facts proved the ruin of non-regulation, for they had gone on four years without regulation, and the result was depreciation and monopoly.

[1] Journ. Cong v. 233. [2] Chastellux, i. 320, note.

The popular agitation and lawless proceedings of this year culminated in the Fort Wilson Riot of October 4. It is said that Morris was one of the persons denounced by the mob, and that he was in Wilson's house.[1] The purpose of the mob was never satisfactorily ascertained. It appears that they were exasperated by the failure of the measures which they had been trying for six months. Some of them had one thing more in mind, some another.[2] Graydon says that the mob set out to mob Wilson's house on account of his professional efforts on behalf of the proscribed tories. The editor of the St. Clair Papers attributes the anger of the mob against Wilson to his professional efforts on behalf of Morris and others who would not observe the price tariff.[3] Others doubt if the mob started with an intention to attack Wilson's house. They meant to support the Committee of Trade. A continental officer showed himself at the window of Wilson's house as they marched past. Firearms were used, and Wilson and his friends repelled the attack. On the day after the riot there was danger of a collision between the militia of Philadelphia and that of Germantown.[4]

On the 10th of June, 1779, an attempt was made in Congress to order Deane not to leave the United States without the permission of Congress, and to order Arthur Lee to return home and sustain his allegations. Both were lost.[5] August 6, Deane was discharged from further attendance on Congress. In a memorial of August 16, Deane complained that he was ruined in fortune, and begged Congress to discharge his accounts and dismiss him.[6] August 26, after trying several votes for different

[1] Westcott, 280.
[2] The documents about this riot are in the Penn. Col. Rec. xii. and Penn. Archives, vii.
[3] St. Clair Papers, i. 488; Graydon, 333.
[4] Reed's Reed, ii. 150, 423.
[5] Journ. Cong. v. 192.
[6] Deane Papers.

sums, they voted to Deane $10,500. He now returned to Europe so much imbittered that he apostatized to the English.[1] In May and June, 1781, the English intercepted letters from him to some of the leading public men in the United States, of whom Morris was one. These letters were published by Rivington, at New York. In the introduction to the pamphlet containing the collection of them,[2] the editor says that Congress was ruled by Washington, the French Minister, and Robert Morris. Many doubted the genuineness of these letters, especially the one to Morris.[3] Deane's friends, among whom were Franklin,[4] Jay, and Morris, were greatly shocked at them.

Paine made a shrewd guess that these letters were written to be intercepted, and not to be sent to the persons to whom they were directed.[5] It is now known that this was the case.[6] The King did not think that they were dramatically well constructed, so as to appear like what they pretended to be. In Deane's address of 1784 he admitted the authorship of the intercepted letters, but ridiculed the idea that he was hired by the English ministry to write them. He maintained that the views were just and reasonable. Their purpose was to show that the American cause was hopeless, and that the wise thing to do was to come to terms with Great Britain.

Jay wrote to Deane in 1780: "I believe you honest, and I think you injured." He urged him to collect evidence to vindicate himself.[7] He did not abandon Deane until he heard that Deane had visited Arnold.

[1] Paul Wentworth wrote, in 1777, that Deane had sought decent excuses to abandon the American cause. He had said: "Nothing but the power of Great Britain re-established can save us from the worst of evils," etc. This is the leading idea of the "Intercepted Letters." (Stevens, 277.)

[2] Paris Papers.
[3] Madison Papers, i. 103.
[4] Franklin in France, ii. 28.
[5] Letters to Robert Morris, 472.
[6] George III. ii. 380 and fg.
[7] Johnston's Jay, i. 455.

Morris wrote in 1782: "Deane has played the fool egregiously, to say no worse. Such conduct as his is ruinous to the man himself, and, however unjustly, to those who have been in his intimacy."[1]

In 1785, after mentioning Deane's account as one of the unliquidated ones, Morris wrote: "As to Mr. Deane, he stands in such peculiar circumstances that it would be odious to say anything in favour of his claim, if the citizens of America were governed by passion and caprice, instead of reason and reflection. But they know that whatever may have been his services and sufferings, or whatever may be his follies and faults, neither can affect the present question. His claim of justice is not mended by his merit nor curtailed by his crime. Whether he is criminal or innocent must be decided on hereafter by that unerring tribunal from which there lies no appeal. But even admitting his guilt, it would be a folly to justify it by withholding his dues. No treason either has operated or can operate so great injury to America as must follow from a loss of reputation."[2] The most just reflection with which to dismiss Deane's case is: "A man driven to despair is to be judged mercifully."[3]

As for Paine, he sought an interview with Morris in January, 1782. He thought that his services had been neglected, and he wanted employment. Morris thought that he might be made useful to act upon public opinion, the immediate occasion being a memorial of the officers about their pay. He and Gouverneur Morris had further conferences about Paine, disclaiming all selfish schemes or plans, but desiring to cause an army to be raised and effectively supported, especially by persuading the States to lay taxes for the army and for the interest on the debt. Washington, Morris, and Robert Livingston agreed to pay

[1] Ford MSS.   [2] Report of 1785, ix.   [3] Sabine, i. 362.

Paine $800 per annum out of the secret service money; but the matter was to be kept secret, lest his writings should lose force "if it were known that the author is paid for them by government."[1]

If we turn back now to the year 1779, we may infer that the quarrels and turmoil of the summer of that year give the reason why Morris was not re-elected to the Assembly. He does not appear to have been regular in his attendance or active in the work of the Assembly during that year. In November, 1778, he voted with the minority for allowing those who had taken the oath of allegiance between the last June and the last election to vote;[2] and in September, 1779, he voted in favour of extending the time for taking the test oath.[3] In these votes, and on other occasions, he showed himself opposed to the rigour against the tories.

This is greatly to his credit. The proscriptions, confiscations, and persecutions of the tories are an indelible blot on American history. No man seems to have raised his voice earnestly and vigorously against this policy. The best men only strove to moderate it; but, as the times went, it was a great merit to do as much as that.

In September, 1779, Morris signed, on behalf of the merchants of Philadelphia, an address to the French Minister on his departure. The merchants promised to develop trade with France in proof of their fidelity to the alliance.[4]

From November, 1779, to November, 1780, is the only period from 1775 to 1784 when Morris was out of the public service. In December, 1780, he wrote to Dumas, agent of the United States in Holland: "After serving my country in various public stations for upwards of four years, my

[1] Morris's Diary in Dip. Corr. Rev. xii. 95.   [2] Penn. H. R. i. 241.
[3] Ibid. 377.   [4] Penn. Packet, Sept. 23, 1779.

routine in Congress was finished, and no sooner was I out than envious and malicious men began to attack my character. But my services were so universally known, and my integrity so clearly proved, I have, thank God, been able to look down with contempt on those that have endeavoured to injure me; and, what is more, I can face the world with that consciousness which rectitude of conduct gives to those who pursue it invariably."[1]

In November, 1780, Morris was once more elected to the Assembly. December 8, he voted with a large majority for the impeachment of Francis Hopkinson, Judge of Admiralty. The Judge was charged with accepting payment for an appointment, and giving false reasons for the condemnation of a prize. Morris was interested in a decision which the Judge had made in that year; perhaps in two.[2] One of his privateers claimed a share in a prize which had been taken while it was in sight. Congress had assigned to Morris a claim which the sovereign might have had under one view of the law. The decision was against him. Hopkinson was unanimously acquitted by the Council, December 26, 1780.[3]

It was in this session that the questions of currency and finance came to a crisis. December 22, a law was passed that the rate of exchange between State and continental paper and specie should be published by authority, and such publications appear in the "Packet" during the winter. It was also provided that creditors might sue, or landlords distress, if debtors were about to flee, or if they refused to give security, or if tenants were committing waste.[4] February 20, 1781, it was voted, by a very large majority, to suspend the State legal tender laws; and on

---

[1] Dip. Corr. Rev. ix. 445.
[2] Hopkinson's Judgments, 393, 395; Penn. Journ. i. 559.
[3] Penn. Col. Rec. xii. 584.   [4] Penn. Journ. i. 561.

the 27th of February the embargo laws which forbade exportation were repealed, as being mischievous to Pennsylvania.¹

It now seemed that the legal tender mania, with price restrictions and embargoes, had run its course, but in the next two or three months the struggle was renewed more vigorously than ever. March 29, a bill was ordered reported by the State Assembly to issue State paper to be a legal tender. An attempt was made to pass an amendment striking out the penalties for selling goods at a lower rate in specie than in paper. It was lost, but the penalty was reduced from a forfeit of twice the value of the goods to a forfeit of once the value. There was also a proposition that if notes were tendered to the creditor and refused by him, they should be paid into the State treasury, and if the creditor did not call for them within four years, they should be forfeited to the State. This was lost.² April 6, the bill was pending to emit bills of credit. Morris tried in vain to strike out the clause which would bar a recovery of the debt if these bills were offered and refused. He was also one of those who entered a protest on the record against the provision for forfeiting the value of the goods, if offered for sale at a lower rate in specie than in paper. The grounds of the protest are, that value rests on confidence, and cannot be created by law; that the law would hurt public credit and violate liberty; that contracts ought to be kept as made; that there was no reason why the paper should not have good credit.³ The next day the bill became a law, and the two parties came to a struggle over the proposition to adjourn. The conservatives, in order to challenge the other party, offered an amendment: " Whether the business under consideration be finished or not." Morris voted for this amendment, with the minority;

¹ Packet, March 3, 1781.   ² Penn. Journ. i. 599.   ³ Ibid. 609.

but the adjournment was carried, in spite of a message from the Governor and Council, remonstrating with them for not providing for the necessities of the State, and half scolding, half pleading with them to do so.[1] The Assembly was reconvened May 3. On the 18th of June a bill was reported providing that all debts contracted since January, 1777, should be settled by the old scale of depreciation. It was recommitted; but upon the request of the Committee, they were discharged and a new one appointed. The new Committee reported on the 20th, when the act to repeal all the tender laws was passed. At this time Morris was not present, although, as we shall see, the Legislature was negotiating with him as Superintendent of Finance for arrangements by which Pennsylvania could discharge its obligations to Congress. He was no doubt, therefore, using all his influence with them to bring about the repeal of the tender laws, but he had now assumed his federal office.

[1] Penn. Journ. i. 674.

CHAPTER XI.

SPECIFIC SUPPLIES.

AT the end of 1779, when it was absolutely impossible to issue any more paper currency, and when the weariness and disgust of the public had alienated them from the recommendations and leadership of Congress, that body, out of utter helplessness, turned to the device of specific supplies. December 11, 1779, they voted requisitions on the States for specific supplies of flour and Indian corn. December 14, they established a system of requisitions and contributions of this kind, Maryland alone voting no.[1] February 25, 1780, an elaborate apportionment of requisitions for such supplies was made. They were to be collected and deposited at the risk of the States, at such place in each State as the Commander-in-chief should appoint. Each State was called upon for the staples which it produced. The requisition for tobacco was planned to obtain an exportable cash article, by means of which those articles could be obtained for the service of Congress which were not produced in the country. This article was therefore put under the direction of the Commercial Committee. At the same time the goods were assessed at prices at which they should be credited to the State, in order to reduce the whole to money in Spanish dollars.[2] According to a report which was made in April, 1781, this project in regard to tobacco was frus-

[1] Journ. Cong. v. 337. [2] Ibid. vi. 22.

trated by the want of ships, and by the blockade of the Chesapeake.[1] November 4, specific supplies to the value of six million silver dollars were apportioned as a tax, upon a very elaborate scheme.[2]

Chastellux describes a convoy of specific supplies which he fell in with in New England. "They were conveying to the army a part of the contingent of provisions furnished by New Hampshire. This contingent is a sort of tax, divided amongst all the inhabitants, on some of whom the imposition amounts to one hundred and fifty, on others to one hundred or eighty pounds of meat, according to their abilities; so that they agree amongst themselves to furnish a larger or a smaller sized ox, no matter which, as each animal is weighed. Their conveyance to the army is then intrusted to some farmers and drovers. The farmers are allowed about a dollar a day; and their expenses, as well as those of the cattle, are paid them on their return, according to the receipts, which they are obliged to produce, from the inn-keepers where they have halted. The usual price is from threepence to fivepence, English, per night for each ox, and in proportion at noon." [3]

The Virginia Papers offer us the best opportunity to trace the system of specific supplies in its practical operation during the critical year 1781. In January of that year the Quartermaster reported to the Governor that the persons in charge of the magazines of provisions prepared for the southern army at Petersburg were giving out the provisions to the militia then in service. The hogs that were to have been made into bacon were being killed and eaten fresh. This would produce calamity the next summer.[4] In July, R. H. Lee reported to the Governor that he was informed by the Collector of the specific tax that

[1] Journ. Cong. vii. App.
[2] Ibid. vi 155.
[3] Chastellux, i. 58.
[4] Va. Papers, i. 433.

there was a thousand bushels of corn and six hundred of oats, with a quantity of wheat taken in the previous year, now about to be ruined by the weevil, unless something was done with it. He speaks of "the ill impression which the sight of these losses makes on the people's minds," and mentions a quantity of grain which had been seized but then left behind, "doubtless overlooked in the confusion of the time."[1] In August, Colonel Davies issued a circular to the collectors of the specific tax, ordering that they should make quarterly returns of the things received by them, stating from whom received and to whom delivered. "The great misapplication of stores in some parts of the country makes it necessary to put a stop to such ruinous irregularities." The State agent reported that he had sent seventy-two barrels of flour to Westham, but there was no one to receive it, and his men left it on the bank of the river without getting a receipt. September 3, he wrote that he was sending more, which he expected would be left in the same way. He referred to some millers "who have thrown the country's flour out of their houses, by which means the flour is ruined." The next day the Quartermaster wrote that there were three hundred barrels of flour at Westham that were spoiled. This, it will be perceived, was on the eve of the siege of Yorktown.

On the day that Washington reached the camp, September 14, the Governor wrote to the Commissary: "The provisions in camp are scarcely sufficient to subsist the present army for three days longer; and should the wished-for reinforcement arrive before a fresh supply of provisions, flour at least, is received, it gives me pain to think of the situation we shall be in."

September 26, Colonel Hendricks wrote to a State officer in Berkeley County: "For God's sake, exert yourself and

[1] Va. Papers, ii. 267.

send down all the flour you can, as our army is in a starving condition." The State officer answered him, a week later, that there was much meat and flour in Berkeley County, left over from the year before, but nearly all spoiled. One Commissioner under the provision law threw up his office in despair on account of the difficulties, in September. Paper money had ceased to pass. "The consequence is obvious that nothing will be obtained without compulsion, which is at best a disagreeable mode of procedure. The provisions now in the county [Hampshire] are fast spoiling, it being flour. Those who have wagons absolutely refuse to carry it away without being paid for their labour, in specie or its real value. The grain, chiefly wheat, on hand for the specific tax, is nearly all destroyed. No barrels are to be had, if it was to be ground up into flour. In short, I see no way left but to make immediate sale of the whole, as a few weeks more will totally ruin both the flour and wheat."

The Virginia line officers addressed a memorial to the Assembly, in November, in which they said that many people believed that they and the soldiers had drawn large supplies from the public stores. "We are persuaded that great expenses on that score were incurred by the State, and we are induced to believe that ample supplies were procured. That they were not appropriated to our soldiers, their unparalleled sufferings have long since taught us. Cold and nakedness have swept off fourfold more of your troops than all the malice of a cruel enemy has ever been able to destroy." They want a strict inquiry as to what became of these supplies. More or less vague allegations of malversation run through the record. In the neighbourhood of Yorktown, after the surrender, we find frequent mention of cattle belonging to the public, which do not appear to have arrived in time to be used by the army. No one would take care of them without pay, and there was no salt with which to salt them. Many were dying. In December there were complaints that the Quartermaster was selling grain of the specific tax to the French.[1]

In January, 1782, Washington wrote to the President of Pennsylvania: "A great proportion of the specific articles have been wasted after the people have furnished them, and the transportation alone of what has reached the army has in numberless instances cost more than the value of the articles themselves."[2]

We have seen, with respect to Virginia, that the people had furnished the articles to a greater or less extent, in 1780 and 1781, but that the army had been in the greatest distress in 1781. If now we enter upon the record of 1782, we find the fullest evidence that these commodities were on hand somewhere, but were neglected, lost, wasted, and spoiled. February 3, the Commissary wrote to the Governor: "There is plenty of grain belonging to the specific tax spoiling, and yet those entitled to it cannot get it." In March, Colonel Davies reported that there was no one in the counties to take charge of the specific supplies; the cattle which had been given in were dying, or the people seized them and then refused to give them up. A great variety of articles were dispersed about the country, and would never be given up by those who had them. "A great deal of grain is at this moment lying useless in the hands of Commissioners, and great numbers of hides are lodged with different people throughout the State, of which no return has ever yet been made." The Commissaries have never yet rendered account. In April he reported the conduct of a Commissioner who had returned cattle collected by him as not fit for use; and when they were

[1] Va. Papers, ii. 336–659.   [2] Penn. Archives, ix. 482.

condemned, had bought them himself for less than their value. In May a miller in Louisa County wrote that two wagon loads of flour had been at his mill since the previous autumn. He fears it will spoil. He never could prevail on the Commissaries to take it away. In May it is stated that the accounts of the Commissioners for the specific tax in Cumberland County, for 1781, could probably never be settled; one of them, who had the papers, having died. In June, Colonel Davies recommended that all the specifics which had been collected should be sold out as soon as possible, lest they spoil, being already much damaged. In July a return of specifics on hand in certain counties showed nearly ten thousand bushels of corn, over three thousand bushels of wheat, a like quantity of oats, over seventeen thousand pounds of bacon, and £472 in cash. Colonel Davies complained to the Governor of the irregularities of the county Commissioners in their mode of collecting and accounting for the specific taxes, thereby causing great confusion, seriously impairing public credit, and adding to the difficulty of supporting the troops. In October it was reported that grain was lying almost ruined by neglect at New Glasgow. The window is open, and forty pigeons have been preying on it, besides ten times as many rats; and the peas have been eaten by weevils.

During the siege of Yorktown, and immediately afterward, the most heartrending complaints and appeals were made by the surgeons and physicians of the hospitals on behalf of the sick and wounded. A French brig having run ashore, in September, 1781, twenty hogsheads of rum were impressed from her cargo, not without remonstrances and some political complications. This rum, which was among the things most earnestly demanded by the doctors, was hauled twenty miles to a storehouse. In July, 1782, we hear that it is still there. In the same month, a Collector of specifics in Dinwiddie County, being ordered to send cattle to York, reported that the drivers demanded three dollars a day; so that for some short distance it cost more to drive the cattle than they were worth. From Albemarle County it was reported, in August, that there were large quantities of grain on hand, much of which was damaged. Warwick County never appointed a Commissioner to collect the specific tax, thinking that they had been so much distressed by the enemy that the Assembly ought to release them. Some other counties did the same. In some counties the Commissioners would not make any reports as to the specifics which they had collected. One State agent declares that he might as well write to an Indian on the subject as to these Commissioners.[1]

The case is perfectly clear. The specific taxes cost the people heavily. The difficulty of collecting and distributing them was excessive. The strain of it on the very best administration would have been very great; but when scarcely any administration could be said to exist, the goods were almost all lost and wasted, and the troops suffered as if nothing had been obtained.

Bancroft says: "When Congress drew supplies in kind directly from each State for its own troops, quotas were sometimes apportioned by the States to their towns, and in towns to individuals. Men of small means in a New England village would club together to buy an ox of a weight equal to their collective quotas, and herds of cattle gathered in this way were driven slowly to camp. All this marked an active spirit of patriotism, reaching to the humblest and remotest, but it showed the want of organized power."[2] That such things occurred upon occasion is true; but if any one understands that a system of this kind was pursued with regularity, over a period of time, so as to

[1] Va. Papers, iii. 52–340   [2] Bancroft, x. 406.

keep the army supplied by this device, he is led into great error. If the statement is taken to cover an illustrative incident from which the temper of those times may be inferred, it is still more delusive.

In October, 1781, Morris declared that "specific supplies are at once burdensome to the people and almost useless to the government." [1]

[1] Dip. Corr. Rev. xi. 489; cf. Washington, viii. 103.

CHAPTER XII.

BILLS ON THE ENVOYS UNTIL 1781.

WE have seen above[1] that, in January, 1777, the Commissioners at Paris proposed that the Secret Committee should pay interest on loans to be contracted in America by means of bills of exchange drawn on the Commissioners. Deane shrewdly objected to this, because he said that Congress would draw every farthing.[2] Congress decided, in September, to adopt this plan, and ordered the interest on loan office certificates to be paid in bills of exchange on the Commissioners in France at five livres for a dollar.[3] Henry Laurens objected to the plan, because the foundation for drawing was unsubstantial, the practice dangerous, and the measure not necessary.[4]

In March, 1778, Franklin complained to Arthur Lee that bills had been presented to him which were drawn to pay an old debt in Canada. "I cannot conceive what encouragement the Congress could have had from any of us to draw on us for anything but that interest."[5]

To draw bills on the Envoys, which they must find means to pay, was a very easy way to obtain resources, and, when once begun, was not abandoned. May 26, 1779, Franklin wrote to the Committee of Foreign Affairs, detailing his expenditures for fitting out ships, etc., in Europe. All remittances to him had failed, "and now

[1] See page 167.   [2] Lee's A. Lee, i. 355.
[3] Journ. Cong. iii. 307.   [4] Gibbes, 89.   [5] Franklin, viii. 249.

the drafts of the Treasurer of the loans coming very fast upon me, the anxiety I have suffered, and the distress of mind lest I should not be able to pay them, has for a long time been very great indeed. To apply again to this court for money for a particular purpose, which they had already over and over again provided for and furnished us, was extremely awkward. I therefore repeated the general applications which we had made when together for aids of money, and received the general answer that the expense of government for the navy was so great that at present it was exceedingly difficult to furnish the necessary supplies, — that France, by sending a fleet to America, obliged the enemy to divide their forces. . . . I at length obtained, as above mentioned, the King's bond for payment of the interest of three million, if I could borrow it in Holland or elsewhere. But though two eminent houses in Amsterdam have undertaken it and had hopes of success, they have both lately written to me that the great demands of money for Germany and for England had raised interest above our limits, and that the successes of the English in Georgia and St. Lucia, and in destroying the French trade, with the supposed divisions in Congress, all much magnified by the British Minister, and the pressing application to borrow by several of our States separately, had made the moneyed people doubtful of our stability as well as our ability to repay what might be lent us, and that it was necessary to wait a more favourable moment for proceeding with our loans."[1]

June 8, before the above letter was received, Congress ordered the Board of Treasury to draw on Franklin for three hundred and sixty thousand livres, in favour of the Committee of Commerce, in order to import military stores.[2] When Franklin heard of this, he replied, Septem-

[1] Dip. Corr. Rev. iii. 87.   [2] Secret Journ. i. 117.

ber 30: "I put into my pocket nothing of the allowance Congress has been pleased to make me; I shall pay it all in honouring their drafts and supporting their credit; but do not let me be burdened with supporting the credit of every one who has claims on the Board of Commerce or the navy."[1]

October 21, he wrote again with respect to another lot of bills, which he had been asked to pay if the drawees should not do so: "I beg that you would not in future have any dependence of that kind upon me without knowing beforehand from me that I shall be able to pay what is desired. I hope you will excuse my giving this caution, which is forced from me by the distress and anxiety such occasional and unforeseen demands have occasioned me."[2]

In the late summer of 1779, Congress seems to have thought that it was impossible to continue drawing so heavily on Franklin, and that they must therefore seek loans in other countries, especially in Spain and Holland.

When France made the alliance with America, it was a matter of very great importance to her that Spain should act in conjunction with her. On the one hand, Spain had the most serious reasons for not doing so, the most important being that it did not behoove her to countenance revolts in colonies, and that the state of her finances did not warrant it. On the other hand, if she did enter into it, she desired to accomplish some of the positive objects which entered into her policy at the time. The attitude of Spain is indeed such as to make the behaviour of France toward America appear Quixotic. Florida Blanca took the position that it was no object to humiliate England.[3] In October, 1777, he wrote a despatch to the Spanish Minister at Paris, which is a sober and sensible criticism of the

[1] Franklin, viii. 383.   [2] Franklin in France, i. 299.
[3] Doniol, ii. 703.

train of ideas which prevailed at Paris at that time. Any precipitate step of Spain, he said, with respect to America, would give a pretext for the enemy to attack two important Spanish interests, — namely, the silver fleet and the forces returning from Buenos Ayres. He did not believe the Americans would keep any arrangement secret. He attached no importance to the threat that the Americans might make peace and form an alliance with England. If what the Americans say is true, they will carry their point alone. The only thing which he thinks it reasonable to do is to advance money; and he offered that Spain would advance seven hundred and fifty thousand francs.[1] At the end of 1778 he was trying to get the biggest price that he could for joining in the war.[2] France and Spain finally made an alliance, April 12, 1779. Peace was not to be made until Gibraltar was recovered by Spain, and it was agreed that France should approve of the exclusion by Spain of the Americans from all the territory west of the Alleghanies. Spain had also most positively determined to exclude every one else from the use of the Mississippi River and to conquer Florida, so as to close the Gulf of Mexico against all other powers.

Jay landed at Cadiz, January 22, 1780, and in April arrived at Madrid.

Henry Laurens was appointed agent to Holland in October, 1779, but June 20, 1780, as he had not gone out, orders were despatched to Adams to go and undertake the business until he should come. Bills are mentioned which were drawn on Laurens on the 23d of November, 1779, and which had been negotiated. Adams was directed to accept them.[3]

Laurens embarked at Philadelphia, August 13, 1780. He had orders from Congress for two frigates to convoy the

---

[1] Doniol, ii. 765.   [2] Ibid. iii. 576.   [3] Secret Journ. ii. 314.

ship. He transmitted his orders to the Captains, and waited four or five days for them, but they did not come; "nor, indeed, did I much expect them, for at that time little regard was paid to orders inconsistent with the Captain's own convenience."[1]

He met with various delays, and was at last captured and imprisoned in the Tower of London, where he lay from October, 1780, to the last day of 1781.[2]

November 23, 1779, Congress voted to draw bills on Jay for £100,000 sterling, and on Henry Laurens for the same amount. There were only five votes against this proposition, and Connecticut was the only State which voted against it. December 27, Congress voted to sell £75,000 sterling of the bills on Jay and Laurens at $25 continental for four-and-sixpence sterling, on condition that the persons purchasing the same should lend to the United States an equal sum at six per cent.[3]

Some of these bills were presented to Laurens in South Carolina. He wrote to Congress somewhat sarcastically, that he had not yet received his commission, and that he supposed they would not draw on him on this side of the water. They took their revenge, perhaps, when he was in the Tower, by letting him lie there. He considered that they grievously neglected him. There is an air about the matter as if he had been deficient in zeal for the business on which he was sent, and as if there had been dissatisfaction with him for lukewarmness.

In 1779, William Lee was endeavouring to negotiate a loan in Holland for the State of Virginia. In September he reported that his preliminary negotiations had succeeded, but that when the power to execute the contract was sent, it contained a specification that the money was

[1] S. C. Hist. Soc. i. 19. [2] Ibid. 22 fg.
[3] Journ. Cong. v. 320, 344.

to be used for arms and ammunition. As this would involve a collision between Holland and Great Britain, the contract was abandoned.[1]

There was a proposition, in 1780, to obtain a loan from Genoa, but France would not guarantee it, on account of the opposition of Neckar.[2]

August 23, 1780, Adams wrote to the President of Congress that he was very sure that if there was an American Minister in Holland, with due authority, he could get loans, and that a contract could be made with strong houses, so that the interest might be paid by sending produce to the West Indies or to Europe.[3] He must have received his commission as such a Minister immediately afterward; but when he tried to obtain the loan, he found it impossible on account of the political obstacles. He wrote to the President of Congress that the bills drawn on Laurens were falling on him. "But I have no prospect of discharging them, or even of deriving my own subsistence from any other source than Passy;" that is, Franklin and the French court. He hoped that Congress would not draw on Holland any more until they knew that a credit had been established for them there.[4]

All through 1780 Franklin had to meet the burden of heavy drafts on himself, besides those which had been drawn on Jay and Laurens. It behooved him to see to it how he could meet these bills and save the credit of the United States from the jeopardy in which Congress had placed it.

November 9, 1780, Congress addressed a circular to the States, in which they said: "An opinion seems to prevail that foreign loans can be obtained, and we perceive with regret that some are disposed to place too great reliance

---

[1] Va. Papers, i. 330.   [2] Dip. Corr. Rev. ii. 429; ix. 73.
[3] Ibid. v. 322, 329.   [4] Ibid. 376, 384.

on this source. Duty compels us to be explicit with our constituents on a subject of such interesting importance. Every effort has been made for the purpose of procuring loans, but without sufficient success to justify a relaxation of our own most vigorous exertions." [1]

Before Laurens sailed, he asked the Committee of Foreign Affairs for a sketch of the contract which had been projected between William Lee and the Dutchman, Van Berkel. They gave him the original, since it had never been read in Congress, and was of no authority. He put it in his trunk with other papers to be assorted at sea. When he was in imminent danger of capture, he threw overboard all his valuable papers, but this trunkful, being regarded as unimportant, remained. The English government regarded these papers, especially the unexecuted contract, as extremely important. The papers were handsomely bound and carefully examined, but subsequently restored to Laurens. The contract, however, was regarded as a hostile action, and became the immediate cause of war between Great Britain and Holland.[2]

April 19, 1781, John Adams addressed a memorial to the States of Holland, in which he made known his character as ambassador, and asked to be received.[3] He was extremely proud of this document, and always believed that it had decisive effect in many directions on the interests of the United States at that moment. It is, in fact, an able document, and there was a vigour and independence about his action in presenting it simply on his credentials from the United States, and not as a protégé of France, which did have effect. The conjuncture, however, was extremely favourable.[4] The merchants and manufacturers of

[1] Secret Journ. i. 178.   [2] S. C. Hist. Soc. i. 18.
[3] Almon, 1781, part i. 357.
[4] From the beginning of the American troubles, the Dutch followed them with great eagerness to anticipate the consequences upon trade, and upon the

the different cities and states of Holland began to discuss the probable effect of American independence, and the steps which should be taken to secure the interests of Holland. In general, the arguments are still on the basis of the old colonial system. The merchants of Amsterdam said: "No man can call in question that England has derived her greatest forces from her commerce with America." They argued that France was better off at the beginning of 1782 than at the beginning of the war, and that the reason was the commerce with America which had been won.[1] All more or less definitely petitioned the States-General to recognize American independence and receive Adams. This step was taken June 15, 1782.

August 6, 1781, Franklin wrote to Adams that he thought no more money could be obtained from France to support American Ministers in Europe.[2]

In an interview which Jay had with Florida Blanca, September 23, 1780, the Spanish Minister mentioned with satisfaction the fact that Congress had allowed provisions to be exported to Havana for the Spanish fleet and army; "that this business was conducted by Mr. Robert Morris in a manner with which he was well pleased." Jay assured him that the greatest confidence might be reposed in that gentleman's abilities and integrity. Florida Blanca said that he had been informed through the French Minister that Congress would yield the navigation of the Mississippi, but that he had been informed later that Congress had changed their mind. He affirmed with warmth that Spain would never yield on this point; that it was the most important object to be attained by the war, — more

rivalries of England, France, and Holland. There is a very interesting series of letters, published in 1777, by Count Nassau la Teck, on the aspects of this question.

[1] Coll. State Papers, 54.   [2] Dip. Corr. Rev. vi. 140.

important than the acquisition of Gibraltar. Throughout these discussions it was often suggested on the Spanish side that the navigation of the Mississippi would be worth nothing to the Americans for twenty-five years to come; and therefore that it might be given up, leaving the future to take care of itself. Jay's reply was that it would be leaving the door open for a war between Spain and the United States.[1]

In the winter of 1780-81 Jay finally obtained a promise of a loan of $150,000 from Spain. He used $34,880 to pay bills drawn on him by Congress, which he had already accepted. In March he sent to the Minister a list of bills due in April. He was told that these could not be paid, but that the rest of the $150,000 would be paid at the end of six months. On this promise he obtained a loan from a banker to meet the April bills, but was obliged to turn to Franklin to provide for the future.[2]

Among the other propositions made by Jay in the hope of inducing Spain to assist the United States, was one that the United States should build frigates for Spain. When the Spanish Minister took up this suggestion, Jay was obliged to respond by explanations which showed, in effect, that such a transaction could be of no use to the United States except to the extent of the profit that might be made on such ships. Still, some inquiries were made as to the terms on which ships could be built in Virginia.[3] April 25, 1781, Jay proposed to Congress to let Spain have one of the ships which the United States had on the stocks but could not finish.[4]

At the beginning of 1781 there was great fear in Amer-

[1] Dip. Corr. Rev. vii. 356, 371, 378.
[2] Ibid. 410.
[3] Bland Papers, ii. 34; Bland to Jefferson, October, 1780.
[4] Johnston's Jay, ii. 27.

ica that peace would be made on the *uti possidetis* basis. This fear caused the southern colonies to diminish somewhat the firm opposition they had made to any concession to Spain about the navigation of the Mississippi, and Jay was authorized to give up the claim to navigate the river below the parallel of thirty-one.[1]

In Jay's long negotiations with the Spanish Minister, he was placed in a most humiliating position. The Spanish Minister constantly held an attitude of expectation, as if waiting to see what offer would be made to him. When no offer was made, he treated the matter as if his time had been wasted, and on one pretext and another evaded an audience. When Jay explained the distressed position in which he was placed by the drafts of Congress, the Minister made no reply, apparently thinking and intending to imply that that was an affair entirely between the American Minister and his own Congress. He employed a go-between at last, who frankly said to Jay, "You offer no consideration."[2]

The total amount obtained from Spain in 1781 was $174,017. The payments extended over the period from January 1, 1781, to March 21, 1782. The amount of bills drawn on Jay over and above those which were detained, lost, or destroyed, was $386,894. Grand paid bills on Franklin to take up those drawn on Jay, to the value of $158,085. His account shows that the amount of money deposited with him to the credit of the Envoys, up to February 20, 1781, was $2,175,925. He paid for supplies furnished $1,298,432; for loan office bills, $1,559,510; and for other bills drawn by Congress on the Envoys, $917,589. Some other small items brought the overdraft up to $1,576,591.[3]

---

[1] Madison Papers, i. App. xix.   [2] Dip. Corr. Rev. vii. 354.
[3] Report of 1785.

"The bills of exchange drawn by order of Congress were not entered when drawn, as they ought to have been, in the treasury books, by the officers of that department, neither were the accounts of the payment of them transmitted from Europe, no regulations for either purpose having been at that time made." Hence Morris could give only a sketch of the banker's account, not a correct return of it.[1]

Bills on the Envoys in 1780 and the first part of 1781 were sold for continental paper, at a rate above the true depreciation, as follows:[2] —

		Face Value.	Sold for	Real Value of which.	Loss.
1780	on Laurens & Adams,	$10,447	$244,811 cont.	$5,378	$5,068
1780	on Jay,	68,386	2,960,582 cont.	44,334	24,051
1780-81	on Franklin,	68,700	contin. worth	57,103	11,596
1780-81	on Jay,	89,091	3,669,052	56,683	32,408
1780-81	on Franklin,	34,800	2,266,000	11,432	23,368
1780-81	on Franklin & Jay,	44,862	specie	31,261	13,600
	Total drawn,	$316,286		Loss,	$110,091

[1] Report of 1785. [2] Report of 1790.

CHAPTER XIII.

THE SITUATION IN 1780; MORRIS BECOMES FINANCIER; HIS VIEWS AND THOSE OF OTHERS ABOUT THE OFFICE.

DURING 1780 American affairs were tending rapidly toward a catastrophe. The people were utterly tired of the war. The financial system had collapsed, and nothing could be put in its place. The specific supply system was a failure.

Washington wrote as early as March, 1779, that some thought the contest over, and thought that there was nothing more to do but make money. "Friends and foes seem now to combine to pull down the goodly fabric we have been raising at the expense of so much time, blood, and treasure." He thinks it an error of the States not to send able men to Congress. The federal government is like the mainspring of a watch. Congress is rent by party. Mason, to whom he was writing, Jefferson, and other such men ought to go into Congress so as to help.[1]

In May, 1780, George III. said that the distresses in America would force the Americans to sue for peace during the summer unless the English met with some disaster.[2] Washington agreed with him. He wrote to the Committee of Congress: "We seem to be verging so fast to destruction that I am filled with sensations to which I have been a stranger till within these three months. The conjuncture requires all our wisdom and all our energy.

---

[1] Bancroft, x. 207.   [2] George III. ii. 319.

Such is the present state of this country that the utmost exertion of its resources, though equal, is not more than equal, to the object." [1]

In September Hamilton said that he would have France told that, without a loan, America must make terms with Great Britain.[2] Arthur Lee wrote that the United States would have to come to terms with Great Britain unless France would grant a loan of thirty or forty million livres at the beginning of the next campaign.[3] A letter from Mrs. Jay shows that there was a general feeling in Europe that affairs were coming to a crisis. She wrote to Mrs. Robert Morris: "The variety of reports circulating here subject me at one time and another to fear, hope, indignation, grief, and in short every emotion of the mind but despair. Far, very far be that from any of us." [4]

In January, 1781, Washington wrote a letter of instructions for John Laurens: "The period of our opposition will shortly arrive if our allies cannot afford us those effectual aids, particularly in money and in a naval superiority, which are now solicited. . . . Without an immediate, ample, and efficacious succour in money, we may make a feeble and expiring effort in our next campaign, — in all probability the period of our opposition." [5] In February Franklin wrote to Vergennes that he felt himself old and failing. He must declare that the conjuncture was critical. . . . "There is some danger lest the Congress should lose its influence over the people, if it is found unable to procure the aids that are wanted, and that the whole system of the new government in America may thereby be shaken." If England should recover the country, no similar oppor-

[1] Durand, 245.   [2] Hamilton's Works, i. 218.
[3] Lee's A Lee, ii. 161.   [4] Boogher, March, 183.
[5] Washington, vii. 368.

tunity would occur again, and she would become intolerably great.[1]

At that time, however, France also was eager for peace. Vergennes tried to make a truce for twenty years, England to keep Georgia and South Carolina and evacuate New York.[2] When this effort failed, France saw no way open to her except to throw herself into the enterprise which she had undertaken, without reserve, and to give the United States both financial and military aid sufficient to establish their independence.

Morris's appointment to the head of the treasury coincided in time with this new infusion of help and energy into the war. So the decisive year 1781 opened with new combinations, the smooth and successful development ot which was very remarkable when compared with the way in which things generally go on in this world when many men and many enterprises must co-operate to a single result.

We are now especially concerned with the reorganization of American finances. Congress had at last been forced to yield the prejudices of inexperience by which they had hitherto been guided.

In 1778 they had directed the Commissioners in France to inform Dr. Price, the inventor of the sinking fund fallacy, that they desired to consider him a citizen of the United States, and to have his aid in regulating their finances.[3] He declined with thanks.[4] In February, 1780, Pelatiah Webster urged the appointment of a Financier, that is, of a competent single officer to take charge of the finances, in place of the committees or boards who had hitherto been intrusted with them. In September of the same year Alexander Hamilton urged the same view, that

[1] Franklin, viii. 536.
[2] Bancroft, x. 244.
[3] Secret Journ. ii. 101.
[4] Dip. Corr. Rev. iii. 64.

there should be single responsible heads of the great departments. "Mr. Robert Morris would have many things in his favour for the department of finance."[1] In December a grand quarrel broke out among the subordinate officers of the treasury, some of whom charged others with neglect of duty, indolence, inattention to the public interests, incapacity, and partiality. A Committee of Investigation reported that the chief charge was the length of time required for business. They cannot tell what time ought to be employed in business, but think it might have been done with more facility " if the present system established by Congress did not necessarily create great delays." Hence they are compelled to acquit the persons charged.[2] There was great confusion in public affairs "not merely from defects in former plans, but from a great negligence in those to whom the execution had been committed."[3] There was no responsibility. Few of the loan office officers had conformed to the regulations about their accounts, and some had made no returns at all.

It was thus by an absolute necessity, produced by the collapse of all former devices, that Congress was driven, in spite of its prejudices, to appoint single heads of the treasury, war, and marine departments. On the 9th of February they fixed the salary of the first at $6,000, and of the others at $5,000 each. They gave to the first the title of Superintendent of Finance, which was generally abbreviated to Financier.[4] On the 20th of February, Morris was elected Superintendent of Finance, without a vote against him, although Samuel Adams and Artemas Ward declined to vote. Samuel Adams refused, because of a "jealousy of delegated powers."[5] He was therefore still

---
[1] Hamilton's Works, i. 215. [2] Journ. Cong. vii. 13.
[3] Dip. Corr. Rev. xii. 487. [4] Journ. Cong. vii. 24.
[5] Wells's S. Adams, iii. 130.

stanchly determined to sacrifice all the real interests at stake for the sake of a dogmatic whim.[1] General Sullivan had Hamilton in his mind for Financier, but did not nominate him.[2] In truth, the minds of all turned to Morris as the one man in the United States for the place. " Our finances want a Necker to arrange and reform them. Morris is, I believe, best qualified of any our country affords, for the arduous undertaking. We shall in a day or two appoint the officers for the foreign affairs and the marine. I wish we had men in these offices as well qualified to execute them as Morris in the treasury."[3] " I have great expectations from the appointment of Mr. Morris; but they are not unreasonable ones, for I do not suppose that by any magic art he can do more than recover us by degrees from the labyrinth into which our finances are plunged."[4] If there had been more people who had taken this sensible view of what could be done, and how it could be done, Morris would have had far greater success as Financier; but the almost universal opinion seems to have been that he did possess, or ought to possess, a magic art for obtaining resources from nothing. The French Minister reported his appointment as follows: " Congress has appointed Robert Morris Secretary of the Treasury, — a merchant who has rendered essential services to his country. . . . Everybody wants him to accept, and it is thought that this post could not be in better hands."[5] Mrs. Jay wrote to Mrs. Morris from Madrid, with respect to Morris's appointment, that Mrs. Morris would not regret the loss of her husband's company if she could see " the universal

---

[1] The French Minister wrote at this time that Samuel Adams was trying to undermine Washington. Adams and his party preached fear of one man's prestige. They held Washington's virtues to be a danger. Their doctrine was: " Distrust is the guardian of republics " (Durand, 234).

[2] Washington, vii. 399. [3] Jones's Letters, 69.
[4] Washington, viii. 71. [5] Durand, 241.

satisfaction it has diffused among the friends of our country; but would you (were you as malicious as myself) even enjoy the confusion of our enemies upon the occasion." [1]

His own understanding of the reasons for his appointment were stated in a letter to Jay in July following: " The derangement of our money affairs, the enormity of our public expenditures, the confusion in all our departments, the languor of our general system, the complexity and consequent inefficacy of our operations, — these are some among the many reasons which have induced Congress to the appointment of a Superintendent of Finance." [2]

The situation did not hold out any pleasant prospects to the man who undertook the charge of the treasury. The members of the Board of War told him that they had not money enough to send an express rider to the army. " The various scenes of distress and the extreme difficulties which presented themselves to my view at that time were sufficient to have deterred any man from the acceptance of such an appointment. But, however unequal to the station, the attempt was indispensable." [3] In his Report of 1785 he said, of the time of his appointment: " The aspect of affairs was not promising at that time, but appearances were more favourable than the reality." There was a floating debt of two millions and a half of dollars.[4]

He kept a diary during all the time that he was in office, of which only fragments have ever been published. The following extract from it shows that he understood, from the experience he had already had of public affairs, what he had to expect. " This appointment was unsought, unsolicited, and dangerous to accept, as it was evidently

---

[1] Boogher, March, 1883. [2] Johnston's Jay, ii. 40.
[3] Carey's Debates, 47.
[4] See the first column of the table in vol. ii. p. 129.

contrary to my private interests, and if accepted, must deprive me of those enjoyments, social and domestic, which my time of life required, and to which my circumstances entitled me; and a vigorous execution of the duties must inevitably expose me to the resentment of disappointed and designing men, and to the calumny and detraction of the envious and malicious. I was therefore determined not to engage in so arduous an undertaking; but the solicitations of my friends, acquaintance, and fellow-citizens, a full conviction of the necessity that some person should commence the work of reformation in our public affairs, by an attempt to introduce system and economy, and the persuasions that a refusal on my part would probably deter others from attempting this work, so absolutely necessary to the safety of our country, — these considerations, after much reflection and a consultation with friends, induced me to write a letter to the President of Congress, dated the 13th of March, 1781."[1]

In that letter he says that, after twenty years of business as a merchant, he was ready for ease, and that he had been so successful that he was prepared to enjoy ease; also that he had no ambition beyond his present situation. His duties as member of the Pennsylvania Legislature have prevented him from making an earlier reply. "Putting myself out of the question, the sole motive is the public good; and this motive, I confess, comes home to my feelings. The contest we are engaged in appeared to me in the first instance just and necessary; therefore I took an active part in it. As it became dangerous, I thought it the more glorious, and was stimulated to the greatest exertions in my power when the affairs of America were at the worst. Sensible of the want of arrangement in our moneyed affairs, the same consideration impelled me to this undertaking,

[1] Dip. Corr. Rev. xi. 351.

which I would embark in without hesitation could I believe myself equal thereto; but fearing this may not be the case, it becomes indispensably necessary to make such stipulations as may give ease to my feelings, aid my exertions, and tend to procure ample support to my conduct in office, so long as it be founded in and guided by a regard for the public prosperity. In the first place, then, I am to inform Congress that the preparatory steps I had taken to procure for myself relaxation from business with the least injury to the interests of my family, were by engaging in certain commercial establishments with persons in whom I had perfect confidence as to their integrity, honour, and abilities. These establishments I am bound in honour and by contracts to support to the extent agreed on. If therefore it be in the idea of Congress that the office of Superintendent of Finance is incompatible with commercial concerns and connections, the point is settled; for I cannot on any consideration consent to violate engagements or depart from those principles of honour which it is my pride to be governed by. If, on the contrary, Congress have elected me to this office under the expectation that my mercantile connections and engagements were to continue, an express declaration of their sentiments should appear on the minutes, that no doubt may arise or reflections be cast on this score hereafter. I also think it indispensably necessary that the appointment of all persons who are to act in my office, under the same roof, or in immediate connection with me, should be made by myself, Congress first agreeing that such secretaries, clerks, or officers, so to be appointed, are necessary, and fixing the salaries for each. I conceive that it will be impossible to execute the duties of this office with effect unless the absolute power of dismissing from office or employment all persons whatever that are concerned in the official expenditure of public moneys be committed to the Superintendent of Finance. For unless this power can be exercised without control, I have little hopes of efficacy in the business of reformation, which is probably the most essential part of the duty." He added that the duties of the Superintendent of Finance, as stated in the Act of Congress, exceeded the powers granted to him, so that he could not be responsible in those matters; but he thought they might be adjusted later.[1]

Congress refused to vote that Morris might maintain his commercial connections. Then the paragraph from his letter was read in which he refused to accept, if he must dissolve his connections; and the vote being taken again, they consented to it. They were also disinclined to grant him the power of peremptory removal, and appointed a committee to confer with him, to whom he addressed a written statement on this point. "I am persuaded that a minister who would venture to execute the duties of his office with vigour without possessing uncontrolled the power of dismission, would in a few months put it out of his power to proceed in his business, and Congress would have full employment to hear and determine between him and suspended officers."[2] March 31, a proposition that the Financier should be authorized to remove, for incapacity, negligence, dishonesty, or other misbehaviour, all persons employed in the expenditure of public money, and all who are unnecessary, during the war, was lost, the only States which voted for it being North and South Carolina and Georgia. S. Adams led the opposition to this, as he did to all the other motions for giving Morris power. At length, on April 21, Congress passed resolutions giving the Financier power to remove, for cause, persons not immediately appointed by

[1] Dip. Corr. Rev. xi. 350.   [2] Journ. Cong. vii. 54.

Congress, also such as were unnecessary; and to suspend persons appointed by Congress, reporting the reasons. In his statement to the Committee of Congress, Morris asserted that the Financier should himself have no accounts with the public, or that, if such became necessary, Congress should from time to time appoint a committee or special board to examine and settle such accounts.

The event showed that he was wise to use the command of the situation which he then possessed to insist upon these stipulations before accepting. One of the old colonial faults was, that the legislative bodies assumed executive functions, and would not allow the executive department its essential powers. This was one constant source of strife with the royal governors, and one of the modes of behaviour which was always construed in England as insubordination to the royal authority, and as effort for independence.[1] It was only with great difficulty that Morris wrested from Congress that sort of executive independence which we should to-day regard as one of the first essentials of a good practical system of government. As we shall see, he only wrested it from them imperfectly, after all.

These negotiations consumed four months; but they being at length finished, Morris formally accepted his appointment on the 14th of May. In his letter of acceptance to the President of Congress, he wrote that he would undertake the duties as soon as possible, but that time would be required to organize the office, to make plans for obtaining money, and to obtain information by which to correct abuses. He must also settle up his private affairs, so as to put them in the hands of other persons. "My necessary commercial connections, notwithstanding the

[1] Chalmers's History of the Revolt is a construction of the whole colonial history from this point of view.

decided sense of Congress, expressed in their resolution of the 20th of March, might, if the business were transacted by myself, give rise to illiberal reflections, equally painful to me and injurious to the public. This reason alone would deserve great attention; but further, I expect that my whole time, study, and attention will be necessarily devoted to the various business of my department." He therefore proposes that the existing arrangement of the treasury shall go on until he can make adequate arrangements for undertaking the duty. "Another consideration of great magnitude, to which I must also pray the attention of Congress, is the present public debts. I am sure no gentleman can hope that these should be immediately paid out of an empty treasury. If I am to receive and consider the applications on that subject, if I am to be made responsible, that alone will, I fear, be full employment for the life of one man, and some other must be chosen to attend to the present and provide for the future. But this is not all: if from that or any other cause I am forced to commit a breach of faith, or even to incur the appearance of it, from that moment my utility ceases. In accepting the office bestowed on me, I sacrifice much of my interest, my ease, my domestic enjoyments and internal tranquillity. If I know my own heart, I make these sacrifices with a disinterested view to the service of my country. I am ready to go still further, and the United States may command everything I have except my integrity,[1] and the loss of that would effectually disable me from serving them more." He therefore wants all outstanding debts funded, so that he may have to provide only for the interest and the eventual discharge of the principal. "I

---

[1] By this he means his commercial credit, the commercial honour of his signature. His anxiety about this, from the beginning of his administration, is to be noted on account of the sequel.

must again repeat my serious conviction that the least breach of faith must ruin us forever. . . . Congress will know that the public credit cannot be restored without method, economy, and punctual performance of contracts. Time is necessary for each, and therefore the removal of those evils we labour under can be expected from time only." [1]

In the diary he made notes of other considerations which were prominent before his mind at the time, especially his reason for not entering upon the office at once. " Particularly it was necessary to retain my seat in the Assembly of Pennsylvania, in order to lay a foundation for such measures as might tend to their support of me in pursuing the public good; not doubting but their example would have proper influence on the Legislatures of the other States, especially in their determination upon general points, such as their repealing those tender and penal laws which in their operations had destroyed all public and private confidence and credit; in passing effective tax-bills that might yield substantial aid to the United States for calling in the paper money that had lost its credit, and in adopting plans of reviving and establishing the credit of such as had been injured in some degree, but which, being necessary in circulation and originally issued on funds sufficient for its redemption, ought not to be given up to ruin, if possible to prevent it." [2]

On the 15th of June Morris wrote to Washington that he had accepted the position, but had not yet taken the oath, for the reasons just given. His objects were, he said, especially to reduce public expenditures, " as nearly as possible to what they ought to be, and to obtain revenues in our own country to meet those expenses as nearly as can be, and then to show foreign nations engaged in the war

[1] Dip. Corr. Rev. xi. 360.   [2] Ibid. 363.

that we must look to them for the balance. And I am very confident, when they shall see exertions on the one hand and economy on the other, they will be willing to assist us all they consistently can.[1]

He had, in fact, already begun the work of his department; and as we shall see, he did set about it with a degree of energy and enterprise which was not manifested by any other person in the revolutionary period in an equal degree. He also profited by his previous experience on the Commercial Committee to introduce careful methods of business into his office, if we may judge from the description we possess of those papers of his which are not now accessible.[2] There is a statement afloat which is often quoted, that two members of the Massachusetts delegation declared that it cost Congress eighteen million hard dollars per annum to carry on the war before Morris was appointed, and after that only four million.[3]

On the 6th of July Congress validated the acts of Morris which he had executed before he took the oath, and approved of his accepting a certain trust and powers from the Assembly of Pennsylvania, in an engagement to be mentioned below. They also authorized him to employ an assistant. For this position he selected Gouverneur Morris. In his diary[4] he speaks very highly of the abilities of his assistant, and there is great reason to believe that Gouverneur Morris was very efficient, and deserves more credit than he has received for his share in the work done in the office during Morris's administration. On the 11th of September Congress reorganized the treasury department, according to Morris's plan.

In the mean time the Assembly of Pennsylvania had been in conference with Morris in respect to measures to

[1] Letters to Washington, iii. 339.
[2] Homes's Sketch.
[3] Waln, 355.
[4] Dip. Corr. Rev. xi. 426.

support his administration. It was afterward charged that he was partial to Pennsylvania; but there is much more reason to believe that he turned first, in his great necessities, to Pennsylvania; so that, if there was any inequality, that State suffered by its nearness and by his familiarity with it. In June the Assembly authorized the Superintendent of Finance to obtain the specific supplies for Pennsylvania. He agreed to accept the agency of the State for this purpose, and promised to pledge his private credit, as far as might be necessary.[1] Especially they authorized him to commute these specific supplies into paper currency. He was to buy the notes which other States had issued under the Act of Congress of March 18, 1780, and with them to pay the four tenths of Pennsylvania. All issues of that State, except that of April 7, 1781, were to be withdrawn by the taxes just voted on the 22d of June.[2] Here was another case where he engaged to execute transactions in the purchase and delivery of commodities on behalf of the State, and in the execution of paper money contracts for the State, which, in view of the fluctuations of the medium, were sure to involve the most delicate questions of integrity and fidelity, — questions which no evidence could possibly solve. He accepted this agency July 20.[3]

He had succeeded in bringing about the repeal of the embargo by pledging himself that there would be no scarcity for the army. It was repealed June 7, 1781.[4] July 2, he wrote to Washington that the ships had been busy carrying flour to the French and Spanish islands, bringing back goods and dollars.[5] There had never been a day when he

[1] Penn. Journ. 681. [2] Penn. Packet, July 2, 1781.
[3] Penn. Archives, ix. 264. [4] Penn. Journ. 660.
[5] A story is given, on the authority of one Reese, who was a confidential clerk of Morris, that the latter imported specie from Havana in 1781 in

could not buy five thousand or ten thousand barrels of flour, and the price had fallen from twenty-eight or thirty shillings to fifteen or seventeen; hence he wanted to enforce the doctrine that "commerce should be perfectly free and property sacredly secure to the owner."[1] When, a year later, North Carolina proposed to lay an embargo, in order to enable the United States to buy supplies on better terms, he gave fuller expression to his views of that policy: "I am to request that all such restrictions be taken off. They sour people's minds, destroy the spirit of industry, impair by a rapid as well as a certain progress the public wealth of the State, producing a dearth of the things embargoed; eventually enhance the prices far more than they could have been increased by any other mode; whereas perfect freedom makes the people easy, happy, rich, and able to pay taxes, and the taxes when paid can be expended amid a plenty of products, and consequently be expended to advantage."[2]

After the revolt of the Pennsylvania line in January, 1781, Congress made a requisition on the States for $879,342, to pay arrears to the army. In April nothing had been paid on this.[3] In a circular to the States, in January, Congress said that the certificates of the commissaries and quartermasters obstructed every plan which had been devised for supporting public credit and carrying on the war. As these certificates were receivable for taxes, the whole revenue consisted of them, so that what little result was produced by taxation and requisitions was all the time dealing with past expenditure, and not producing resources for the future. At this point of time everything that could possibly be "anticipated" had been

casks, mixed with sugar, and that Reese helped him to take it out secretly (Mag. Amer. Hist. xi. 442 n.). On Morris's public attempts to get specie from Havana, see below.

[1] Letters of Morris, 465.   [2] Dip. Corr. Rev. xii. 282.
[3] Journ. Cong. vii. App.

anticipated by the paper devices of the previous years, while no adequate measures had been taken to deal with them at maturity. In 1780 there had been an attempt, as is above shown, to remove the continental currency by a sweeping and enormous taxation. This would have been a remedy if it could have been carried out; but it could not. Therefore we find Morris, when he comes into office, demanding that the past shall be past, and that he shall only be charged to provide for the interest on the debt previously contracted; and we also find him complaining of the quartermaster's certificates and loan office certificates which robbed him of current revenue. He also wanted to use "anticipations," which would have required that he should start anew from the time when he took office and deal only with the future, on a new and reformed system, with adequate taxation as its basis. The outstanding paper was a clog upon every step. November 12, 1781, Congress repealed the provision that certificates given for supplies by quartermasters and commissaries should be receivable for taxes.

One explanation of the trouble about requisitions is that there was no assessment. It was therefore impossible to know how much each State ought to pay, and there was no adequate publication of the facts as to what each State had paid. Being in the dark as to the facts, each State maintained that it had paid more than its share; or, whenever there was a proposition in any State to pay, it was immediately rejected, because the doubt and fear arose whether such State might not be running beyond the others. Thus every motive which was brought into play, instead of stimulating zeal, crushed it out. By 1781 also the States seemed to have reached the point where they believed that they might content themselves with no answer, or a negative answer, to the demands of Congress.

The modern reader wonders that the members of Congress did not go home and prevail upon the States to comply with the requisitions; but it would have cost popularity to do this. John Adams was credited by Morris with having persuaded Massachusetts to adopt the impost.[1] Alexander Hamilton exerted himself in 1782 to persuade New York to lay taxes. Other instances of effort of this kind are not known to us. The governors of the States could not urge taxation and zeal upon the legislatures without a painful and unpopular contest. The members of a legislature who laid taxes must expect to return to their constituents to face grumbling and popular dissatisfaction.

In July, 1780, Washington wrote to Reed to urge him to use his power as President of Pennsylvania. He argued that it would be good policy for Reed to do so, and win the reputation of an efficient war governor. Reed made a very sensible reply, the strongest point of which was that an efficient and successful governor must have a party behind him. His reply shows very clearly that a man could not, as governor, be popular with the army and the citizens at the same time. To please the former he must favour burdens on the latter. To please the latter he must save them as much as possible from burdens on behalf of the former.[2]

In 1782 Morris wrote to Franklin: "Many who see the right road and approve it continue to follow the wrong road, because it leads to popularity. The love of popularity is our endemial disease, and can only be checked by a change of seasons."[3] Congress could not be blamed for inexperience, although perhaps they could be for the obstinacy of inexperience which would not learn; but they

[1] Dip. Corr. Rev. xii. 427.
[2] Reed's Reed, ii. 220; cf. also 300.
[3] Dip. Corr. Rev. xii. 267.

were to blame for flinching from their duty for fear of unpopularity. If we are astonished at this cringing to popularity, we must notice that in the society of the period the dependence of a man for comfort and success upon the active good-will of the little community in which he lived was far greater and more direct than anything with which we are now familiar.

We can now see what Morris's plan of action was. He agreed, in his view of the situation, with those who desired that he should take the office. He was no doubt flattered by their assurances that he was the one man in America to set things right. He thought that he saw just what ought to be done. In the first place, he must cut off the old system. If taxes and requisitions brought him in nothing but masses of old continental paper, his case was hopeless. The war was still going on, — was, in fact, at its highest strain. He must provide for the present and the future. He therefore wanted taxes laid in specie which would give him a revenue, and these taxes must be *federal*. This revenue would pay the interest on the debt. Then he wanted requisitions paid in by the States as a reliance for war expenditure. When he went into office he had no reliance on money to be drawn from France, but hoped to contract loans with which to supplement his domestic measures. He proposed to introduce a system of retrenchment and economy; for it is doubtful if the waste, extravagance, and folly of the previous financial management can be paralleled in history. He knew that the country possessed ample means of defence; that the people had not suffered on account of the war; that the lack of organization had prevented the resources from being used; and that the lack of administrative method had produced exasperation and resistance, without bringing out power. The schemes for a bank and other devices were subsidiary measures by which to support his main plan. He wanted system, order, regularity, and punctuality.

He was obliged immediately to modify his stipulation about back debts with respect to those which were due to one class of persons. In the report of 1785 he said: " When the Superintendent of Finance was appointed, the treasury was so much in arrears to the servants in the public offices that many of them could not, without payment, perform their duties, but must have gone to jail for debts they had contracted to enable them to live." Hence, although he had stipulated that he should pay no back debts, he was obliged to do it with this class of people. He could not discriminate between those who could pay their debts and those who could not. Therefore he paid them all.

CHAPTER XIV.

THE TASKS OF THE FINANCIER; HIS MEANS, PLANS, AND DEVICES; HIS APPEALS TO THE STATES, AND PROPOSALS TO CONGRESS.

IT is astonishing to notice what heterogeneous tasks were at once laid upon the Financier or undertaken by him. May 3, he proposed to the President of Congress to import some specie, saying that he had heard that Congress had been obliged to obtain hard money " on terms inconsistent with the dignity of government, and not very consonant to the public interest."[1] June 23, Congress authorized him to launch and equip the ship "America," at Portsmouth. July 3, they authorized him to export goods on account of the United States, and to import supplies as he might deem useful for the public service. On the 8th of September he accepted the office of Agent of the Marine, in order to save expense to the United States. On the 12th he was authorized to fit out and employ the ships of the United States. On the 21st he wrote to Congress, calling their attention to the "idleness, waste, and extravagance" in the hospitals. Professing ignorance of this matter, he selected three physicians as a committee, and referred to them the papers, begging them to form and recommend a plan of economy.[2] On the 9th of November he proposed to Congress that the President of Congress should have a salary.[3]

---

[1] Dip. Corr. Rev. xi. 365.
[2] State Dep. MSS. No. 137, i. 141.   [3] Ibid. 223.

In the management of the specific supplies also, which now fell upon him, he had to undertake great enterprises in the collection, transportation, and exchange of commodities. Writing to Schuyler, May 29, he states the motive which had led him to undertake his office, and his need of support. He begs Schuyler to buy and forward a thousand barrels of flour to Washington at once. He has the means of raising hard money to pay for the flour; but he wants as long credit as he can get, and asks Schuyler to employ his own credit. "For your reimbursement you may either take me as a public or a private man; for I pledge myself to repay you with hard money wholly if required, or part hard and part paper, if you so transact the business. In short, I promise, and you may rely that no consideration whatever shall induce me to make a promise that I do not see my capability to perform, that I will enable you to fulfil your engagements for this supply of flour."[1]

We also find him making arrangements to exchange flour in one State for flour in another, so as to save the expense of transportation.[2] His functions as Financier, therefore, included nearly everything which could come under the general head of business.

In the midst of all this he found time to write to some of the leading Quakers, in July, begging them to loan money to the United States, at five per cent, which could be applied to the relief of refugees from the Southern States. He promised to keep secret the fact that he had made this application, in order that they might reply to it with perfect freedom; for if it should be known that he had applied, and they should think fit to refuse, they might fear odium and abuse. They declined to lend, being impoverished by hard times, unjust laws, and frauds of debtors,

---

[1] Dip. Corr. Rev. xi. 368. [2] Journ. Cong. vii. 106.

while their expenses for charity within their own body had increased.[1]

What resources then had the Minister of Finance at his disposal for his numerous and difficult tasks?

When Morris came into office in June, he had no domestic revenue to depend upon, but the balances due on the old requisitions. He wrote to Jay, July 4: "The various requisitions of Congress to the several States, none of them entirely complied with, create a considerable balance in favour of the United States, and the claiming this balance is delivered over to me as revenue; while on the other hand, the dangerous practice of taking articles for the public service, and giving certificates to the people, has created a very general and a very heavy debt. The amount of this debt is swelled beyond all reasonable bounds, nor can the extent of it be at present estimated. These things need no explanation, but it may be proper to observe that if the certificates were not in my way, there is still an infinite difference between the demand of a balance from the States and an effectual revenue."[2]

In a report which he made to Congress, August 28, 1781, he stated the requisitions which Congress had made on the States before March 18, 1780, with the specie value of the same according to the official table of depreciation, as follows:[3] —

January 1, 1778	$1,250,000	$857,222
April 1, 1778	1,250,000	621,423
July 1, 1778	1,250,000	412,864
October 1, 1778	1,250,000	268,472
January 1, 1780	60,000,000	2,042,500
February 1, 1780	15,000,000	451,041
March 1, 1780	15,000,000	401,450
		$5,054,972

[1] Penn. Hist. Soc. Coll. i. 131.   [2] Dip. Corr. Rev. vii. 422.
[3] Ibid. xi. 447.

May 22, 1781, the treasurer of the United States was directed to draw on the States, at thirty days' sight, for their quotas under the vote of August 26, 1780, which should have been paid in before the last day of the last December; and to give notice that he will draw for other quotas as they become due. The States were called upon to provide for these bills.[1]

According to the Treasury Report of May 4, 1790, the amount credited to the States for drafts on the State treasuries in 1779, 1780, and 1781, which had been paid, was, in thousands of dollars: —

New Hampshire	123	Pennsylvania	188
Massachusetts	447	Delaware	41
Rhode Island	66	Maryland	116
Connecticut	375	Virginia	278
New York	98	North Carolina	73
New Jersey	46		

When Congress drew on Franklin, he had to find means to pay their drafts. When they drew on a State, it paid little or no heed.[2]

Magazines of provisions were to be formed of the arrears of specific supplies, and now we find that the treasury was to be supplied with the balance of unpaid requisitions.

By a resolution of June 4, 1781, Congress ordered to be transferred to Morris bills of exchange on Franklin, Jay, and Laurens, then held as follows:[3] —

	Franklin livres.	Laurens bank guilders.	Jay dollars.
By the paymaster under the Board of War	57,000	2,750	57,993
By the loan officer of Pennsylvania		40,958	25,782
By the Pennsylvania Bank		655,050	62,388
By Ichabod Burnet[4]	49,000		
	106,000	698,758	146,163
In dollars	19,629	279,503	
Total in dollars			445,295

[1] Journ. Cong. vii. 84. [2] Ibid. vi. 16.
[3] Report of 1785. [4] For the Southern army, see vol. ii. p. 82.

Of these bills, part were thrown overboard from the "Trumbull" to prevent capture; part were cancelled, especially those drawn on a man who was in the Tower of London. Morris negotiated of them

	Livres.	Bank guilders.	Dollars.
On Franklin	57,000		= 10,555
On Laurens.		40,958	= 16,383
On Jay			25,782
			52,720[1]

This, therefore, is the amount which was put at Morris's disposal, even in bills drawn on "the pump at Aldgate." It is doubtful whether he ever drew any bills on the envoys. He drew on the bankers, who were to be provided with funds, it is true, by the loans obtained at the solicitation of the envoys; but the bankers interposed another credit, and the bills were, in form, regular.

On the 8th of June Morris wrote to Le Couteulx & Co., bankers at Paris, to open an account with them.

Franklin remonstrated mildly against the selection of this banker. He said that Grand had acted ever since the Commissioners had been in Paris, and had been very accommodating. Both bankers were used from this time on. Le Couteulx seems to have been Morris's banker. They had business interests in common. It was sometimes alleged or suspected that Morris's relations with him were like those which Necker was said to have had with his own bank while he was Finance Minister.[2]

Morris began by depositing half a million livres which he had obtained from the French treasury; namely, bills on

---

[1] As we have been obliged to convert many sums which are not converted in the Report, and to make combinations, for our purpose, different from those in the Report, and have always neglected fractions, discrepancies occur sometimes in the first figure.

[2] Cf. Dip. Corr. U. S. iv. 97.

Franklin.[1] It was with this, and not with any domestic resource, that he began his administration; and we shall see below,[2] that the appropriation of this sum was disputed. In the next month we find him driven to the same old devices of trickery with paper money. He wrote to Franklin that Pennsylvania had just issued £500,000 in paper [under her Act of April 7], so secured that there could be no doubt of its redemption. Nevertheless the notes rapidly depreciated when only £130,000 were out, and a tax was laid in order to absorb all the paper and bring in some specie. The £500,000 were put in Morris's hands in order to pay to Congress the balance due on the resolution of the 18th of March, 1780, and to pay for specific supplies. He had been trying to do this gradually by the receipts from the tax which were put in his hands, without making any new issue, and to appreciate the paper. The United States, however, had drawn for the balance due them, and the holders of drafts issued by Congress against this debt of the State were clamorous for payment. He must therefore provide the State officers immediately with means. It will be observed here that he was standing between the State and the Union, and acting for both, in order that he might gain all the possible advantages of balancing accounts and so restraining the issue of notes. He now tells Franklin that he has hit upon a new device. He will sell bills on the French bankers for specie only, while he borrows the paper with which to pay the drafts drawn by Congress on the State. Then he will draw bills on Franklin for 400,000 livres at six months' sight or more, for which he expects to get 400,000 paper dollars. Then he will draw on the bankers in favour of Franklin at sixty days' sight, winning three or four months for his operations, the bills on the bankers in favour of Franklin being sent on

---

[1] Dip. Corr. Rev. xi. 372.   [2] See vol. ii. p. 82.

three months later than the bills drawn on Franklin, within which three months he hopes to appreciate the paper.[1] Here, then, we find the Superintendent of Finance driven to the most vulgar kind of bill-kiting before he had been two months in office.

The most serious fact of all was that he convinced himself that there was, in this kind of an enterprise, some legitimate field for financial finesse.

In the Report of 1785 he speaks of his negotiations in paper money as made with a double view of counteracting the losses on bills of exchange, when the cash for which they were sold in America was compared with the sum given in payment of them in Europe, and also of "restoring to its expressed value that paper which was then greatly depreciated. This, which is commonly called appreciating money, although difficult, may be performed. The paper in question was raised from so low a rate as six for one to that of two for one, and it would have been brought nearly, if not entirely, to par, had not some measures intervened which, though well meant, were not judicious. Indeed, an operation of this kind is so delicate that the least derangement or interference proves fatal." This undertaking to restore the paper money of Pennsylvania "was the more necessary because the Legislature had assigned it as a fund for the purchase of specific supplies, formerly called for by Congress, when they appointed the Superintendent of Finance their [*i.e.* the State] agent for that purpose. The gain made on those negotiations in paper was by selling bills of exchange for that paper, and afterwards paying it [out] at a smaller rate of depreciation than that by which it was received. And at each successive operation, the rate was lowered by accepting it on the same terms for bills of exchange at which it had been pre-

[1] Dip. Corr. Rev. xi. 396.

viously paid. It was never applied to the purchase of the specific supplies, because it was checked in the progress towards par, as has been already mentioned, and therefore, if it had been paid out in any quantity from the treasury, those who received it would have suffered by the consequent depreciation. And if the measures determined on for calling it in had been pursued, it might again have risen in value so as that the State would have been obliged to redeem at par what had been issued at one half. In a word, the view of those evils which inevitably follow from the issuing of paper money, and which always have attended that measure in a greater or smaller degree, rendered it most advisable to purchase for the State with specie, and supply the want of cash by the use of credit, until sufficient funds could be raised by the taxes then levying."

However, these transactions never entered into his plans except in the most incidental way. He addressed himself immediately to the governors of the States, urging them to comply with the requisitions and to pay up the balances due.[1] On the 25th of July he sent out a circular to the governors, in which he used argument and exhortation: " It gives me great pain to learn that there is a pernicious idea prevalent among some of the States that their accounts are not to be adjusted with the continent. Such ideas cannot fail to spread listless languor over all our operations. . . . If once an opinion is admitted that those States who do the least and charge most will derive the greatest benefit and endure the smallest evils, Your Excellency must perceive that shameless inactivity must take the place of that noble emulation, which ought to pervade and animate the whole Union." He therefore solemnly promises that the accounts of the States with the United States shall be speedily liquidated, if he can possibly effect

[1] Va. Papers, ii. 221.

it. " It is by being just to individuals, to each other, to the Union, to all; by generous grants of solid revenue, and by adopting energetic methods to collect that revenue, and not by complaining, vauntings, or recriminations, that these States must expect to establish their independence, and rise into power, consequence, and grandeur." He does not appear to have had any accounts before him, for he urges the States to report to him immediately the moneys, supplies, transportation, etc., which they have rendered as an offset to the requisitions which have been made upon them. He also asked for copies of the several Acts passed by the States since March 18, 1780, for the collection of taxes and furnishing of supplies or other aids to the United States, and of the results produced by them. He asked for a report as to the State issues of currency, and closed with an eloquent appeal.[1] Two days later he issued another circular to the States which had not complied with the recommendation of Congress for the five per cent impost. He complained of the conditions which had been inserted by those States which had complied. " The faith of the United States is pledged to the public creditors. At every new loan it must be pledged anew, and an appeal is now made to the States individually to support the public faith so solemnly pledged. If they do, it is possible the public credit may be restored; if not, our enemies will draw from thence strong arguments in favour of what they have so often asserted, — that we are unworthy of confidence, that our Union is a rope of sand, that the people are weary of Congress, and that the respective States are determined to reject its authority." [2]

We have one case of the explicit reply which he received to appeals of this kind. It is dated a little earlier, and perhaps was in his mind when he wrote these circulars.

[1] Dip. Corr. Rev. xi. 400.   [2] Ibid. 408.

It is from the President of Pennsylvania, who wrote: "We have long since given up the hope of liquidating any account of the State with the continent. We consider every advance as an absolute disposal of the money, and upon this principle have deemed it safest to guard in the first instance, rather than trust to the precarious hope of future settlements and discounts."[1] This one voice may be taken as expressing the feeling of every Governor and every State.

Morris turned to Congress likewise. August 28, he addressed to them a memorial on the situation. He urged a settlement of the accounts with the States as the only way to overcome their feeling that the accounts never would be settled, or that one had done more than the others. If this is not done they will become every day more negligent. "A dangerous supineness pervades the continent; and recommendations of Congress, capable in the year 1775 of arousing all America to action, now lie neglected." They all consider everything not furnished as so much saved. The basis of the quotas ought to be revised, for if they were equitable in 1775, they are not so now. The States, it is true, have expended something for supplies, but no taxes have been laid, and the sums they have expended have come partly from the continental treasury, and partly from the State currencies which tended to depreciate the continental paper and impede its circulation. He proposes that an adjustment of the debtor and creditor balances be made up to the 18th of March, 1780. Many object to the resolutions of that date, but they have been enacted and partly acted upon, and it is impossible to recede from them. "The precedent of disobedience once established, our Union must soon be at an end, and the authority of Congress reduced to a metaphysical idea." The certificates given by public officers "have anticipated the

[1] Penn. Archives, ix. 288.

revenue and brought us to the brink of destruction." He objects to receiving these certificates for taxes, because it would deprive him of revenue. They are issued by officers "who are compelled to the melancholy duty of plundering their fellow-citizens." They try to make up by the amount of the certificates not only for the value of the goods, but also for the vexation of the mode of taking, so that the certificates are issued in an extravagant amount compared with the value of the goods. He proposed that they should not be receivable for taxes, but should be scaled down to the specie value of the goods, and converted into six per cent scrip, payable in one, two, three, four, and five years, to bearer, and receivable as cash for continental taxes at their maturity.[1]

October 19, he issued another circular to the States. He stated the cost of the war, according to the best information he could get, at about twenty millions a year. In order to overcome the difficulties, "the first proper step is to state them fully to the people through their representatives. It shall therefore be a part of my study to prepare every transaction for the public eye, so that the meanest individual may be in due time informed of those affairs in which, as a free citizen, he is interested." Various publications "have conspired to infuse an opinion that every power in Europe is favourable to us, — that great sums of money are already advanced to us, and that still greater may be obtained. Whatever may be the fate of my administration, I will never be subjected to the reproach of falsehood or insincerity. . . . The public opinion as to the conduct of other princes and states [besides France and Spain] has greatly injured us by relaxing our exertions; but the opinion as to pecuniary aid has been still more pernicious. People have flattered themselves with a vi-

[1] Dip. Corr. Rev. xi. 442.

sionary idea that nothing more was necessary than for Congress to send a Minister abroad, and that immediately he would obtain as much money as he chose to ask for." But every reasonable man should see that people will not part with their property without the prospect of repayment. "Have the efforts to borrow in this country been so successful as to ground any hope from abroad? or is it to be supposed that foreigners will interest themselves more in our prosperity and safety than our own citizens?" All the bills drawn on the agents in Europe have at last been referred to France for payment. "This has done us injury by anticipating the aid which France has been disposed to afford us, and at the same time has justly alarmed and greatly embarrassed the French Ministry." As soon as the estimates for the next year can be made, he will advertise for contracts "as the most effectual mode of husbanding our resources." France has given the plainest notice that she will render no more pecuniary assistance. How then can more be expected, "when, to every request, the short answer can be made, by asking what we have done for ourselves. . . . The neglect of funding the public debt has introduced a practice of issuing loan office certificates for the interest due on other loan office certificates. This I have absolutely forbidden, nor will I ever consent to it. . . . It is high time to relieve ourselves from the infamy we have already sustained, and to rescue and restore the national credit. This can only be done by solid revenue. Disdaining, therefore, these little timid artifices which, while they postpone the moment of difficulty, only increase the danger and confirm the ruin, I prefer the open declaration to all of what is to be expected, and from whence it is to be drawn." Hence he tells the creditors that they cannot be paid until the States provide revenue.[1]

[1] Dip. Corr. Rev. xi. 499.

December 11, he wrote to the Governor of New York, urging taxation, blaming the system of foraging, and calculating how many rations could be paid for by the sums given in New York State for bounties.[1] The sums paid for bounties throughout the war were in strong contrast with the expenditures for the efficiency and comfort of the troops after they were enlisted. In December he issued still another circular to the governors, asking for information about the laws of the States, their finances, taxes, and so on. An earlier appeal of the same sort had been entirely fruitless. Commenting on this, he wrote to Franklin: " When I tell you that I am not much deceived in my expectations, you will readily form a proper conclusion as to the relaxed habit of administration in this country."[2] In the following winter he continued to send out circular after circular of the same general character, urging the States in every possible way to grant financial support. Between November and May he issued nine such circulars, without any apparent effect whatever, except to arouse enmity against himself.[3] He very naturally used stronger and stronger language as he went on, until it did seem that he was hectoring the States. From the modern standpoint, it appears that the most effective remedy would have been publicity. If the sessions of Congress had been held open to the public, if its debates had been published, and if these circular letters of Morris had been published in the newspapers, there must have been some effect upon the popular sentiment, which needed educating. As it was, Morris wrote one of his long and enthusiastic circulars, committed it to the mail, and sat down to wait for

---

[1] Dip. Corr. Rev. xii. 65. [2] Ibid. 29.
[3] In June, 1782, Hamilton wrote to him that the people in New York were angry with him for a letter of the previous winter, reflecting on their exertions (Hamilton's Works, viii. 69).

results. The mail was slow and uncertain at best: the distances were long;[1] when the circular reached a Governor, if the Legislature was not in session, he placed it on file. If the Legislature was in session, he transmitted it to them. They adjourned and went home as if nothing was the matter, or as if they had no responsibility. It would be ludicrous if it were not so pitiful, to watch these proceedings of the Minister of Finance. He might almost as well have scattered a handful of waste paper upon the wind, in the hope that it would bring him relief.

His letters of this winter show how heavily the whole situation weighed upon his mind. To Washington he wrote in January, 1782: "To increase the means of payment by retrenching every other expenditure is my constant object. To increase the means of payment by grants of money, the States alone are competent to."[2] To the President of Congress he wrote, a month later: "We have reason to apprehend a continuance of that shameful negligence which has marked us to a proverb, while all Europe gazed in astonishment at the unparalleled boldness and vastness of our claims, blended with an unparalleled indolence and imbecility of conduct."[3] In the midst of the obstacles, which hedged him in on every side, the one idea that seems to have been most prominent, as suggesting a remedy which he could himself enforce, was that of retrenchment. He computed the salaries of the commissaries in the Middle and Eastern States at $10,525 per month, which, at the rate paid for rations at West Point,

---

[1] To show the time required for news to be transmitted, it may be noted that the news of the battle of Lexington was sent from Wallingford, Conn., to Charleston, S. C., by relays of express riders, in seventeen days (Drayton, i. 249, 276). The Governor of Rhode Island wrote a letter to the President of Congress, at York, November 8, 1777, which was received December 31 (R. I. Col. Rec. viii. 370).

[2] Letters to Washington, iii. 470.   [3] Dip. Corr. Rev. xii. 104.

would have bought 3,278 rations per day; and inasmuch as the salaries were not the only expense, he calculated that five thousand soldiers were being fed for what it formerly cost to support the issuers of provisions. This retrenchment he had effected since he came into office.[1] In February he issued notes to the officers of the army, redeemable in six months, in specie, for two months' pay, in order that they might supply their great need of clothing. He had, when he did this, hopes and expectations that the loan in Holland would prosper, and that France would grant a subsidy of 12,000,000 livres.

[1] Dip. Corr. Rev. xii. 116.

CHAPTER XV.

BORROWING IN EUROPE BY THE STATES; APPEALS OF CONGRESS TO FRANCE; MISSION OF JOHN LAURENS; THE YORKTOWN CAMPAIGN.

MAY 26, 1779, Franklin addressed a remonstrance to the Committee of Foreign Affairs against the attempts of the States to borrow in Europe. They often offered greater rates of interest than Congress. The European view is that if these applications are proper, they ought to come through Congress. Three States have applied to the French court for arms, ammunition, and clothing or money, and one has applied for naval stores and ships of war. They have supposed that it was his business to help them.[1] In answer to a request from the Governor of Virginia to help William Lee to obtain arms and stores, he said that he had found three merchants willing to provide the goods, but that Arthur Lee took up the business, whereupon quarrels ensued and complaints to Franklin. "But I cannot remedy them, for I cannot change Mr. Lee's temper."[2] In 1779, when William Lee was trying to negotiate a loan in Holland for Virginia, he met with the difficulty, besides the political obstacles, that the bankers "desired some clear and certain information, by some public Act, how far any particular State was authorized, by the terms and articles of the general association or Union of the thirteen United States, to borrow money

---

[1] Dip. Corr. Rev. iii. 91.   [2] Franklin, viii. 320.

Finances of the American Revolution. 293

on its own single securities; but they rather wished to have the guarantee of Congress added to that of the particular State for which the money was borrowed, as one State might be conquered by, or make some accommodations with Great Britain, and the rest remain independent."[1]

In 1780 Mazzei, or, as he is called, Mazzie, was sent out on some sort of a mission to Tuscany by Governor Jefferson. He likewise was drawing and spending money.[2] He had an idea of opening trade with Italy and demanded aid of Franklin. Franklin discountenanced the project: therefore he complains of Franklin.[3] Penet likewise tried to raise loans for Virginia, and asked Franklin's aid. "I was told by him," writes Penet, "that a great number of people, having been commissioned by different States to raise such loans, far from succeeding happily in their negotiations, prevented other gentlemen to obtain success on account of the prejudices they had excited in being importunate."[4]

In 1781 Mr. Searle was sent to Holland to borrow money for Pennsylvania. He failed.[5] In the same year the painter Trumbull tried to get a loan in Holland for Connecticut.[6]

The assistance of France, until the end of 1780, consisted in supplies, or in money which could be expended for supplies, or for the payment of interest on the loans contracted in America. November 22, 1780, Congress adopted a long memorial to the King of France, setting forth their distress and begging for money.

At about the time that this memorial was being prepared in America, Franklin was informing Vergennes of

---

[1] Va. Papers, i. 330.   [2] Ibid. 335.   [3] Ibid. 346.   [4] Ibid. 353.
[5] Dip. Corr. Rev. xi. 416 ; Reed's Reed, ii. 450.
[6] Trumbull, 80.

the drafts which had been presented to him, and was begging for help. The Minister replied: "You can easily imagine my astonishment at your request." Still he promised help for the next year.[1]

In January, 1781, it was decided to send a special messenger to France to give fuller explanations, and to support the appeal which had been prepared in November. This action proceeded from some dissatisfaction with the course of things in France.[2] It will be seen, however, that it was a very unfortunate step; for Franklin had not only proceeded, out of the independent necessity of the case, to do what the memorial of November called for, but he succeeded before the special Envoy arrived, in obtaining all the help which was obtained. The proceedings of the special Envoy and his agents only availed to traverse Franklin's arrangements, and introduce such confusion as to frustrate nearly all the benefit which should have been obtained from the help of France.

Colonel John Laurens was selected as special Envoy. He was a son of Henry Laurens, who was President of Congress in 1778, and agent of the United States in Holland, but a prisoner in the Tower of London while his son was on this mission. John Laurens was only about twenty-six years of age, and aid on Washington's staff, a friend of Lafayette and Hamilton, and full of chivalric enthusiasm for the cause.[3]

[1] Franklin in France, i. 387. [2] Reed's Reed, ii. 295.

[3] He is one of the most admirable personages in the history of the Revolution. It is narrated of him by Custis, that he was married to Miss Manning, daughter of a director of the Bank of England. Being in London when the war broke out, he hid in the ballast of a ship, in order to get from England to America. He was killed at the end of August, 1782, in a trifling and unnecessary skirmish with a foraging party in South Carolina. Washington said of him: "He had not a fault that I could discover, unless it were an intrepidity bordering on rashness;" and Hamilton said of him, "Laurens's heart realized that patriotism of which others only talked" (Works, viii. 87).

Congress provided him with a list of supplies wanted, among which were eight plain but elegant silver-mounted small swords. We are not surprised to learn that Vergennes protested against this list.

Paine says that Laurens did not want to go, and this is quite in accordance with his character. He wanted to stay and fight. He asked Paine to go with him, which he did.[1] They were as strangely mated as any couple who ever travelled together.

About February 1 news was received from Franklin that he had taken up the bills on Laurens. "You cannot conceive how much these things perplex and distress me."[2] He had obtained supplies to the value of $400,000 by giving bills on Congress to be paid in supplies for the French army. These bills fell on Morris just as he took office in June. He could not pay them. "It is not easy to convey to your mind," he answered to Franklin, "an idea of the pain I suffered. I felt for you, for Congress, for America."[3] This is the one case in which the Commissioners ventured to draw the other way, and the bills were promptly dishonoured.

Franklin referred to it somewhat bitterly afterward.[4]

March 10, an answer was received from the King to the petition of Congress of November. He was touched at the description of their distress, and would assist them as far as the enormous expenses of the war would permit.[5] March 24, Luzerne sent a message to Congress. He warned them that they could rely only on themselves for the expenses of the coming campaign. The King had gone further than he ought already. The French court "was exceedingly surprised on being informed of the step

---

[1] Letters to Morris, 476. [2] Dip. Corr. Rev. iii. 179.
[3] Ibid. xi. 398. [4] Ibid. viii. 57.
[5] Secret Journ. ii. 409.

which Congress had taken in disposing of bills drawn on their Minister, although they could not be ignorant that they had no funds for discharging them. This is a conduct totally inconsistent with that order which his Majesty is forced to observe in his finances, and he has no doubt but in future Congress will most studiously avoid a repetition of it. He has, nevertheless, resolved to discharge the bills which became due last year to the amount of one million livres, and it is probable his Majesty will be able to provide funds to the amount of three million for the discharge of those which will become due in the course of the present year. The King's Ministers have also procured for Dr. Franklin, whose zeal, wisdom, and patriotism deserve their utmost confidence, the sums necessary for the purchase he is ordered to make. These expenses, joined to those occasioned by sending a fleet and army to this continent, far exceed what Congress had a right to expect from the friendship of their allies; and the Chevalier de la Luzerne is persuaded that from this moment Congress will abstain from that ruinous measure of drawing bills of exchange without the previous knowledge and consent of his Majesty's Ministers." It is proposed that Congress shall provide the supplies for the French fleet and army, and receive pay in bills on France.[1] In consequence of this, they voted, April 11, to prepare magazines of supplies. May 25, they ordered that these magazines should be formed of the arrears of the specific supplies of 1780.[2] The specific supplies had been little. The arrears were nothing.

About May 1 came a letter from Franklin, stating that he had applied to the French Minister for a loan of twenty-five million livres (say five million dollars). The Minister replied that this was impossible, but the King would, for the year 1781, give six million livres as a present, would

[1] Dip. Corr. Rev. x. 459.   [2] Secret Journ. ii. 399 fg.

lend four millions more, and would guarantee a loan for ten millions more if it could be obtained in Holland. The subsidy granted was to be drawn by General Washington. This last stipulation was a reflection on Congress. Franklin tried to get it changed, but was told that it was his Majesty's order.[1] Congress was alarmed at the danger of a "dictator." Luzerne managed to interpret his instructions to mean Washington "or some other person."[2] When Morris entered on his office, June 4, he wrote to Congress that no Act had been passed to give him control of the French subsidy.[3] The same day they passed such an Act.[4] Bayley[5] says that it is supposed that the drafts went out signed by Washington.

Colonel Laurens arrived in Paris in April. His father was informed of it in his prison, and was told that the presence of his son in Paris on a public mission would hurt his own case.[6]

Colonel Laurens submitted a memorial to Vergennes, which is dated in March, and therefore seems to have been prepared in advance.[7] He argued to Vergennes that it was the interest of France to press the war energetically, and he pushed this argument indiscreetly, so that it verged on a threat that America would not support France. Vergennes instructed Luzerne to tell Congress that Franklin's method of diplomacy was more effective.[8] The young staff officer was far more soldier than diplomat. It is hard to understand Franklin's meaning, when he told Laurens that he could not ask him to quit the army, otherwise he would be glad to see him in Paris again as his successor.[9]

[1] Dip. Corr. Rev. iii. 192.
[2] Washington, i. 23, note.
[3] State Dep. MSS. 137, ii. 37.
[4] Secret Journ. ii. 585.
[5] Loans, 10.
[6] S. C. Hist. Soc. Coll. i. 36.
[7] Dip. Corr. Rev. ix. 215.
[8] Durand, 248.
[9] Franklin in France, i. 454.

Vergennes exclaimed vehemently against the exorbitance of the demand submitted to him by Laurens. Laurens cut down the list, making allowance for the lost cargo of the "Lafayette" as well as he could. He argued that the United States were exhausted, and that France must now give them decisive support or lose all that had hitherto been fought for. The answer was that the demands of Congress were excessive; that the United States ought to make greater exertions; that France was under enormous expenditures; that French credit was being strained; that the administration of the American finances did not inspire confidence; that the resolution of the 18th of March, 1780, was pernicious; that the application of Congress was tardy and sudden.

Laurens evidently exerted himself to the utmost to send off the supplies. His eagerness to do this was what led him to accept the "South Carolina" frigate,[1] and to fill out her cargo by purchases in Holland. He sailed on a French frigate, carrying a sum in specie, and with the "Cibelle" and "Olimpe" under convoy, on the 1st of June, and reached Boston on the 25th of August.[2]

Laurens reported to Congress, April 24, that he had chartered the ship which had been hired by the State of South Carolina, and which was detained for debt at Amsterdam, partially loaded, under command of Captain Gillon. He paid the debts, took the cargoes for Congress, and was very proud of the negotiation.[3] In June, however, Adams wrote from Amsterdam that Major Jackson was

---

[1] This ship, originally called "L'Indien," was owned by the Prince of Luxembourg, but was bought and fitted out by the American Commissioners. The expense was found to be more than they could bear. She was transferred to the King of France, and then rented to Gillon, as agent of South Carolina, after which she was called the "South Carolina" (Paul Jones, ii. 269; cf. Dip. Corr. Rev. iii. 132).

[2] Dip. Corr. Rev. ix. 236, 242.   [3] Ibid. 227.

there, under instructions from Colonel Laurens, preparing the goods and cash which were to be shipped to the United States by the ship "South Carolina."[1] Over £50,000 worth of goods had been bought, but Franklin would only pay for £15,000 worth, fearing that his money would not suffice for his obligations.

September 2, Laurens reached Philadelphia and prepared his report. He no doubt informed Morris of all his doings in Europe.

In September, Luzerne transmitted to Congress the substance of long despatches from Vergennes, written in May, during Laurens's visit. "Though we would wish to avoid every disagreeable intimation, friendship and common interest oblige me to speak without reserve and with perfect sincerity, that the King has done on this occasion what he can do no more." Colonel Laurens ought to be satisfied with the success of his mission, although he has not obtained all he demanded. "The Court of France hopes these demands will not be renewed, for how disagreeable soever to refuse allies whom the King sincerely loves, necessity would oblige him to reject pecuniary demands of any kind whatsoever." Luzerne was to tell the Americans "that it is time for them to relieve His Majesty from the heavy burdens of a war which he has undertaken and carries on for their sake." France confidently expects that no bills will have been drawn after April 1. Vergennes thinks that the King's benevolence has been abused, — all the bills on Adams, Jay, and Henry Laurens having been thrown on Franklin, that is, on France.[2]

June 27, Franklin ordered back the specie which had been sent to Holland to be shipped in the "South Carolina."[3]

---

[1] Dip. Corr. Rev. vi. 75.
[2] Ibid. xi. 15; Secret Journ. iii. 36.
[3] Dip. Corr. Rev. iii. 221.

Jackson protested that Laurens obtained this money, and that Franklin had no right to interfere with it. He was determined to arrest it in the hands of the banker. Franklin replied that this money was part of the six millions which he had obtained as a gift before Laurens came. What Laurens obtained was a guarantee of a loan of ten millions, to be contracted in the money market of Holland. Franklin supposed that the specie which Jackson was preparing, and which Gillon was to take, was a part of the Dutch loan. He learns that that loan has produced nothing, and that the specie taken to Holland is a part of the six millions which he had begged, and on which he relied to pay bills which he had accepted, being those which had been drawn on Henry Laurens and Jay, and on which he relied also to pay for Jackson's purchases in Holland. Laurens had already taken two and a half million livres out of the six millions with him in specie, besides leaving many orders for supplies for which Franklin must pay. " I applaud the zeal you have both shown in the affair, but I see that nobody cares how much I am distressed, provided they can carry their own point."

The French Court retained five million livres from the loan of 1781, with which to replace the ship "Lafayette." The amount of specie ordered back from Holland was 1,430,000 livres. The cost of sending and returning it was 19,539 livres.[1]

Laurens's mission was productive of very little good. He brought specie to the amount of not quite four hundred and seventy thousand dollars, and on this Morris was able to practise his "magic art" of reflecting specie by paper until he manifolded it. Laurens was credited, however, with inducing France to order the fleet to North America.[2] John Adams thought that his memorial to the States of

---

[1] Report of 1785.   [2] Dip. Corr. Rev. vi. 262.

the Netherlands greatly aided Laurens, and furthered all the other events favourable to America at this juncture.[1]

Morris had scarcely taken office when he was called upon to provide means for the most important campaign of the war. Washington had cherished a plan of attacking New York, with the help of the French, but they objected on the score of expense. Morris, in July, 1781, urged the same objection.[2] August 2, Washington wrote to Morris that the attack on New York was impossible; that he wanted to attack the English in Virginia, and he asked Morris to find out what means of transportation could be obtained at Philadelphia or Baltimore to carry the troops down the Bay.[3] Congress appointed Morris and Peters a committee to confer with Washington, especially in regard to the expense.[4] Washington wrote to Morris that the troops must have a month's pay before they went South. He begged Morris to provide it, also to furnish five hundred guineas for secret service. Morris replied that money matters were in the worst situation possible; exchange down to five shillings, and unsalable at that. Hence he gave little encouragement.[5] In August he visited the camp. On his return he recorded in his diary: " During my stay at camp I had constant applications for money from almost everybody, as all had claims on the public. I took with me only one hundred and fifty guineas, and finding so many demands, I thought it best to satisfy none of them; therefore brought the money back."[6] This reasoning shows that he had high qualifications for the Financier of the Revolution.

Washington, however, wrote again a few days later: " I must entreat you, if possible, to procure one month's pay in specie for the detachment which I have under my com-

[1] Dip. Corr. Rev vi. 265.   [2] Ibid. vii. 429.   [3] Ibid. xi. 417.
[4] Letters to Washington, iii. 381.   [5] Dip. Corr. Rev. xi. 431.   [6] Ibid. 433.

mand. Part of the troops have not been paid anything for a long time past, and have upon several occasions shown marks of great discontent. The service they are going upon is disagreeable to the northern regiments; but I make no doubt that a douceur of a little hard money would put them in proper temper. If the whole sum cannot be obtained, a part of it will be better than none, as it may be distributed in proportion to the respective wants and claims of the men."[1]

The movement to Virginia having been resolved upon, a very important share in carrying it out fell to Morris. On the 28th of August he wrote to Washington: "I directed the Commissary-general immediately on my return from camp, to cause the deposit of three hundred barrels of flour, three hundred barrels of salt meat, and twelve hogsheads of rum, to be made at the head of Elk, and pointed out the means of obtaining them. . . . I have written to the Quartermaster of Delaware and Maryland to exert himself in procuring the craft. . . . I have written to the Governor and several of the most eminent merchants in Baltimore to extend their assistance and influence in expediting this business. Foreseeing the necessity of supplies from Maryland and Delaware, I have written in the most pressing terms to the Governors and agents to have the specific supplies required of them by Congress in readiness for delivery to my order. . . . Still I fear you will be disappointed in some degree as to the shipping, and that I shall be compelled to make purchases of provisions, which, if it happens, must divert the money from those payments to the army that I wish to make. I have already advised Your Excellency of the unhappy situation of money matters, and very much doubt if it will be possible to pay the detachment a month's pay, as you wish. Therefore it will be best not to raise in them any expectation of that kind. Should it come un-

[1] Dip. Corr. Rev. xi. 438.

expectedly, so much the better." It does not appear that the movement of Washington to the southward was kept a secret; for Morris says here, " I have had occasion to lament that too many people have, for some days past, seemed to know Your Excellency's intended movements. This city is filled with strangers, so that Colonel Miles cannot procure private lodgings; and my family, being chiefly at Springetsbury, affords me the opportunity of appropriating my house in town to your use. I believe we can accommodate your aids, etc., with mattresses, but our beds are chiefly in the country, and as what I have cannot possibly be appropriated to a better use, I beg Your Excellency will consider and use my house and what it affords as your own." [1]

On the 30th Washington and his suite reached Philadelphia, and dined at Morris's house.[2] On the 5th of September Morris recorded the negotiations by which he secured means to pay the soldiers. He applied to Rochambeau for twenty thousand hard dollars, promising repayment at any time he should name. He met Luzerne, Rochambeau, and Chastellux at Luzerne's house. Their military chest was low, and, although they had money at Boston, it would take six or eight weeks to get it to Philadelphia. Money was also on the fleet of De Grasse, but its arrival was uncertain. Moreover the consent of the Intendant and the Treasurer was necessary, and they had set out for the head of Elk. The whole party rode thither to see them. The troops had shown great discontent on marching through Philadelphia. Morris and the Frenchmen met an express from Washington, bringing news of the arrival of De Grasse. Rochambeau thereupon consented to lend twenty thousand dollars, Morris promising to repay it by the 1st of October.[3]

[1] Letters to Washington, iii. 394. [2] Diary, Dip. Corr. Rev. xi. 462.
[3] Ibid. 463.

Morris believed that the French army was supported at a larger expense than was necessary. He desired to make contracts for supplying them.[1] Of the specific supplies obtained from Pennsylvania in 1781, he sold to Holker, for the French army, flour to the value of $19,424, on which the profit was $6,883. These figures show what margins there were for operations to be made by a man in a commanding position; for what he did for the Congress upon occasion he could do for himself nearly all the time. His public position need not have given him anything more than the knowledge where the opportunities were.

He also thought that the bills of exchange drawn by the French army agents, and his own bills on the bankers in Paris, unduly depressed the exchange, and that, if he had the management of both, he could lessen the loss from this cause. The French agents said that they meant to buy with specie, but that, if they used bills, they would allow him to negotiate them. The accounts show that he did this, and, as he thought, with success.

Another of his enterprises which came to nothing, but which shows the energy and enterprise with which he devoted himself to the work of his office, is a scheme to convert the outstanding certificates. He wrote to Franklin that, from the best returns he could get, there were $7,200,000 due on six per cent certificates, interest payable in France at five livres for a dollar, but greatly depreciated. He wishes he could buy in these certificates. He could do it with 15,000,000 livres, and if that could be borrowed at five per cent, the six per cent interest which France is now paying on those certificates would pay the five per cent and sink the principal in ten years.[1]

Unfortunately, this scheme, like nearly all the others, was a proposition that France should assume the load of the enterprise.

[1] Dip. Corr. Rev. xii. 44.   [2] Ibid. xi. 380.

Finances of the American Revolution. 305

The money which had been provided to pay the soldiers did not prove sufficient. September 7, Washington wrote that $20,000 would fall far short of the sum necessary, but that he had received 500 guineas for secret service. On the 10th, Morris wrote to him: "I am a good deal disappointed and put to inconvenience by the money at the Elk falling short of the object, which obliges me to send money thither that was absolutely necessary to fulfil my engagements here. I must struggle through these difficulties; but the doing so requires that attention and time which ought to be bestowed upon greater objects."[1] Johnson,[2] arguing to diminish the merit of Morris, says that he possessed the "art or abuse of dazzling the public eye by the same piece of coin multiplied by a thousand reflectc ." The charge was not without foundation, but it will b admitted that he needed such an art, if ever man did.[3]

It was so obviously the proper move to make, that everybody expected Clinton to prevent the junction of Washington and Rochambeau, or to invade New Jersey. Arnold wanted to attempt the first of these enterprises,[4] and it was expected at New York that Clinton would attempt the second.[5] There was great alarm at Philadelphia during the last two weeks of September.[6] Congress called on Pennsylvania for 3,000 men to defend the city.[7] This meant more trouble for the Financier. He did not believe that the danger was real, and he dreaded the expense; but he consented to the measures taken on account of the alarm

---

[1] Dip. Corr. Rev. xi 467 [2] Johnson's Greene, ii. 254.
[3] A week before Cornwallis surrendered, the Quartermaster-general of the American army could not obtain from the post-office despatches on public business, because he could not pay the postage (Pickering's Pickering, i. 306).
[4] Jones's New York, ii 207. [5] Ibid. 467.
[6] Va. Papers, ii. 413, 488. [7] Penn. Archives, ix. 397.

of the people.¹ It was at this time that Paine proposed a tax on the rental of Philadelphia.²

It does not lie within our province to narrate military history; but no one can do justice to the Financier unless he takes note of the features of the time. The Virginia Papers show that Virginia was in anarchy in 1781, not by the acts of the enemy, but by the inefficiency of the administration.³ There were 50,000 militia in Virginia east of the Alleghanies,⁴ and only 3,500 at Yorktown when Cornwallis surrendered. It is true that they were treated with contempt and derision by the military men. Washington set part of them at work building a road.

A French officer who was with the army during the Yorktown campaign, and who kept a diary, wrote as follows: "I cannot too frequently repeat how much I was surprised at the American army. It is beyond understanding how troops who were almost naked, badly paid, composed of old men, negroes, and children, could move so well, both on the march and under fire."⁵ The modern student is constantly astounded at the same paradox.

In the following May, Livingston, in a circular to the governors, thus passed judgment on the Yorktown campaign and the American share in it: "We have at no period been in a situation to second fully the endeavours of our allies to serve us. We either neglected to assemble our army in time, or to provide the means for supporting or moving them. A feather would have turned the balance last year, notwithstanding the powerful aid we received abroad. Providence blinded our adversaries. To their temerity we owe our success. . . . The inferiority of

---

[1] Penn Archives, 414, 420; Dip. Corr Rev. xi. 473.
[2] See page 34.   [3] See pages 140, 241.
[4] Va. Papers, ii. 219.
[5] Balch, Les Français en Amerique, 124.

our army in point of numbers to that of our allies,[1] while they acted at Yorktown, has been considered in Europe as a proof of the assertions of Great Britain, and has been urged as an argument of our weakness, our weariness of the war, or our internal divisions. A moment's reflection will show the advantages that this affords our antagonist in a negotiation; how much it weakens the claim we make, and how many important benefits may be lost forever by our appearing in Europe to receive our independence rather as a gift than to have established it by our exertions." [2]

In truth, the Yorktown campaign is a striking example of the effect of concord on one side and discord on the other. The French and American forces co-operated in the best possible manner, while Clinton and Cornwallis were acting at cross purposes, animated by jealousy and spite.

Cornwallis surrendered, October 19. On the 18th, Morris made a report to Congress on the state of the treasury.[3] He could not command more than one twentieth of the sum necessary for the current expenses of the year. He had not since his appointment received a shilling from any State but Pennsylvania, and from that only paper money for the four tenths under the Act of March, 1780, and £7,500 in specie, which must be expended for contracts in the State, and did not equal the sum expended for specific supplies for the State. He is told that ten thousand suits of clothes must be bought for the next winter, which will cost at least $200,000. He adds a statement of his immediate cash obligations. The first item is the sum due the French military chest, $26,000. The second is $10,000

---

[1] The French had 7,000 regular troops at Yorktown; the Americans had 5,500 continentals and 3,500 militia. The French had two fleets; the Americans had not a ship
[2] Va. Papers, iii. 147.   [3] Dip. Corr. Rev. xi. 491.

due the French for flour taken at New York to be replaced in Virginia. The next is $15,000 for transportation on the Chesapeake and Delaware during the late movement of the army. After many other items he closes with $12,000 due to himself for cash advanced. The total is $201,000.

There is a story often repeated that Morris advanced $1,400,000 for the outfit of Washington's army for the Yorktown campaign.[1] Sometimes it is said that goods to that amount were bought with his notes, and sometimes with his own money. Other statements may be met with in regard to advances of his own money made by Morris from time to time while Financier.[2] The present is the only occasion known in the record where he actually made any advance of his own means, and we here see the exact amount of it. Of course it was a loan and was repaid. Two years later he wrote to Greene: " While I was in advance, not only my credit, but every shilling of my own money, and all which I could obtain from my friends, to support the important expedition against Yorktown, much offence was taken that I did not minister relief to the officers taken prisoners at Charleston."[3]

As to the money he had borrowed of the French, promising to pay it again on the 1st of October, he wrote to the French Minister on September 20, that all his means had been absorbed in the Yorktown movement. He begged a delay until the money which Laurens had just brought to Boston could be brought forward. This Luzerne granted.[4]

Marshall[5] says that if Morris was not perfectly successful, he certainly did more than could have been believed possible, and that it was due to him that the Yorktown campaign was not frustrated by lack of means of transpor-

---

[1] Hazard's Reg. ii. 251.   [2] Phillips, ii. 189.
[3] Dip. Corr. Rev. xii. 369.   [4] Ibid. 471, 484, 491.
[5] Life of Washington, iv. 474.

tation and subsistence. Under the terms of the capitulation he was authorized by Congress to take such supplies as were needed by the United States from the stocks of the British traders at Yorktown and pay for them with tobacco to be shipped under flag of truce to New York. This led to a new set of suspicions and charges that he was trading where others were forbidden to trade.[1]

If the Americans had estimated the victory at Yorktown as highly as the English did, it seems that they might have disbanded their army, stopped expenses, and left the English to depart when they got ready. The news of Cornwallis's surrender produced the greatest confusion and distress at Court and in Parliament.[2] It was recognized as a fact that America could not be reduced to obedience again, and in February it was resolved that the war should be continued only in a defensive manner. It had become a current notion, however, that Lord Shelbourne was dishonest and could not be trusted. We find it reiterated by all kinds of people. It was, therefore, believed that the armament here must be kept up, and that the United States must be on their guard against insidious schemes.

[1] Va. Papers, iii. 393.   [2] Walpole's Last Journals, ii. 474.

END OF VOL. I.

www.ingramcontent.com/pod-product-compliance
Lightning Source LLC
Chambersburg PA
CBHW020331240426
43665CB00043B/220